LII

2025

The Yearbook of
The Society for the Study of Midwestern Literature

MidAmerica, a peer-reviewed journal of The Society for the Study of Midwestern Literature, is published annually. We welcome scholarly contributions from our members on any aspect of midwestern literature and culture. Except for winners of our annual poetry and prose contests, we do not publish poems, short stories, or creative nonfiction.

For submission guidelines, see ssml.org. Please direct questions to the editor, Patricia Oman (poman@hastings.edu).

For permissions and back issues, please contact Marcia Noe (marcia-noe@utc.edu).

To

Janet Ruth Heller

May her memory be a blessing.

CONTENTS

Bibliography

Awards

Calls for Proposals

PREFACE

Patricia Oman

As this issue of *MidAmerica* was nearing completion, I learned of the passing of longtime SSML member (and past president) Dr. Janet Ruth Heller, a poet and scholar who regularly participated in SSML's annual symposium and who contributed many pieces to SSML's journals *MidAmerica* and *Midwestern Miscellany*. We are fortunate that she chose to be part of SSML's community and will miss her. This issue of *MidAmerica* is dedicated to Janet.

Based on the contents of this issue, it seems that SSML members have been thinking a lot lately about power and perspective.

The issue begins with the prize-winning entries of this year's creative writing contests. Lynn Domina's "Of Copper" is the winner of the Gwendolyn Brooks Poetry Prize and Caitlin Horrocks's "Locked Out" the winner of the Paul Somers Prize for Creative Prose. Both pieces explore memory and perspective, Domina's poem reflecting the hidden costs of a common metal and Horrocks's short story exploring the uncrossable boundaries between mother and son, adult and child.

The critical essays in this issue focus on a variety of midwestern authors and span almost a hundred years, but they all address authors who challenge established power structures. Michael Steiner's essay, "Meridel Le Sueur and the Crafting of Proletarian Regionalism in the Midwest in the 1930s, 1940s, and Beyond," for example, describes radical writer Meridel Le Sueur's complex relationship with the Midwest, emphasizing the need to understand the region's contradictions and intertwining power structures. In "'How to Survive': The 'Little Black City' and Columbus's Elastic Redevelopment in Works by Aminah Robinson and Adrienne Kennedy," Jared Hackworth writes about two experimental Black artists from Columbus, Ohio, who show how community can resist external structural redevelopment of neighborhoods. And Keriann Kaufmann's "'Like Dinosaur Blood': Cyclical Trauma in Donald Ray Pollock's 'Discipline' and 'Real Life'" argues that two stories from Pollock's 2008 collection *Knockem-stiff* reveal the failure of the American Dream for those in the twenty-first century who have no access to economic mobility.

Review essays in this issue evaluate a new collection of scholarly essays edited by Jon K. Lauck and Catherine McNicol Stock, *The Liberal Heartland: A Political History of the Postwar American Midwest,* and two recent full-length collections of poetry by longtime SSML members, Mary Catherine Harper and Margaret Rozga. Rozga, as it happens, is the winner of the 2026 Mark Twain Award.

Rounding out the content of this year's issue is the "Annual Bibliography of Midwestern Literature" for 2023.

I look forward to seeing what directions SSML members' interests take them in the next year! A good place to start might be to check out the Calls for Proposals at the very end of this issue. Guest editors for upcoming issues of *Midwestern Miscellany* are seeking proposals on several topics, including "Reading and Writing the Midwest," "New Perspectives on Midwestern Working-Class Literature," and "Midwestern Drama." The 2026 SSML Symposium (May 28–29 at the Kellogg Center in East Lansing) might be a good place to workshop some of these ideas.

Hastings College

OF COPPER

Lynn Domina

In human bodies, it heals
capillaries, influences genetic
transmission.

Always the miners

Her patina glistens
and catches my breath
every time my plane descends
above New York harbor.

the one whose leg shattered

Walking into the auditorium,
I notice tympani,
anticipate this majestic symphony's
rolling crescendo.

the one decapitated

Which most resembles
a piece of wire:
a lamb, a globe, a penny, a window:
the most difficult question
on our sixth-grade IQ test.

Later, Bill Anspach said, *They're both*
made of copper.

death more common than payday then

Cephalopods bleed blue
because in them copper
carries oxygen
from cell to cell
to cell.

even now their bodies stil!

My mother humming as she scrubs
a saucepan, soap bubbles
refracting evening light
until I can no longer
distinguish the copper bottom
from this autumn sunset.

pummeled

My favorite necklace:
a thin disc,
Lake Superior's silhouette
laser cut
from its center.

Northern Michigan University

LOCKED OUT

Caitlin Horrocks

Perhaps the urgency of that Christmas Eve felt to her like the rush of school mornings, the desperate push to get all three kids out the door with backpacks and bags of winter gear, wondering whether the plow had made it yet to the lake road, tossing granola bars into the backseat for their breakfast. Christmas Eve was a race to fetch the presents she'd hidden in the shed outside, fill the stockings, wrap the last gifts, before Isabelle, who wouldn't sleep alone, woke and noticed her mother was no longer in bed with her. The Christmas-frenzy felt like morning-frenzy, which was maybe why, Meryl told herself later, she'd reached behind her and reflexively pulled the door shut.

She tried the knob, which confirmed, as she knew it would, that the door had locked behind her. On a school morning she would have had her keys, phone, would have been wearing a coat and boots. Now? Red and black checked flannel pajamas, underwear, a stretched-out bra, a thick purple bathrobe. Rubber-soled slippers, fleece lined. They weren't open-heeled, but that was the best she could say for them. She'd left them on because the path to the shed was shoveled, a neat ribbon of smooth-packed snow. The minute she stepped beyond the path she'd be calf deep, and the slippers would let it all in. It was twenty-something degrees, and would keep dropping through the night. An ordinary night, but cold enough to kill her.

Putting the Santa presents in the shed had seemed like the only way to outwit Gavin, who'd found all the same potential hiding spaces in the small two-bedroom cottage that she had. He considered himself a real Sherlock Holmes/Odd Squad/Nate the Great-type, a burgeoning child-detective, and he seemed more outraged by his failure to anticipate his parents' separation than by the separation itself. "But WHY," he kept asking Meryl, wearing a pretend police hat and pointing a magnifying glass at her accusingly. "What were the clues? I didn't see any clues!"

She didn't have a good answer to give him, because she wasn't sure herself. She could think of clues, sure, but Ian had been the one to decide the marriage was over, and his "why," the howling heart of the matter, was still a mystery to her.

When Meryl and Ian had argued over who would have the kids on Christmas morning, Gavin had yelled over them both, questioning the existence of Santa Claus, boy-splaining distance and reindeer speeds to his sisters and sounding, to Meryl's ear, entirely too much like his father. She'd been looking forward to seeing Gavin's little face light up on Christmas morning, not just with the magic of the holiday, but with the realization that he hadn't, at age six, figured out the whole world. That there were mysteries and miracles yet unexplained and maybe his mom knew at least something about something after all.

What she knew right now: that she had, like the "incompetent bitch" Ian had recently accused her of being, locked herself out of the house on Christmas Eve with the kids inside.

There were no neighbors. Duckweed Lake was a seepage lake barely bigger than a pond, maybe fifteen acres. It was shallow and muddy and sprouted huge patches of floating green duckweed in the summer. It was "serene" and "peaceful," and the fall colors were beautiful, but unless you really loved fishing and didn't mind only ever catching black crappie, it took some positive thinking to see it as "fun." The entire north shore belonged to a rich Chicagoan who had added and added onto his summer home until he bought a mansion on a "better" lake closer to Lake Michigan and put this house on the market for more money than anyone was willing to pay to summer on Duckweed Lake. The south shore was a defunct church camp, a haunted-looking assemblage of wooden tent platforms with no tents and a lodge whose ripped screens waved like bats in and out of the windows. There were a handful of houses and cottages along the west and east sides, nearly all seasonal, like hers was supposed to be.

Her hands were shaking, more from panic than cold, as she balled them into the pockets of her robe. If her slippers were doomed to end up snow-filled, maybe she should spare her socks now. They were bad socks, fuzzy acrylic with blurry pictures of cats and pizza slices on them. She did not understand these socks, or why her daughter Lina had thought she'd like them, but they'd been a gift, so she wore them. She took them off standing one-legged, placing each bare foot carefully back in its slipper. Now she had mittens. That was something.

With a deep breath she stepped off the porch and into the snow, which immediately poured in around her ankles. She pushed up on each window at the south side of the cottage, though she knew they were all latched against the cold. At the west side was a deck on wooden supports, overlooking the lake. She climbed over the railing where it met the wall, carefully inserting her feet between the balusters to get up on the deck, then flinging herself over. The slider door? Also closed and locked. Her parents had had it replaced a couple of years ago, and the locking mechanism was new and sturdy. She yanked hard. It didn't budge. Back over the railing, she slid partway down the slope before catching herself. She climbed back up to the other side of the cottage, where her children were sleeping.

Curtains and plastic hung over the bedroom windows, plus additional blankets she'd draped over the curtain rods, trying to stop the single-pane windows from hemorrhaging the warmth from the electric baseboards. She couldn't see anything. But she assumed from the silence Isabelle was still asleep. They shared the master bed, where Isabelle frequently groped for Meryl's warmth, stretched out her hand to touch her mother's cheek, jabbing her in the eyes or sticking her fingers in Meryl's mouth, and Meryl half-woke multiple times per night, wincing. Isabelle wasn't seeking reassurance amidst the upheaval of the separation: she had always been this way, as had Lina at that age. Meryl hadn't slept through the night in years.

Gavin and Lina, who were in kindergarten and pre-K this year, were on bunk beds in the kids' room, which had peeling Disney decals on the walls and a trunk of ancient toys that had been there since Meryl was a child and this was her grandparents' cottage. Then it belonged to her parents, and she'd once assumed they'd sell it to help finance their retirement. But they'd sold the regular house instead, and bought a condo in Florida to become snowbirds.

When Ian had announced in September that he wanted a divorce but didn't intend to leave their house, her parents had already left Michigan for Tampa. The weather had held warm and golden, and living in the cottage had felt like a great solution, like something other than pique and humiliation. The forty minutes back down to Cedar Springs where the kids went to school was doable. Tiny Tots Early Childhood Center needed morning shift assistants so badly they found a spot for Isabelle in one of the toddler rooms, and put Meryl to work in the other. Even with the employee discount, Isabelle's care ate much of Meryl's wages, and gas money much of the rest. Other people's kids drained her patience for her own, but Lina and Gavin both finished school at 2:30, so a full-time job was impossible. She hadn't worked since Gavin was born, when she'd quit a warehouse job she'd never liked in the first place. Their money had always been Ian's money, and she didn't really understand what he was planning to do with it. He hadn't yet officially filed. Was there hope of reconciliation, or was he torturing her, or lazy, or waiting to spring some additional trap? She felt suspended, locked in to this performance of confident independence she'd started back when the weather was warmer and the roads clear. The neighbors all left and shut down their cottages, draining and blowing out the pipes, cutting the power and adding antifreeze to the toilet tanks.

Like theirs, her family cottage had not been built for year-round habitation. She piled the beds with electric blankets and brought in additional space heaters that kept tripping the fuses, and she didn't know how she'd pay the utilities, but the children still complained, and she couldn't tell if they were complaining in the way they complained about the cottage's laggy video streaming, or if they were truly cold.

The crux wasn't even the children but the water lines. She'd thrown insulation and heat tape at the problem, done all the things she could do with the credit limit she had and the ground already frozen, received a succession of laughably high estimates from contractors. She was battling winter, and winter, they told her, always eventually won.

She tried the windows quietly, then returned to the door, where she turned the knob one more time for good measure. She ran through everything she knew about locks, which didn't take long. There were things you could try with credit cards or hairpins, but she didn't have a credit card or hairpin or remember what she should try. She couldn't think of a way to break in that wouldn't involve literally breaking a door or window, terrifying the children and making the cottage colder and less habitable than it already was. She had pjs, bathrobe, wet slippers, and—whatever was in her car? There was a winter emergency kit in the trunk, with shiny silver space blankets, a flashlight, a small metal shovel she could use if she did need to break a window. She stepped into the driveway to try the car, but nope—that was locked, too.

Apart from the presents, what else was in the shed? She stood sideways at the shed door to let enough porchlight fall on the lock to see what she was doing. The combination was her parents' wedding anniversary, which was six more grains of salt in an abraded wound every time she had to spin it. Once inside, she stumbled into the humped black garbage bags filled with Christmas presents. The snow in her slippers had already turned the fleece spongy with melted water. They squelched as she walked, and her feet burned.

She thought, as she periodically did, of an afternoon when she was hugely pregnant with Isabelle and home alone with Gavin and Lina, ages three and two. She'd been trying to empty the dishwasher as quickly as possible, carrying a leaning tower of drinking glasses that tipped out of her hand and shattered. She was barefoot, surrounded by a huge corona of broken glass. The kids came running at the crash. "Stay out of the kitchen!" she yelled, in the very-serious-business voice that only sometimes discouraged them. They paused but didn't leave. "Go back to your video," she said.

"It's the Groke episode. It's too scary."

She'd put on *Moomin*, a show she'd watched on DVD as a kid but now seemed to be available only on a 24/7 livestream on YouTube. The Groke was dark purple and kind of like a giant ghostly Grimace if Grimace had only arms instead of legs, groaned constantly, and froze everything it touched. Meryl couldn't in good faith say the Groke was not scary.

Lina had picked up on the fact that her mother seemed to be trapped by some kind of glittery barrier. She darted forward and giggled, feinted at Meryl with a stick. Why was there a stick in the house? Lina wagged it at Meryl like her mother was a zoo animal, safely behind bars.

"Get out, Lina, I'm serious," she said, trying to do with tone and words what she couldn't do with her body. But Lina was two, and when had "I'm serious" ever convinced any toddler of anything? Meryl tried to pick different words. "Go away. You need to go away." She stretched out her arms, but they didn't reach to the edge of the glass. She couldn't physically push Lina away without stepping into it.

Lina grinned, and Meryl could tell she was about to dart forward. So Meryl moved first, swooping Lina up into her arms. She couldn't make herself take another step, could barely make herself keep breathing, didn't understand how John McClane had done it in *Die Hard*, but Lina was safe, and from the middle of the glass Meryl could place her back on clear floor. She braced a hand on the counter and took a slow lunge out of the worst of it. She whimpered as pieces were pushed further in, and something in the sound finally convinced the kids to back away. On a clear patch of floor, Meryl slid down with her back to the cabinets, turning her feet on their ankles, soles pointed inwards. She managed to pull out a few pieces, tried to channel her inner yippee-ky-yay, but started feeling so nauseous she wasn't sure she could keep going. There was more and more blood obscuring her view. She asked Gavin to bring her her phone, and called Ian.

She'd been humiliated to do it, but in the time it took him to get home, she'd crawled to the living room, switched away from the scary Groke to *Gabby's Dollhouse*, given the kids a snack, wrapped her feet in dishtowels, and elevated them on a footstool. The kids had been quiet, mildly concerned, but not alarmed. She was feeling like an action hero.

But Ian hadn't seen it that way. "Jesus Christ," he'd said, at the roomful of glass, the bloody footprints, sounding not impressed, nor even concerned, but angry.

The obvious thing to do, she recognized, was pound on the door or windows and terrify the kids, have them let her back in. But what would she say about why she'd been outside? She pictured Gavin's gimlet eye. She'd had him take the trash out already, right before bed. If she said she'd left something in the car, he'd ask what, and there was nothing convincing in the car to produce. If she said she wanted something from the shed, which was true, he'd see the presents. If she said she was investigating a suspicious sound, he'd ask why she wasn't wearing boots. For anything she could think of, she heard already his rebuttal, and the additional question: "On *Christmas Eve*? You expect me to believe that on Christmas Eve?" This would happen in front of his sisters. She'd be dropping three kids off to Ian on Christmas afternoon who'd learned prematurely that Santa Claus wasn't real because their mother had locked herself out and needed her children to rescue her.

No, she thought: that was the last resort. It was *a* resort, obviously, and preferable to freezing to death and inflicting some real *Gremlins*-level trauma on the kids, but was it absolutely the only remaining choice?

She rued the fact that she'd never hid a spare key in the shed, but maybe someone else had? Maybe she'd find one dangling on a lanyard behind the kayak, glowing like the little silver bell in *The Polar Express*. She shoved her way in, fell over a pile of scooters and knocked lifejackets off the wall. She found a flashlight in a crate on a shelf, but the light flickered and almost immediately died. By turning it on and off like a strobe light she searched as best she could, but found nothing useful and no key. A key. The Visser house? She exited the shed and looked across the lake, to the one house she knew for sure was occupied year-round. She saw a rectangular light, promising a bank of lit windows rather than an exterior floodlight. She couldn't be sure of more because she wore glasses to drive, to see at a distance, and those too were locked inside the house.

Because the Vissers were the only permanent residents, they often agreed to keep an eye on things for neighbors, which had turned into keeping an eye on things for AirBnBers. She remembered her mother on the phone once, telling a guest who'd locked the key inside to go to the Vissers for the spare. But the cottage's days as a rental property had been limited. Her parents found cleaning between short-term guests a pain, and the guests themselves a bigger pain. They got particularly disgruntled over the amount of duckweed in Duckweed Lake and once her dad responded publicly to a review by typing only "ya can't fix stupid." The listing got flagged for review and he took the whole thing down in a huff.

Even if the Vissers didn't have a key, they could lend her a coat, footwear, a ride back to her cottage and maybe some casual locksmith expertise. Bill Visser was a retired carpenter who had always given the impression of no-nonsense competence. Their families had known each other for four generations. Maybe he had a key to the Chicago mansion, and latitude to invite her to stay there. Maybe one of his kids, all grown and flown, happened to have a whole spare house.

That was ridiculous, but she'd been on her own with the one option she'd thought of for three months now without coming up with any better ones, and she thought of Bill and Magda with longing. It would feel so good to sit in their kitchen, with the Bible verses painted on old washboards hung over the top row of cabinets, the red enamel tea kettle, the ceramic fish refrigerator magnets. She could remember the room precisely, from rowing across the lake with her brother and eating cookies with the Visser kids. Across the lake. It was a short, straight shot. As they'd gotten bigger, the kids had dared each other to swim across, until that got too easy to merit a dare. The road jagged sharply away from the lake at both the north and south sides, adding distance and time and danger of frostbite. It had been so cold, and the lake was so small. Surely it was frozen enough by now to walk straight over.

She started patting her pockets for her phone—some hardy subreddit of ice fisherman must have figured this out for her—before remembering that her phone was inside. She looked down the slope to the lake. There were no dark spots, no obvious holes or indentations, but without her glasses, she couldn't trust her eyes. She seized on the memory of the ice fishing shanty she'd noticed yesterday driving past Bittern Lake. No—two shanties. One might be someone overeager or ignorant. But two suggested some consensus, about the thickness of the ice. Bittern Lake was bigger, deeper, spring-fed. If Bittern had frozen thick enough for shanties, surely Duckweed was frozen enough for one average-sized adult to walk across.

She listened in the stillness for anyone awake in the house. Nothing. She grabbed a kayak paddle from the shed, and half-walked, half-slid, down the slope to the shore. She tapped the cloudy ice with the paddle, using it like a makeshift spud bar. She'd had a boyfriend once who'd invited her out ice fishing, and she'd been bored out of her mind but grateful now to have witnessed the basics. One hard tap with no sound and no water meant you could walk. Three hits meant you could stay and sit. She didn't need to sit. She just needed to get across. She walked out a few more paces, in easy reach of the shore, and tried jumping. Her feet shot out from under her and she fell hard on her ass. The impact knocked a sound out of her, but nothing out of the ice, no creaking or groaning. She walked a few more paces, trying to gauge the point where the muddy bottom dropped off, trying to imagine markers like her dock and her neighbors' boats, all erased in this season. She kept walking until she knew she must have passed it, must be standing where the water got as deep as it ever got. The ice felt more solid than the under-insulated floors in the cottage. More solid than her marriage, ha ha ha! her brain offered up, and she realized she felt punch-drunk, not so much from cold, but adrenaline, fear, the strangeness of the situation. Tonight felt simultaneously more fiercely real than her regular life and like it couldn't possibly be actually happening.

She noticed that her legs, where snow had crept up her pajama parts, stung in a way her feet no longer did. She understood that this was not, objectively, good, but she could appreciate the blankness, the lack of discomfort. She could ignore her feet, prioritize other problems. She could triage her body like she'd been triaging her life: what pain could be shelved, ignored, turned away from?

The day her feet had been full of glass, Ian had taken the kids to a neighbor's house, then silently cleaned the kitchen. She switched from *Gabby's Dollhouse* to *Outlander*. She almost never got to watch anything she liked. But the theme song summoned Ian to the family room. "Seriously? You're going to watch TV while I clean up the mess you made?"

"What else do you want me to do?" she asked, gesturing at the dishtowels wrapped around her elevated feet. If he'd given her a clear answer, she'd have done it, or tried. She could imagine how the sound of the show grated, the way it grated on her when he sat doing who knows what on his phone while the children screamed at each other. But he just rolled his eyes and went back to the kitchen, and she kept watching.

He broke his silence in the car. *Irresponsible*, to have stepped in the glass, *ineffective*, to have had no other way of stopping Lina, *incompetent*, to have been carrying too many glasses at once. He'd never hit her, but that day in the car she realized that she was leaning as far away from him as she could get, her shoulders tensed so tightly she felt the twinge of them even over the pain from her feet. He wouldn't do anything while he was driving, she thought, and then they'd be at the ER, and he wouldn't do anything there either. But how long had her body been afraid of him? She remembered clearly a time that his body meant only good things to her—safety, pleasure, satisfaction both with him and with being the person he'd chosen. Those things were all still there, which made her fear all the more confusing.

In the middle of the lake, the ice still thick and silent and generous, she allowed herself to stand for a moment and look up at the stars. In a scrap of good luck, it was a clear night; the usual grey winter cloud cover had broken up, and there were stars and most of the moon lighting her way. If Gavin were here he would make her estimate its size, because that's what he'd been doing lately, on the car ride home in the evening, and around this time last month she'd said, "Two-thirds."

"But what percentage?"

"Seventy," she said, because that's the amount of moon she saw.

"Wrong!" he yelled, so loudly she jumped and the steering wheel shivered. "Two-thirds is 66.6!"

They'd been driving alongside Bittern Lake, and she almost pulled hard towards the guardrail, because it was too late, everything was too late, Ian had ruined her children, had taught them to set traps instead of speak. But maybe the girls were salvageable, she thought, continuing to drive, maybe they still knew how to pose actual questions, and listen to the answers, and then she reminded herself that Gavin, too, was still a small, salvageable child, whom she loved fiercely, and who was Ian to take any of that from her? She thought about responding that it was actually 66.66666666666666 etc. but she couldn't remember the name of the symbol that indicated the sixes went on forever, and by the time she looked it up she knew the moment had passed, that she'd look ridiculous if she tried to dunk on her six-year-old's math knowledge.

She thought of *Moominland Midwinter*, from the book series she'd liked even more than the show, but which Gavin had rejected entirely. The Moomin family, who all looked like wholesome little bipedal hippos, hibernated through the long Finnish winters, but in one book, Moomintroll woke early. He ventured out alone, leaving his sleeping family, and found his whole world transformed by snow. She took comfort in the memory of the illustrations, the intrepid Moomintroll under an expanse of stars. He made friends. He came to no harm. He had an adventure, then crept back into bed. She tried to remember whether there was an explanation for why he'd woken alone, which made her remember Isabelle, and she hurried, no longer bothering to tap the spud bar.

At the ER at least one of the nurses clearly thought she'd been day drinking. How else had she ended up with feet full of glass? Plenty of people dropped things, but stepping into the pieces was apparently something else. "Fuck yeah, something else. Something heroic," she told herself, but couldn't recapture her bravado. She felt dumb and afraid of what they thought of her. She watched the glass come out of her foot with a sense of vindication: all clear, tiny shards, no beer bottle brown or wine bottle green.

"Jam jars," she said, which the family used as water glasses, but then she wondered if that made it sound like they couldn't afford to buy regular glasses. "From the fancy jam company. With the French name." She was feeling woozy again. Now what if she'd made it sound like they spent all their money on fancy jam instead of child gates for the kitchen? "Not like, *that* fancy. We just buy it at Meijer."

"Bonne Maman?" the doctor said.

"What?"

"The moderately fancy brand of jam."

"Right. 'Good mother'? Isn't that what it means?"

The doctor shrugged, and she regretted saying anything, because she felt like a walking Rorschach test of whether she had or hadn't been a "good mother."

"Literally yes," Ian said, and her heart perked up with relief at the verdict, but he was staring at his phone, where he'd looked up the translation. "But the phrase is used to mean 'grandma.'"

"Granny jam," the doctor said. "Sounds better in French."

In the moment, the doctor's laconic delivery as she plucked another splinter of glass from Meryl's foot seemed very funny, and Meryl tried to make it into A Thing, a family in-joke for anything that looked better at a distance. "It sounded better in French," she said a few days later, about the crinkle fries the kids wouldn't eat from Culver's. She was having trouble standing long enough to do much cooking.

"I *told* you you should just go to McDonalds," Ian said, not playing along.

"Don't pretend these burgers aren't better."

"To *you*. You got them because *you* like them better."

She realized that was actually true, but why shouldn't she have something she wanted every so often? She never got to watch what she wanted. She never got to sleep how she wanted, without someone kneading her face, never got to sleep in, or ignore nighttime wakeups, because Ian had to get up in the morning for work at the Newaygo County Sheriff's Office. He was a traffic enforcement deputy, but Gavin could not be dissuaded from picturing him as a detective.

She made it to the wooden stairs that lead up to the Vissers' house. They were slick, and she climbed carefully. The windows in front of her were warmly lit, but no people were visible, just a plaid couch, two matching recliners in front of a blank TV. End tables and a coffee table free of mugs or crumb-covered plates, opened books or devices. No signs of life. She politely walked around the house to the front door and rang the bell, then knocked. No one came. She didn't see a camera, but waved just in case, trying to look hapless and harmless, which was easy since she was wearing a bathrobe in the snow.

Nothing, and she looked behind her at the garage, and stumbled towards the windows. No car inside, or in the drive. She thought she could see the strips of tire tracks, but covered with a layer of accumulated snow. It was Christmas Eve. It was not hard to imagine the Vissers spending the holiday at one of their children's houses. Or doing what her parents had done, and disappearing to Florida. She trudged around to the back of the house, where she spotted a clock inside that read 9:59. As she got ready to knock on the glass, the lamps all went off at once. They were on a timer.

She could break this window, she supposed, as she hadn't broken her own. There'd be spare winter gear left in the closets, at least something better than what she had on. She could warm up for a minute. She could use their phone to call an emergency locksmith, if she could find such a thing on Christmas Eve. If she could even find a number. Even find a phone. No guarantee the Vissers hadn't gotten rid of their landline once cell service at the lake became more reliable. She'd have to tell the Vissers, and pay for the damage, and she supposed it was still breaking and entering, even if you were freezing, and they wouldn't press charges, but she didn't know what Ian would do with evidence of honest-to-God criminal activity. She didn't want to find out. The walk across the lake had been easy. Easy enough to do again, and wake the kids like she'd tried to avoid. She turned back towards home. She couldn't feel her feet, but they were still working.

Then she fell down the stairs. She flung out her arm with the paddle as she slid, jamming it through the balusters, stopping her fall but wrenching her shoulder. She hung like that for a minute, splayed on the stairs, trying to catch her breath. She got herself seated squarely on a step and tried to let go of the paddle, but her fingers wouldn't open. She looked at the cats and pizza slices and thought, "open," and her fingers just … didn't. She leaned her mouth down to them, hooked her top teeth over her fingertips, tasting snow and polyester, and pulled up. She thought of Isabelle's little fingers jabbing into her mouth. Once she loosened the grip her hand opened, and her heart slowed a little. She scooted the rest of the way down the slope on her butt, next to the stairs, which only had a railing on one side. She left the paddle, too afraid to ask anything else of her hands, lest she realize they couldn't do it.

Her shoulder hurt, badly, and her right ankle. But she could walk on it. The fall could have been worse. She kept moving forward into the darkness, trying to make sure she was angled correctly toward her cottage, before realizing that that shouldn't be difficult. Her windows should be lit, should be the only lit thing on that whole side of the lake, shining like a beacon. Just like the Vissers' house, her cottage's living room, where the kids had laid out their stockings by the small artificial tree (too small, too artificial, the children had complained), had a view of the lake. The lights had been on. Surely they'd been on? But if they'd been on, who had turned them off? If the kids had woken, why were they sitting in the dark? Or the space heaters had tripped a fuse again and plunged the house into dark and cold, and her kids were huddled up not knowing what was happening or where she was. Or the space heaters had started a fire she couldn't yet see and her children were dying of smoke inhalation.

She lurched forward as quickly as she could, which was not quick. On the ice, her limp was hard to manage. The tiny, even steps that warded against slipping were agony. When she hopped forward on it, putting as little weight on her right ankle as possible, she nearly slipped. She did slip, several times, and fell once, but kept moving. She considered whether crawling would be worth the slower speed to minimize risk of further, incapacitating injury. She tried it and felt over-dramatic, imagined Ian rolling his eyes and saying, "You know you can still stand," and she didn't want his voice in her head, but it didn't go away until she stood and resumed walking.

"What's his deal?" she'd wondered aloud one night to friends, on a rare girls' night out. They tried to get together more often, but their kids were too small and needy, their jobs too inflexible, their husbands too tired, their houses just far enough apart. But that night they'd met at Main Street Pub, near Grand Valley State University, where a few of them, though not Meryl, had gone to school, and they thought they'd feel nostalgic but they only felt old, even though they were only 30.

"He's probably cheating. That's his deal," her most I'm-not-mean-I'm-just-honest-friend said, and Meryl froze, thinking Jani had actual evidence, and Jani didn't, just speculation, and Jani was in fact often mean, but in this case she turned out to be right.

His story was that he'd accidentally reactivated a years-old profile on one of the apps, idly swiped through the matches out of curiosity, said something casual to a girl he recognized from high school and hadn't seen in the twelve years since. They'd had sex more than once but less than a lot. Meryl believed parts of this. She was pretty sure the two weren't still together, if they'd ever actually been "together."

"*You* left," he said, and when she asked what that meant he told her she'd disappeared, and when she asked what *that* meant he went on about how she'd disappeared into the kids, into momming, into Gavin's insufferability and Lina's pickiness and Isabelle's bed, like Meryl wanted to spend her nights having her face kneaded, like there was anyone else who was going to do any of this shit, because Ian sure wasn't.

"So we've got a kid who won't sleep, one who won't eat, and one who never shuts up. You've made being a mom, like, your entire personality, and you're not even good at it."

This had cut her so deeply, and she couldn't think of a soul to tell. Partly because she was afraid of someone agreeing with him, but also because if they ranted right along with her, said all the right things, really raked Ian across the coals, it would be harder to explain if she ever got back with him. Because she knew she'd take him back. If he wanted her back she'd go, eagerly, because she didn't know what else to do, or where to go, or who to be. If she moved on from the cottage she was admitting that the separation had gone from something angry and temporary and ripe for revision, to something more permanent. Everyone said not to make any big decisions in the first years after having kids, because everything was chaos and misery and people weren't really themselves, and she'd waited, for Ian's patience to return, his charm, his love, and only gradually realized that maybe they wouldn't, that whatever he'd felt for her wouldn't in fact ebb and flow but had been finite, and had worn down to nothing.

Mostly all that was in her head at this moment was *forward. Forward.* But part of her was reflecting in a detached way that the current situation seemed to be clearly not the result of A+ decision-making. She could look back and feel that she'd made defensible choices, but here she was, in a pretty indefensibly dangerous situation. The cloud cover had thickened, so the radius of darkness around her had tightened. The wind had even picked up, like this was the part of a movie where things got really dire. Her whole body was shaking, making it harder to balance on her bad ankle. She knew shivering was her body trying to warm itself, that she should be more afraid of it stilling in surrender, but the lack of control was terrifying.

"Mom? Mom!" The sound was not in front of her, where she'd thought her house was, but ahead and to her left. She contemplated and then discarded the idea that the voice was Gavin: the kids had always called her "Mama." But really, who else was out here? Hadn't Gavin been trying out "Mom" occasionally, now that he was a mature kindergartner and permanently mad at her? It had to be Gavin. This chain of thought took a very, very long time to work its way through her brain, and when she opened her mouth what came out was nothing that would reassure a child, or even call him to her. But there was a flashlight bobbing towards her, and she thought about waiting for it to arrive, but was worried she couldn't start moving again if she stopped.

He was too short to lean on, when he got to her, but they both tried. He pushed his flashlight into her fingers but she couldn't hold it. "I'm okay," she tried to say, and the sound of it made clear that she wasn't. They arrived at the shore below a neighbor's house, but closer to home than she would have been without him. She'd lurched far off course. He kept close as they climbed the stairs, and his warmth was miraculous. That it had arrived here, beside her, that he'd brought it with him out into the cold, no, that it *was* him, that living warmth, and here was this human she'd spun out of nothing and that had spun away from her and back.

He sat her on the couch, wrapped her in blankets, helped elevate her ankle. She'd played patient before to the children's pretend doctors, but they both knew this was for real. He had already gotten the flashlights out of the junk drawer, and the lantern from the closet. He reminded her of Ian once again but the good parts, like his confidence and competence. Nothing smelled hot or smoky and she hoped this was only another tripped fuse. That would also match with Gavin's story, which was that he'd woken in the dark, with both nightlight and space heater off, and gone to look for her. He'd hunted everywhere as his sisters slept, and finally through the window he'd seen something, or someone, moving out on the ice. "I didn't know if it was you or not," he said. "I thought maybe it was the Groke. But I decided to check."

"That was very brave of you."

"What were you doing out there?" he asked, and she understood what an insult it would be, to lie now to this brave and competent little human, and she told him the truth: the shed, the presents, the door, the worldwide parental conspiracy. He took the Santa news well, even triumphantly, his suspicions confirmed.

"You're okay with—not believing?"

Gavin tilted his head, like he didn't understand what there was or wasn't to be okay with, and Meryl wasn't quite sure, either. Like it was a choice, to know something or not know it? Like if it felt bad to not believe in Santa, you could return to a time when you did? This seemed ridiculous but familiar. It seemed like what she'd been trying to do with Ian.

Gavin stood and rezipped his coat.

"What are you doing?"

"Getting the presents."

Meryl wanted to protest, to say she could take it from here, but she suspected that if she tried to stand she wouldn't be able to walk.

He seemed able to tell what was for who, filling the stockings, and Meryl felt like she'd done something right. He made occasional suggestions—Lina, he said, liked Jelly Bellies much more than Lifesavers, which was news to Meryl. Should he swap them?

"Sure," she said. "Do what you think is best. Or swap them with one of my candies if you want to. Just not the liqueur ones," she added, when Gavin looked up at her slyly.

Gavin started to rearrange, reallocate. Meryl couldn't really complain about his decisions.

"Do you remember the book *Moominland Midwinter*?"

"Is that the one where Moomintroll wakes up and goes outside by himself?"

Meryl nodded. "I don't think we ever made it all the way through. You thought the pictures were scary."

"The pictures *were* scary. It was dark and he was all alone."

Meryl managed to stand and hobble to the stove, was relieved to find her hands steady enough to heat and pour water for decaffeinated tea, for her, and hot chocolate for him.

"Was it scary, outside?" he asked her.

"Yeah," Meryl said.

I was grateful for that, her honesty, her admission of fear. It was a nice antidote to everything else about that year. We didn't hear Lina stir, only her footsteps, already coming down the hall. There was no time to hide the stockings laid out and half-filled, me doing the filling, a Bluey figurine in my hand that was clearly meant for her, since I didn't like Bluey.

"You're opening my presents?" she said, with a tone of profound betrayal.

I couldn't think of any way to defend myself other than what I did, which was to tell her I wasn't taking presents out, but putting them in. "I'm being Santa," I said. "He was in a hurry and he left everything in a big pile and I'm putting them in the right stockings."

"You're lying."

What could I say? I was.

"Mom bought all the presents and hid them in the shed and then when she went to get them she locked herself out and almost died."

Lina blinked at me. "Stop teasing."

We both waited to see what our mother would say, but she said nothing at all, like she'd been spinning stories since the separation (*It will be an adventure to live in the cottage! Maybe we'll all be living together again soon!*) and she'd finally run out.

"Did you buy the presents?" Lina asked.

She admitted it.

"Because we were bad? We were too bad for Santa to bring us presents?"

"No, honey. You weren't bad."

I'd walked us to the edge, and then she took us over. I did not think of it this way at the time, but I can imagine my mother thinking of that circle of glass she'd told us stories about, of no good way forward but through. Lina did not take it well. There were ugly, snotty tears, "I hate yous," questions about whether reindeer existed, too. She shrieked so loudly she woke up Isabelle, and I went to comfort her but she didn't want me, she only wanted our mother, and squeezed her face in satisfaction when they lay down together, and I finished setting out the presents and went back to bed, where I lay awake for a long time.

The next day our mother loaded us into the car, along with our new presents, to take us to our dad's. I remember that she was limping, and that she didn't seem to want us to notice, so I didn't say anything. There were probably a lot of things I really didn't notice, but kids are kids. Parents are aliens. Neither sees the other, not really. At some point maybe I noticed that she never wore sandals, but I didn't think much of it. I had a girlfriend by then who insisted she had ugly feet, though I didn't think so. She scraped at her heels with this gray rock while we watched Netflix, and even paid for some special spa service where fish ate off her calluses, which I thought was even grosser, and I wondered if my mother was similarly neurotic about her feet.

I knew that however gross my girlfriend's feet fish were, I didn't want to hurt her by saying so, that I didn't want to talk to her the way my dad talked to my stepmom, which was probably the same way he'd talked to my mother, although I couldn't really remember. My memories were fragments until the Christmas Eve I was six, which I remembered vividly. I wrote a story for my high school English elective about a lady who locks herself out of her house on a winter night and almost dies. The neighbors save her. "Wow! Really powerful sensory details (brr-rrr!!!)! but I never quite understood why she couldn't just pound on the door and wake the kids up to let her in," my teacher wrote, and I realized I didn't really understand either, and I wrote another version trying to figure it out, and another one, and I still wasn't sure I had it right, but my teacher suggested we send it off to a scholarship competition and I won $500, and she suggested I submit it to a literary magazine, which I also did, but when it was accepted I started sweating, rivulets literally streaming down my sides, because I was a thief. I'd stolen my mother's life, and I couldn't imagine letting her read it. I withdrew the story.

I drove the kids to her house one afternoon years later, so my wife and I could get away for a date night. My mother had gotten very into gardening after she'd bought her own place way out in the country, with the money she'd made from opening and running her own Tiny Tots location. She had a huge set of raised beds with chicken wire walls to keep out the deer. My mom was doing the watering in flipflops instead of rubber garden boots. She was missing the little toe on her left foot, the fourth and fifth toes from her right. I couldn't stop staring. Her feet looked terribly wrong, but also neat and smooth, with soft flat spaces that toes had once protruded from.

"When?"

She tilted her head, like the answer was so obvious she couldn't be sure I was really asking what I seemed to be asking. How had I not noticed for thirty years that she was missing three toes? But then, she'd put effort into preventing me from noticing, and I felt that old sense of being trapped, of being punished for not knowing things no one had told me, had actively not wanted me to know.

"That Christmas we spent at the cottage. When I got locked out. Frostbite. It wasn't clear they needed to come off until later."

"Did it hurt?"

"The surgery? Some. Not too bad."

"But then. At Christmas."

"Not really, actually. I couldn't feel much. It didn't hurt until later."

And I wondered what I had and hadn't understood, what secrets she'd revealed and what she'd kept, and how I was never going to know her, not really. I could have published that story after all, I thought. It would have slid right off of her, a kid's story, like Santa.

I don't think she ever would have read Moomintroll books, though. I never encountered them as a kid. I didn't know they existed until my wife, born in Japan, talked about how much she'd loved the tv show as a kid. She read them to our kids in a Japanese translation, which our kids put up with for a while until they started to ask more and more often for English, which I could tell gutted my wife but she didn't want to make too big a deal about it. Who wants to be the bad guy all the time? Who wants to be the bad guy about your own language? I took over bedtime stories, read through the English translations, and never totally grasped the appeal. Maybe you had to have first visited Moominvalley as a kid. The book that got me closest was *Moominland Midwinter*, where Moomintroll ventures out into the wide and unforgiving world. He thinks he's alone, in the towering dark. But maybe when Moomintroll went out exploring, Moominmamma woke up too, and watched him from the window, without him ever knowing. Maybe she had her own adventures. Even if she only slept, she slept her own dreams, and Moomintroll would never know, not really, what they were.

Grand Valley State University

"How to Survive"
The "Little Black City" and Columbus's Elastic Redevelopment in Works by Aminah Robinson and Adrienne Kennedy

Jared Hackworth

"Elastic Redevelopment" may be the best phrase to describe Columbus, Ohio's urban character. Columbus's twentieth-century history is marked by *elasticity*, an urban studies term denoting patterns of rapid expansion and redevelopment not impeded by natural or manufactured boundaries (Rusk 10–11). With a population of 913,175 in 2023, Columbus's rapid expansion shows remarkable elastic growth (US Census). Columbus's neighborhoods have faced much elastic redevelopment, particularly on the city's Black East Side.

Culturally, the Columbus region has gained a reputation as being "flyover country," conventionally assumed to be several steps behind cutting-edge cities on the coasts. However, the art produced in Columbus testifies to the city's culture and community, just as sophisticated and original as that found in New York or Los Angeles. The evocative multimedia artist Aminah Robinson and the transgressive playwright Adrienne Kennedy find creative ways to exploit the artistic possibilities of Columbus's elastic redevelopment and spotlight traditionally overlooked neighborhoods. Robinson and Kennedy, well known in Ohio, are rarely studied outside of Columbus, mainly due to their work's midwestern focus and experimental nature. Robinson, who lived from 1940 to 2015, grew up in the housing project Poindexter Village and remained in the area her entire life. Kennedy, who was born in 1931, grew up in Cleveland and attended The Ohio State University in Columbus. She then relocated to New York City, but her work never left Columbus; many of her plays feature characters from Ohio modeled after her youth.

Robinson's and Kennedy's works take up the pieces left by elastic urban growth and model the benefits of having a community that can withstand structural redevelopment. An examination of Robinson's and Kennedy's relationship to place necessitates both a turn to theories of urban elasticity and original archival research on the history of two successive neighborhoods on Columbus's Black East Side: the Blackberry Patch and Poindexter Village. Bringing scholarly attention to these previously overlooked neighborhoods helps shine a light on the way that residents responded to forces of elasticity in the mid-twentieth century. Both Robinson and Kennedy take up their neighborhood's history and pinpoint the exercise of power that enables the city's elastic redevelopment at the expense of its disenfranchised residents. Robinson's art depicts joy and adaptive responses to structural inequality in community life, while Kennedy calls attention to the danger of urban isolation. Robinson and Kennedy provide ways to represent Columbus in the face of the erasures threatened by elastic urban growth and pass on lessons learned in the city through the arts. The art this produces is itself uniquely elastic in form, creating a style distinctive to the often overlooked, mid-size city it represents.

Aminah Robinson: Elasticity and Form

Elasticity, characterized by rapid expansion, redevelopment, and suburbanization, sets Columbus apart from other midwestern cities. David Rusk defines elasticity as a city's ability to grow by encompassing new land when it is not hemmed in by natural resources or independent suburbs blocking its growth. Inelastic cities, by contrast, cannot expand outward, trapped between natural boundaries and pre-existing suburbanization (9). Columbus displays elastic growth through aggressive annexation, as Kevin R. Cox observes, so that "the city's tax revenues have expanded on a regular year-in, year-out basis" (15). Columbus's constant redevelopment and sprawl, unimpeded by natural barriers or expansion-resisting satellite communites, resembles a southern Sun Belt city much more than its northern Rust Belt neighbors.[1] As such, Cox sees Columbus as "out of place" and "out of step" with Rust Belt and Sun Belt cities, stuck somewhere in between (11). Urban elasticity has shaped Columbus's idiosyncratic character, creating tensions between its location in the Rust Belt and its Sun Belt–style suburbanization and uncontained growth.

While scholarly research has examined Columbus's elastic growth models, no studies have yet examined the impact of these patterns of development at the neighborhood level. The history of Columbus's Black East Side is often condensed to a footnote indicating the Blackberry Patch's demolition to make way for the construction of Columbus's first housing project: Poindexter Village. The Blackberry Patch had a thriving economy and social scene from its founding in the late 1890s until its destruction in 1940. Examining how Poindexter Village grew out of the Blackberry Patch provides the necessary historical and urban context for reading Robinson and Kennedy's work.

Nestled between Hawthorne Avenue and Milk Alley from 1890 to 1940, with a booming Black economy and unique development model that blended the Sun Belt and the Rust Belt, the Blackberry Patch resembled no other northern neighborhood. Resident Anna Bishop writes in her community history *Beyond Poindexter Village: The Blackberry Patch* that the neighborhood "looked exactly like the Cabin towns that people lived in down south" (Part 1, 4). Bishop reports that the new residents built a city in the North that looked like the South, with southern materials like scrap wood, pot-bellied stoves, and outhouses. This re-manufacturing of the land grew into a "little Black city," transforming the region (Bishop, Part 1, 4). Bishop interviewed Delsa Lattimer Grant, who remembered the economic prosperity of the little Black city in which everything she could want was "within walking distance" (Bishop Part 3, 18). Nimrod Allen, executive secretary of the Columbus Urban League, commented in 1922, "There are nearly one hundred business enterprises on East Long Street and vicinity," as the Blackberry Patch stood out as a bustling urban neighborhood (qtd. in Giffin 97).

In the late 1930s, Columbus officials took advantage of a new Federal Housing Administration program that funded redevelopment by demolishing the Blackberry Patch and constructing the public housing project Poindexter Village in its place.[2] Columbus's local housing authority heralded the change between the Blackberry Patch and Poindexter Village, celebrating elastic redevelopment for the good of the city. The Bulletin of the City of Columbus announced the end of the Blackberry Patch on January 8, 1940; Roger N. Addison, the President of the City Council, declared that the project would "vacate certain streets and alleys," a change that people were "praying" for (qtd. in Bishop, Part 4, 36). In 1940, when construction began on Poindexter Village, public housing was primarily a northern project.[3] However, the village style and expansive size of Poindexter Village suggest a Sun Belt elasticity distinguished from other northern, high-rise housing projects. The two-story brick buildings that constituted Poindexter Village blended into the nearby neighborhood despite adding over four hundred units. The neighborhood did not fulfill the statuesque stereotype of American public housing. Instead, it had standard-size windows and doors, front yards, sidewalks, brick streets, and buildings with only four to six units. During construction, in front of the village stood a sign stating, "On This Site Poindexter Village, A Low-Rent Housing Project, is being developed by the Columbus Metropolitan Housing Authority, Under Loan Contract with the Federal Works Agency, United States Housing Authority" (*Poindexter Village* 152). The government-issued sign, supported by a poured-concrete base, proudly announced a new neighborhood marked by elastic growth through a northern development program. Even though Poindexter Village was filled with many residents of the Blackberry Patch, many longed for their old homes while settling into the new, state-created neighborhood.

Visual artist and Poindexter Village native Aminah Robinson responds to the city's elastic growth patterns with expansive formal choices that highlight the continuity of community life across urban instability.[4] In her handmade monograph *The Ragmud Collection*, Robinson portrays the history and community of the Blackberry Patch and Poindexter Village with fold-out pages, handwritten text, paintings, descriptions, buttons, and thread. Made up of smaller chapbooks, the work is a collage of images, brief anecdotes, and historical scenes.[5] Robinson's *The Ragmud Collection* makes the distinctive elastic growth of Columbus explicit with its formal elasticity, using inventive materials and storytelling methods that draw their style from Columbus itself. Robinson takes up the tension between old and new neighborhoods, making art that showcases individual experiences of elastic redevelopment's imposed transformations.

Robinson demonstrates the unity of the Blackberry Patch's community through her visual art. In her piece "The 1930 Sit-In's by the Women of the Blackberry Patch" in *The Ragmud Collection*'s chapbook "Life and History of Afro-Amerikans," Robinson's buildings and color palette in the painting emphasize the Blackberry Patch's uniqueness (Figure 1). Robinson discusses the women of the Blackberry Patch, elevating their work to stand with the more typical titans of Black history. Robinson depicts these women in an eight-panel fold-out, giving their resistance to Columbus's local housing authority more space than any other historical figure in the chapter. All the text in the

Figure 1. Aminah Robinson, "The 1930 Sit-In's by the Women of the Blackberry Patch" in *The Ragmud Collection*, 1987–2008; Toledo Museum of Art, Ohio; digital reproduction by institution.

piece is handwritten, as Robinson's use of handwriting visualizes the importance of localized community knowledge in Columbus's redeveloping environment. The simplicity of handwritten script embossed upon the art makes local wisdom visible, standing against the loss of community life in rapid, elastic urbanization. She crafts a textual object that stresses the necessity of community information within Columbus's constantly shifting landscape. The streets are a brilliant yellow, and the homes are red and yellow, emanating a vividness of life and energy inside the community. At the same time, the sky darkens, a sign of a gathering storm. Robinson juxtaposes the vitality of the neighborhood and the gathering darkness behind it as the city government ignores the protests against Poindexter Village's construction.

In her illustration of the protest, Robinson depicts five women, proud of the "little Black city" they have built, holding a sit-in to protest the demolition of the Blackberry Patch. With dignified expressions, the women sit outside, protesting the change with cardboard signs reading "I Am A Private Property Owner—I have Rights! Amendment V" and "We Are The Rock!! Stay" (Figure 1). With this language, Robinson portrays a battle from within the Blackberry Patch. Their neighborhood was not a slum to be prayed for, but their chosen home. Sitting in wooden kitchen chairs and holding wooden signs, the women are only partially anchored, and the futility of their protest registers in the fragility of their materials. One woman sits on a small blue stool in the face of this redevelopment; her position in the piece momentarily impedes demolition despite her social and spatial precarity. In contrast to this stands the Poindexter Village sign put up by the Federal Housing Authority. While the women protest with homemade signs, the city pours the concrete foundations of redevelopment. Through these visual elements of vibrant color and the breakable materials of the residents' protest, Robinson exhibits the vitality of life in the Blackberry Patch and the insufficiency of its residents' Black-led protest against Columbus's urban planning decisions.

After the Blackberry Patch's demolition and Poindexter Village's construction, many Blackberry Patch residents began new lives in the neighborhood,

built upon the rubble of the old. Robinson leans into the promise of Poindexter Village's elasticity through her poetic imagery, idiosyncratic syntax, and
mixed-media construction in her text *A Street Called Home*. Robinson writes,
"The rooftops of Poindexter Village are as crowded with pigeons as the street is
with people. The people are the traffic. It's hard to see everything going on at the
same time" (1). With this image, Robinson develops the constant motion of an
elastically ever-expanding city—people blur into traffic, which becomes incomprehensible motion. Robinson utilizes pigeons on a roof to figure the crowds
in the street; both parts of the simile represent urban life. In this blurry view
of a rapidly expanding neighborhood, "[t]here's the drugstores, the shoe shops,
the beauty parlors, the schools, the churches, the theaters and hotels, the open
air markets. The nightclubs and musicians, the newspapers and restaurants—
they're all part of the street called home" (1). Robinson's idiosyncratic syntax
furthers the expansive quality of her list; the places begin to appear in pairs con-
joined with "and." Robinson builds momentum with this grammatically unnec-
essary conjunction—the street is bursting with a life that cannot be contained
in a sentence or traditional list structure. Envisioning a street with grit that stays
put despite redevelopment, Robinson writes, "that was a self-sufficient street; it
knew how to survive" (1). The street bursts with vitality: "People wove in and
out with their horses and carts and trucks; you could hear the street cries; people
bartered and bought and sold; people played and danced. Everything you could
need you could find on Mount Vernon Avenue" (1). Robinson's introduction
depicts urban space characterized by constant expansion and change.

The formal aspects of Robinson's work mimic the city's elasticity. Robinson's *A Street Called Home*, while fitting in a 9.5-inch by 10.5-inch rectangle
when on the shelf, folds out into a twenty-eight-panel narrative of the neighborhood. The medium of the book itself becomes elastic for Robinson; the form of
the street cannot be contained in a traditional book shape. Robinson crams figures into the scene, visualizing the immense blur of the city she discussed in the
introduction. The line quality captures the expansion of Columbus. (See Figure
2 for a representative excerpt of Robinson's street painting style, in "Life Throbs,

Figure 2. Aminah Robinson, "Life Throbs: Blackberry Patch" in *The Ragmud Collection,* 1987–2008; Toledo Museum of Art, Ohio; digital reproduction by institution.

Blackberry Patch," which depicts the neighborhood on the verge of transformation.) Robinson's forms lack neat edges and sometimes appear almost unnatural, such as the children bent sideways below the Mount Vernon sign and the dense crowd curving in on itself. Robinson's visualization of the street's pace allows her to represent the feeling of a rapidly expanding, elastic city, even while correctly recording every street's name.

Robinson's use of mixed media also highlights the importance of community ties that began in the Blackberry Patch and still survive in Poindexter Village despite rapid elastic growth. While the street is cramped, Robinson makes the community's connection literal with the thread going through their sightlines and interconnections—they have become part of the fabric of the city and the buildings. The buttons, tied directly to the people walking in the city, also tie directly to the street itself by helping to compose it. Like her images of protest, these images of Mount Vernon Avenue's bustling street life show the continuity of the Blackberry Patch and Poindexter Village, where community life becomes a strategy of resisting elastic redevelopment.

In *The Ragmud Collection*, Robinson pairs two pieces to underline that Poindexter Village's folklife requires the pre-existing foundation of the Blackberry Patch. Robinson centers the histories of redevelopment, noting the past is needed to interpret the present. The front cover of one chapbook proclaims "Folklife in Poindexter Village" (Figure 3). In this visualization of Poindexter Village, the title is enclosed, locked together to tell the folk stories of the block surrounded by buttons and thread that tie the community together. "Folklife" itself is of interest, with community self-definitions again taking center stage through her handwritten text. Robinson highlights the foundational nature of the Blackberry Patch in the second example. On that cover, the title "Blackberry Patch, Legends Hand Me Down" is surrounded by the same birds, repeating the pattern from the front cover, with stitching, birds, and figures. Robinson frames this story of elastic redevelopment as the legends of the community passing down the lessons they have learned. Painted lower on the page, nestled between a menagerie of animals and two Black figures, echoes the refrain

Figure 3. Aminah Robinson, "Folklife in Poindexter Village" and "Blackberry Patch: Legends Hand Me Down" in *The Ragmud Collection*, 1987–2008; Toledo Museum of Art, Ohio; digital reproduction by institution.

"Hand Me Down," as the community itself is passed on. Robinson proposes that the folklife of the Blackberry Patch has been handed down to Poindexter Village, creating a culture that survived neighborhood demolition. Her form echoes this—the button and thread that makes up her sweeping landscapes tie the neighborhood together in an elastic representation of Columbus's form.

Aminah Robinson's work establishes community life as a means of survival in elastic cities through her narrative painting. Despite the forced redevelopment of the Blackberry Patch into Poindexter Village, folklife and culture thrive through a network of relationships that survive elastic redevelopment. As stories and legends are passed down from the Blackberry Patch to Poindexter Village, the community fortifies itself against decisions from the local housing authority. The city's government may destroy their homes, but residents' community and culture cannot be uprooted. Robinson's art ultimately identifies how a community can resist forced urban redevelopment by preserving networks and inscribing history, representing the Blackberry Patch and Poindexter Village for generations to come. Her work depicts resilience and, at the same time, is itself an example of resistance. She develops a model for building and maintaining community life in the face of an elastically redeveloping Columbus.

Adrienne Kennedy: The Violence of Redevelopment

In contrast to Robinson's tight-knit community in *The Ragmud Collection*, Adrienne Kennedy's 1991 play *Ohio State Murders* unveils how Black outsiders lack the tools to survive Columbus's elasticity, facing isolation and violence. In the play, the Black writer Suzanne Alexander returns to The Ohio State University in the 1990s, where she gives a lecture about violence in her work. The lecture recounts her experiences as a student in the 1950s: she took literature courses, had an affair with white professor Robert Hampshire, gave birth to their twins, and was expelled from the university. Hampshire refused to interact with Suzanne or his children after their birth, and after Suzanne moved to the East Side, he murdered both of his daughters.[6] The plot of Kennedy's play could not be more different from Robinson's uplifting of community life, yet the two authors showcase the dangers of Columbus's redevelopment. Kennedy's play ceaselessly maps the destructive force of Columbus's elasticity, which destroys those not tethered to community.

Kennedy's play takes place on Ohio State's downtown campus, surrounding wealthy neighborhoods, and the East Side by Poindexter Village. Starting in the 1940s, Columbus and Ohio State utilized the East Side as a social research laboratory, conducting studies on the neighborhood. Cox writes that the changes in Poindexter Village were "led by major institutions like universities or hospitals that want[ed] to fortify themselves by, in effect, getting rid of 'them' from the surrounding neighborhood" (198–99). The university, wishing to assert regional dominance, worked to research poverty in Poindexter Village and create barriers for people from the East Side to have mobility to Ohio State's campus.

The relationship between Poindexter Village and Ohio State in the mid-twentieth century was tenuous at best. At the time, Ohio State was not fully integrated; many Black students lived in boarding houses in Black neighborhoods, predominantly in Mount Vernon and Poindexter Village.[7] This policy resulted in a double bind; students who lived in Poindexter Village did not fit in with white university culture or Poindexter Village's local Black culture. Poindexter Village residents were suspicious of anyone affiliated with the university. Most Black students arrived from out of town, stayed for a few years, and never developed community connections. Their days were spent on the North Side, returning to Mount Vernon boarding houses only for meals and lodging. Ohio State used the neighborhood for research and for housing Black students but also held the ultimate authority for the neighborhood's redevelopment.

The published criticism on Kennedy is wide ranging, largely focusing on her literary allusions, autobiography, and play with temporality.[8] Esther Beth Sullivan's recent article "To Be Free of Air: Narrative and Negation in the Alexander Plays" examines the intertextuality and negativity of Kennedy's text through an Afropessimist lens. For Sullivan, "the dramatic tension of Kennedy's play is not found in the story itself, but between *what* is uncontrollable about past events and *how* control is performed in present recollection" (162). Natalia Vysotska's "'Don't Go Away Mad': Adrienne Kennedy's *Ohio State Murders* as a 'Funnyhoused' *Medea*" explores Kennedy's intertextuality and autobiography in a similar light; the play's violence is a manifestation of the racism Kennedy faced in her own time as a student.[9] Vysotska asks similar questions as Sullivan: asking not "what?" but "how?" in Greek tragedy, moving to a "why?" in the play's final scenes (135). The critical landscape's insights into Kennedy's questions can be expanded with a turn to setting in addition to temporality. This urban studies intervention expands Sullivan and Vysotska's scope as Kennedy explores the how and why of both temporal narrative and the city's elastic character.

Kennedy's Columbus is a city with immense discriminatory elastic redevelopment. She depicts a cold, unfeeling city that remakes itself at every turn, eliminating people and segregating neighborhoods as it sees fit. Throughout the play, Suzanne Alexander is constantly remapping the spaces of Columbus. She is unable to grasp the city and encounters an everchanging landscape to which she cannot lay hold. The play's setting is "Night" (239). Set apart as its own line, Kennedy privileges the darkness and disquiet of evening. From this darkness emerges "Stacks: hundreds of books on 'O' level beneath the library at Ohio State. A window high in the distance from which can be seen University Hall, a vast dark structure" (239). Underground, the only site in view is "vast" and "dark"; the imposing environment can be understood only through its magnitude and illegibility.

Kennedy's urban mapping of Columbus constantly expands and reworks itself but never escapes the opening's illegible darkness. As Suzanne begins her speech in the present, she reflects, "When I visited Ohio State last year it struck me as a series of disparate dark landscapes, just as it had in 1949, the autumn of my Freshman year" (239–40). The city's cold, unfeeling landscape remains constant; it is an alienating "series" that remains dark and ungraspable (240). Throughout the play, she describes the campus as a "barrack-like structure," and she writes an "essay on loneliness and race at Ohio State" (241, 244). As a student, she grew "to dread the blocks bound by the stadium, the High Street, the vast, modern, ugly buildings behind the Oval, the dark old Union that was abandoned by all except the Negro students" (256–57). Every facet of the elastically shape-shifting campus is disorienting to Suzanne. To cope, Suzanne maps the campus. She "used to write down locations in order to learn the campus," recording,

> the Oval, behind the green, the golf hut, behind Zoology, the tennis courts beyond the golf hut, the Olentangy River, the stadium off to the right, the main library at the head of the Oval, the old union across from the dorm, High Street at the end of the path, downtown Columbus, the Deshler-Wallick, Lazarus, the train station. The geography made me anxious. / The zigzagged streets beyond the Oval were regions of Law, Medicine, Mirror Lake, the Greek Theater, the lawn behind the dorm where the white girls sunned. / The ravine that would be the scene of the murder and Mrs. Tyler's boarding house in the Negro district. (240)

The elastic, changing geography of Ohio State's campus disorients Suzanne and demonstrates the university's authority; she cannot interpret the landscape because of its rapid redevelopment. Suzanne says, "The geography made me anxious" (240). She experiences a campus constantly in flux, listing actual campus locations, such as "the Oval," and places known only by what they are not, such as the space "behind Zoology" (240). Robinson's lists in *A Street Called Home* take the same form; both authors gravitate towards listing and mapping as ways to represent the city's elasticity. The differences in their lists, Robinson's making space in a redeveloped neighborhood and Kennedy's distress in this ungraspable space, yield the same final result: a depiction of Columbus's elasticity that redevelops neighborhoods as it sees fit.

Kennedy's map of the disorientation and redevelopment of an elastic city is always uniquely tied to race. In this constantly changing city, the violence of segregation imposes strict boundaries even while the space itself is in constant flux.

Suzanne's Columbus is segregated; there are places for the white girls to "sun" while the boarding house is in the "Negro district" (Poindexter Village) (240). Prior to her expulsion, Suzanne lived in a dorm where "there were six hundred girls. Twelve of us were blacks. We occupied six places, rooming together two in a room" (242). The girls have places in the dining room at "tables where the Negro girls sat" (245). Sometimes, "the white girls gave parties in the dorm. But we were never invited" (252). The campus is segregated explicitly by dorm and implicitly by social codes. In the city,

> Very few Negroes walked on High Street above the university. It wasn't that you were not allowed but you were discouraged from doing so. Above the university was a residential district encompassed by a steep ravine. I never saw this ravine until the two days I visited Bobby at his house (the ravine was where the faculty lived). A year and a half later one of my baby twin daughters would be found dead there. (242)

Kennedy's Columbus is rigorously segregated by neighborhood—Suzanne's daughter is killed when she crosses the boundary. Kennedy notices the strict limits on its Black residents without community ties produced by the city's environment. There are places one can and can't go; there are places white families live and Black children are murdered. Kennedy writes, "The police now referred to Cathi's drowning as the Ravine murder," as even the murdered child becomes known only by her transgression of racial boundaries (257). Kennedy notes that violence against a Black child matters only on the white North Side; the location matters more than the dead child's name.

When Suzanne moves to Mrs. Tyler's boarding house on the Black East Side, Kennedy places Suzanne as an outsider. Suzanne reflects, "Sometimes Mrs. Tyler's neighbors shunned me" (251). Indeed, the descriptions of community life on the East Side, from Vernon Avenue to Poindexter Village, are surrounded by silence in the play. Suzanne lives there, yet is ostracized from community life entirely; she does not even attempt to map the neighborhood. Marked by Ohio State, she is distrusted by both her neighborhood and her university. Suzanne reads and reflects that "[a] city should have a sacred geography never arbitrary but planned in strict accord with the dictates of a doctrine that the society upholds" (247). Kennedy reveals Columbus's geography is planned against Suzanne; caught between Ohio State and Robinson's Poindexter Village, she cannot belong to either. Instead, her relationship to both is marked by violence—with Ohio State, the murder of her daughters, and with Poindexter Village, a painful, shunning silence.

The play is framed as Suzanne's lecture on violence in her work, a motif that stems from her daughters' murder. Suzanne opens her lecture by saying, "I was asked to talk about the violent imagery in my work; bloodied heads, severed limbs, dead father, dead Nazi, dying Jesus. The chairman said, we do want to hear about your brief years here at Ohio State but we also want you to talk about violent imagery in your stories and plays" (239). Kennedy opens the play with a connection between the violence of her fictional writing and years at Ohio State—the mention of the university is surrounded on both sides by descriptions of violent imagery. That the chairman is implying that there is no connection between her Ohio State years and violence could not be more false; for Suzanne, the two are deeply intertwined.

As the play reaches a climax, Hampshire, the father of Suzanne's twins, murders his other daughter. He masquerades as a graduate student researcher to murder Carol, allowing Kennedy to critique Ohio State's power in Poindexter Village. Suzanne says,

> Right after Easter Mrs. Tyler told me a grad student from Ohio State was coming that evening. He was doing a study of Negros in the Columbus area and had heard from campus housing that she kept students and was also a native of Columbus and knew a great deal about the depression years there and the development of the neighborhoods. (261)

With this, Kennedy sets up a standard trope of a graduate student—an unassuming, if annoying, researcher of the neighborhood. Research provides the best cover story for a white person to enter a Black neighborhood and commit a violent crime; the authority of Ohio State allays any suspicions. With this inclusion, Kennedy critiques the violence of Ohio State, constantly observing and experimenting on the neighborhood to the point that the intrusion has become invisible. And, with Ohio State–sanctioned neighborhood research as an invisibility cloak, Hampshire murders Carol and then kills himself. That Hampshire was "posing as a researcher" provides an excuse for his presence in the neighborhood; his tie to the city's most dominant institutions of the city protects him from suspicion. Even after his murder-suicide, "[t]he university protected Robert Hampshire for a long time. Nothing of the story came out in the papers. There were stories that a white professor had wandered into the Negro section of Columbus and was killed" (262). Kennedy's passive tone of "had wandered" and "was killed" serves to remove all blame from Hampshire himself and the university, implying that a neighborhood resident caused this death. Kennedy reveals that Ohio State's reputation is more valuable than the truth.

Kennedy's play ends with a return to Suzanne's creative work, allowing storytelling to serve as a resistance to violence even without the type of embedded, generational community knowledge that Robinson depicts. Suzanne ends the play saying, "Good-bye, Carol and Cathi. / Good-bye … / (Pause.) / And that is the main source of the violent imagery in my work. Thank you" (263). For Suzanne, the entire city is a place of institutional danger. Ohio State continues to hold power over Columbus, redeveloping and segregating its neighborhoods at will. And yet Kennedy is not silent; she chooses to write work that attends to this violence. Her work provides a resilient voice that interprets the dangers of urban redevelopment. Even though she lacks Robinson's community knowledge of neighborhood turnover, Kennedy's invitation back to speak at the university provides the opportunity for storytelling to respond to dominating power structures. Suzanne's narrative provides a strategy of resistance in the face of the invisible, dark dangers lurking behind urban design.

Conclusion

Robinson and Kennedy's works engage with Columbus as formal inspiration that provides new ways of meaning-making. Robinson builds representations of the Blackberry Patch and Poindexter Village that cultivate the history of redevelopment. Her mixed-media work reproduces Columbus's elasticity—as the city infinitely stretches out, so too do her unfolding book constructions. Kennedy treats the expanse and constant shift of the city differently, using references to elastic urban forms that expose the violent and isolating effects of the city's existing authorities. For her, institutions reshape the city's landscape regardless of the community's desires or rights. Both artists cultivate a style of elasticity unique to Columbus that critiques the city's redevelopment. Robinson's expansive form, with its lists, buttons, and threads, pulls the community together in resistance, even as Kennedy's mapping and violence underscore the danger that occurs when one is isolated from community. The destruction of Columbus's history and the redevelopment of its land inspire these authors' methodologies, enabling their tools of protest and resistance. Robinson and Kennedy resist elastic redevelopment that would erase their communities and repurpose urban forms in ways that preserve and continue the neighborhood's stories, creating models for life in a mid-sized, in-between city.

University of Illinois, Chicago

Notes

1. Rust Belt cities, located in the Northeast and Midwest, are characterized by dense early-twentieth century industries and now face declining populations, slowing economies, and inelasticity. Sun Belt cities, conversely, are located in the South and Southwest and exhibit sprawling suburban designs, skyrocketing populations, and elasticity (Cox 7).

2. From 1937 to 1950, three main policy shifts in public housing occurred: the 1937 Wagner-Steagall Housing Act, the 1940 Pause, and the New Housing Act of 1949. The 1937 Wagner-Steagall Housing Act prioritized density reduction, arguing that housing with an inappropriately high population density should be demolished and replaced with low-density housing (US Con-

gress). World War II resulted in the 1940 pause on public housing. When housing projects resumed in 1949, density restrictions were removed, with public housing often taking the form of high-rise buildings instead of single-family homes (McDonald).

3. Federal Housing Administration data reveal that 73,000 public housing units were built in the United States in 1940. Of these, 38,100 were single-unit buildings, and 11,700 were double-unit buildings—only 31% of public housing had three or more units, compared with over 50% having three or more units in 1960. The first year that the Federal Housing Administration collected regional data, in 1949, 84.3% of public housing units were built in the Northeast, with only 4.4% in Central states, 4.4% in the West, and 6.3% in the South (US Department of Commerce 23).

4. The critical work on Robinson has largely focused on her visual artwork, with catalogs published by the Columbus Museum of Art and the Toledo Museum of Art. See *Raggin' On: The Art of Aminah Brenda Lynn Robinson's House and Journals*, edited by Carole M. Genshaft.

5. Robinson's multimedia work is housed in the Toledo Museum of Art; this essay explores the facsimile the TMA published in 2010.

6. The 1992 play, as written, features a present Suzanne and a younger Suzanne, though the production's 2022 Broadway debut featured Audra McDonald in both roles, a later revision that Kennedy endorsed. As such, this essay does not routinely distinguish between the two Suzannes.

7. Individual academic departments decided whether to admit Black students at Ohio State. While Black students could attend the university, the psychology and English departments, among others, rejected Black students (Albright et al.).

8. See foundational earlier research in Philip C. Kolin's *Understanding Adrienne Kennedy*, in which he describes the autobiographical nature of the play, Ohio State as "a landscape for racial hatred," the division into two Suzannes, and the role of Hardy's novels (133). For Kolin, the play works by "reversing chronological time" (140). See also *Intersecting Boundaries: The Theatre of*

Adrienne Kennedy, edited by Paul K. Bryant-Jackson and Lois More Overbeck. The collection examines Kennedy's works in depth, from director's notes from past productions to critical essays.

9. Vysotska notes that "the action continuously zigzags among various points on the time axis" but is grounded by allusions to Hardy and classical works, especially *Medea* (121).

Works Cited and Consulted

Albright, Thomas, et al. "A Ruckus on High Street: The Birth of Black Studies at The Ohio State University." *Journal of Race and Policy*, vol. 9, no. 1, spring/ summer 2013, pp. 23–46. *Project MUSE*, muse.jhu.edu/article/933623.

Bishop, Anna. *Beyond Poindexter Village: The Blackberry Patch*. Ohio State University, 1982.

——. *Beyond Poindexter Village, Part 2: Heroes of the Blackberry Patch*. Ohio State University, 1982.

——. *Beyond Poindexter Village, Parts 3 & 4*. Ohio State University, 1991.

Blackford, Mansel G. *Columbus, Ohio: Two Centuries of Business and Environmental Change*. Ohio State UP, 2016.

Bryant-Jackson, Paul K. and Lois More Overbeck, editors. *Intersecting Boundaries: The Theatre of Adrienne Kennedy*. U of Minnesota P, 1992.

Cox, Kevin R. *Boomtown Columbus: Ohio's Sunbelt City and How Developers Got Their Way*. Trillium, 2021.

Genshaft, Carole M., editor. *Raggin' On: The Art of Aminah Brenda Lynn Robinson's House and Journals*. Ohio UP, 2020.

Giffin, William W. *African Americans and the Color Line in Ohio, 1915–1930*. Ohio State UP, 2005.

Kennedy, Adrienne. "Ohio State Murders." *Collected Plays & Other Writings*, edited by Marc Robinson, Library of America, 2023, pp. 239–63.

Kolin, Philip C. *Understanding Adrienne Kennedy*. U of South Carolina P, 2005.

McDonald, John F. "Public Housing Construction and the Cities: 1937–1967." *Urban Studies Research*, 2011. doi.org/10.1155/2011/985264.

Opam, Kwame. "Overlooked No More: Aminah Brenda Lynn Robinson, Whose Art Chronicled Black Life." *New York Times*, 26 Feb. 2021, www.nytimes.com/2021/02/26/obituaries/aminah-brenda-lynn-robinson-overlooked.html.

Poindexter Village Construction Journal, vol. 2, 1942. Columbus Metropolitan Library Digital Collections, digital-collections.columbuslibrary.org/digital/collection/african/id/25005/.

Robinson, Aminah Brenda Lynn. *The Ragmud Collection: Books by Aminah Robinson*. Toledo Museum of Art, 2010.

——. *A Street Called Home*. Harcourt Brace, 1997.

Robinson, Aminah, et al. *Symphonic Poem: The Art of Aminah Brenda Lynn Robinson*. Harry N. Abrams, 2003.

Rotella, Carlo. *October Cities: The Redevelopment of Urban Literature*. U of California P, 1998.

Rusk, David. *Cities without Suburbs: A Census 2010 Perspective*, 4th ed. Woodrow Wilson Center Press, 2013.

Sullivan, Esther Beth. "To Be Free of Air: Narrative and Negation in the Alexander Plays." *Theatre Journal*, vol. 74, no. 2, 2022, pp. 151–72. doi.org/10.1353/tj.2022.0043.

US Census Bureau, "Population Rebounds for Many Cities in Northeast and Midwest," 2024. www.census.gov/newsroom/press-releases/2024/subcounty-population-estimates.html.

US Congress. Public Law 75-896. 1937. www.govinfo.gov/app/details/COMPS-10348.

US Department of Commerce, Bureau of the Census. *Housing Construction Statistics: 1889 to 1964*. US Government Printing Office, 1966.

Vysotska, Natalia. "'Don't Go Away Mad': Adrienne Kennedy's *Ohio State Murders* as a 'Funnyhoused' *Medea*." *Complexions of Race: The African Atlantic*, edited by Fritz Gysin and Cynthia S. Hamilton, Lit Verlag Münster, 2005, pp. 121–36.

"Like Dinosaur Blood"
Cyclical Trauma in Donald Ray Pollock's
"Discipline" and "Real Life"

Keriann Kaufmann

Donald Ray Pollock's *Knockemstiff* (2008) is part of a proud tradition known as the short-story cycle. Situated in small-town Ohio, there are obvious comparisons to be drawn between it and the great *Winesburg, Ohio* by Sherwood Anderson; but *Knockemstiff* is a different text born of a different time. Unlike in *Winesburg*, there is no "normal" George Willard to ground the grotesqueness of the other residents. *Everyone* in Knockemstiff is damaged. There is no Winesburgian desperate respectability in Knockemstiff; instead, its residents seem to wallow in their depravity. The stories are loosely connected by place but also by some characters that make cameo appearances in each other's stories as well as some characters who are featured in more than one piece. The Knockemstiff of the stories is a bleak place with little economic development, social mobility, or entertainment. The people presented are shallow and self-serving but with a depth of pain that can be truly shocking.

There is more to *Knockemstiff* than its relation to Anderson. *Knockemstiff* stands as a portal into the minds of those forgotten by the American Dream—the belief that upward economic mobility is possible through sheer hard work and devotion to a capitalist society, regardless of birth or station, but also that the lack of success is a symptom of laziness and moral failing—and in doing so allows the reader to experience by proxy and exorcise the ghosts that haunt us still.

Pollock's *Knockemstiff* operates through what I term *cyclical trauma*—a pattern in which parents inflict their own psychological wounds upon their children, who then perpetuate these destructive behaviors onto the next generation. This cycle is both symptom and cause of the American Dream's failure in places like Knockemstiff. When the Dream's promise of upward mobility through individual effort proves impossible—economist Eunji Kim writes "absolute intergenerational mobility rates … have fallen by more than 40%" in recent decades—the resulting shame and frustration must be placed somewhere (39). In *Knockemstiff*, that displacement targets the next generation.

The Gothic serves as the perfect perspective through which to observe *Knockemstiff*. Though not writing about Pollock's work, Steven Bruhm states that "the Gothic has always been a barometer of the anxieties plaguing a certain culture at a particular moment in history" and the primary anxiety in *Knockemstiff* is the death of the American Dream (1). Bruhm writes that in contemporary Gothic "unconscious desires center on the problem of a lost object," which in *Knockemstiff* is the promise of economic mobility itself (3). However, the gothic elements in Pollock's work manifest as psychological hauntings rather than supernatural ones—parents become psychologically possessed by their own failures and project these traumas onto their children.

In the book *The Cambridge Companion to Gothic Fiction*, Jerrold E. Hogle introduces more elements to help define the Gothic tale, stating that it "usually takes place (at least some of the time) in an antiquated or seemingly antiquated space" and that "within this space, or a combination of such spaces, are hidden some secrets from the past" that "haunt the characters, psychologically, physically, or otherwise at the main time of the story" (2). In *Knockemstiff*'s psychological gothic, the "secrets from the past" are not supernatural but deeply personal—failed dreams, broken promises, and shattered expectations that parents cannot escape. Rather than an antiquated space, sometimes the characters are haunted by an antiquated mindset. Inherited trauma haunts, and parents pass on their pain to their children along with the behavior that pain promotes. The American Dream itself becomes a form of haunting when it transforms from promise to impossible burden, trapping families in cycles where children must fulfill what their parents could not achieve.

The chapter entitled "Discipline" takes the concept of cyclical trauma to Ouroborosian extremes. Narrated by Luther Colburn, this story follows the tragic tale of father and son. Luther was a body builder in his youth and entertains hopes of his son being named Mr. South Ohio. To reach this end, he plies his son, Sammy, with steroids and puts him through a grueling diet and exercise routine. One day while driving in the car, they encounter Sammy's main rival, Bobby Lowe, out showing off his routine in front of a wild crowd. Bobby approaches Sammy some days later to invite him to join him in a free competition in front of the McDonald's. Luther is vehemently against the idea and works Sammy all the harder for entertaining it. Eventually, Sammy sneaks out to participate in the competition, suffering a fatal heart attack during it. Luther attempts to go back to his routine, but he mourns the loss of the Mr. South Ohio title, and his son. Luther then decides to follow Sammy's example, going out to perform a body-building routine in the freezing cold on the spot where his son passed and ends up dying himself. In this way, Luther creates and concludes a cycle in which son follows father in his ambitions, and father follows son into the grave.

"Discipline" is haunted by its past, down to the very setting. Most of the story takes place in Luther's gym, an old gas station. Luther goes so far as to comment that "on rainy nights the fumes raising out of the oil-stained cement smelled like dinosaur blood" (120). In a sense, Luther has a good bit in common with the oil. Both come from a past greater than their present and both find themselves contained and forgotten in an old, run-down gas station. Luther looks at his past as a thing of glory, despite never winning Mr. South Ohio—greatness with a tragic end, much like the dinosaurs themselves. Luther's psychological haunting centers not on some distant historical past, but on his own personal failure—his inability to win the title that defined his sense of worth. The idea of a person or place being possessed by the past extends beyond Luther and the gym; in fact, it extends past one lifetime. Sammy is held captive, not by his own past, but by his father's.

Luther obviously sees Sammy as a reflection of himself, a second chance at living out his dream; but he also fears that his son takes after someone else: his wife. Luther worries that Sammy has a smaller frame, like his mother, telling the reader, "I kicked myself a thousand times for not knocking up some fat-ass Amazon with big bones" (121). The irony here is that he insists that Sammy sacrifice everything in pursuit of the Mr. South Ohio title, but Luther allowed himself to make a "subpar" decision in regard to relationships, likely because he had a preference for smaller women—if calling anyone who wasn't a "little bird of a thing" a fat ass is anything to go by (121). He did not sacrifice everything the way that he expects Sammy to. Indeed, when Sammy breaks from Luther's routine, the latter rages that "the little faggot was going for the easier, softer way, just like his mother always did" (121). Clearly, Sammy is never his own person in his father's eyes. He is either Luther or his mother but never Sammy. No matter what he does, he is plagued by his parentage, doomed to follow either his mother "who kept sneaking cigarettes and coffee until the cancer got her"—a death defined by weakness in the eyes of Luther—or his father, a life dedicated to strength that inevitably leads to decay anyway (121).

Pollock shares very little about Sammy, which is odd for a character so integral to the story. He says seven words in the entirety of the piece, never really getting to establish himself as a character. Instead, Sammy serves as a kind of looking glass for Luther. He serves as the blank wall on which his father projects his hopes and dreams. The reader never finds out if Sammy wants to be Mr. South Ohio or simply to please his father. In fact, the story, told from his father's perspective, is set in such a way that any agency the young man does show is almost immediately punished. With the way Luther tells the story, Sammy's disobedience is what ends up killing him. By choosing to go and join Bobby Lowe, Sammy is struck down seemingly out of the blue. The reader can recognize that Sammy's restrictive diet led to his death when the doctor says Luther's "son had a heart attack … and his cholesterol was … 600 to be exact" (123). Luther, however, in the light of this discovery, simply claims, "No, he was healthy as a horse. Shit, you saw him" (123), showing that Luther cannot accept that Sammy's death is more related to the conditioning Luther had been putting him through than to his disobedience. When Luther describes Sammy's dietary regimen, it comes across as nothing short of abusive:

> Every two hours I meted out creatine and fat burners and liquid protein.
> For breakfast, he got a spoon full of oatmeal; for dinner, a sliver of baked

fish. At night, I gave him wooden clothes hangers to chew on. "Shit, son, we're mostly powder anyway," I'd tell him whenever he started to cramp. "South Ohio!" I screamed every time he puked. (121)

Sammy was barely fed. While he may have been 18 at the time of his death, he had been in training for years, meaning that Luther had been habitually starving his son. Considering Luther has a habit of binging and purging, it is miraculous that Sammy didn't also have bulimic tendencies, if not full-fledged bulimia. When the doctor shares Sammy's cause of death, Luther cannot comprehend that Sammy was unhealthy because he was so muscular. Like his obsession with external gratification—such as the Mr. South Ohio title—Luther cannot see beneath the surface in terms of his son's health or even the relationship they have with each other.

There is nothing inherently wrong with seeing yourself in your child; however, Luther takes it to an extreme. He is haunted by his past of failure and projects that past onto Sammy, fulfilling the Gothic trope of haunting. In addition, he is fixated on one individualistic, narrow view of success, much like the American Dream. He fully views Sammy as a reflection of himself—the problem with that being that a reflection is not a person, it is an owned thing. Luther views Sammy as a kind of puppet that he can manipulate into achieving his dreams. The issue is that Sammy is a square block and Mr. South Ohio is a round hole, which is a fact Luther feels he needs to remedy. In the first line of the story, Luther says, "I fixed up my son, Sammy, right there in the parking lot of the Gold's, one cc in the hip" (117). Notice the verb used there, "fixed"—he sees Sammy's natural state as something that is broken and needs to be mended with steroids, maybe because of his smaller frame. Sammy as himself is not enough. This point comes to a head when they see Bobby Lowe flexing in front of the McDonald's—Luther says, "I suddenly realized that Willard Lowe's son was going to beat Sammy for the South Ohio, him of all people in the goddamn state. Willard Lowe was my one true enemy; I'd hated that prick since we used to fight over the plastic weight set in fourth-grade gym class" (119). Here the reader learns that it is not just Mr.

South Ohio that Luther craves but to beat a specific person for the title. We also see his insecurity with Sammy's ability to fulfill his dream. The interesting thing is that, just like Sammy, Bobby Lowe is defined by his parentage and not as his own person. Luther makes this even more clear when Bobby comes to his gym to suggest the competition:

> "Hey, Dad," Sammy said, "I think—"
>
>   "Shut up!" I yelled and then turned back to Bobby. "Look, I know what you're doing. Your old man was the same way, always fucking with me. Him and that goddamn stupid grin of his. Now get the fuck out of my gym!" (120)

We don't know what Bobby's intentions were, but, because of who his father is, Luther immediately jumps to conclusions and shuts him down. Interestingly, he also shuts down Sammy in this moment, refusing to allow the young man to express his opinion on the matter. This is also more than half the words Sammy says in the whole story, and he isn't allowed even a complete sentence. Reflections are to be seen and not heard, and as such Sammy doesn't get to have an opinion that differs from Luther's. He doesn't need to speak because Luther does all the talking for him.

Luther is convinced he never won Mr. South Ohio because he "looked like a starving rat clamping down on a chicken neck" when he smiled (119). As seen in the passage where Bobby visits the gym, Luther is maniacal about the smile. It is his one shortcoming as a body builder, and he envies Willard Lowe his smile. That makes it significant when, just before Sammy dies, Luther reports, "Then I saw it. It stretched across his face, gleaming like a toothpaste ad. I'd never realized Sammy could smile like that" (122). One might think Luther would take the time to reflect on *why* he had never seen Sammy smile like that, maybe consider his son's happiness for a moment, but instead his mind goes straight to Mr. South Ohio. After the paramedics stop attempting to resuscitate Sammy, Luther exclaims, "'Jesus Christ, that boy's the next South Ohio,' I said, grabbing the man

by the throat. 'He's got a smile that can beat the world. He can't be dead'" (122).
He does not say, "That's my son, he can't be dead!" He says, "That's Mr. South
Ohio." It is tragic that Luther's first thoughts go to the achievement of his dream
and not the wellbeing of his son, just as when he first saw the smile his thoughts
went to the competition and not to how happy his son appeared flexing in the
parking lot of a McDonald's. A page later, Luther does show some more feeling:
"'He's only eighteen years old,' I said, kneeling down beside the gurney and running my hand over my son's dead body" (123). Acknowledging Sammy's youth
is a step towards regarding him as a separate person. Notably, this is also the first
time that we see Sammy's body referred to as his own. Luther says "my son's
dead body," which hits hard both in the sense that a parent should never have
to bury their child but also because the corpse belongs to Sammy. It is not an
instrument for reaching Luther's goals or a reflection of the physical perfection
that he strived for but rather simply what it is: a body that once belonged to a
young man.

   After Sammy's death, Luther still finds himself stuck in the cycle of hauntings. Like any good Gothic protagonist, he is unable to escape from the past. Luther's habits lead him to follow his son as he "went back to [his] routine" (123).
Luther has spent more of his life single-mindedly fueled by one thing, one goal,
and with Sammy gone, so is the dream. He sees no other way to live than to continue as he had been, at his gym soaked in dinosaur blood. The notable excep-
tion here is that instead of being himself, he decides to reflect Sammy:

> I pulled on some old sweats, ate some aspirin. After sticking a stack of
> Sammy's Megadeth CDs in the stereo and cranking it up, I just start-
> ed doing set after set after fucking set. I pumped iron for eight hours
> straight, a personal best. Then around 2 AM, I took a scorching shower,
> shaved off all my body hair and greased myself down. (124)

He chooses to use Sammy's music to work out. He does the reps himself, not as
a trainer but like a trainee, setting his own personal best from the days when he

himself was a body builder. Then he acts not as a coach but as a contestant by shaving his entire body and applying grease to himself. He is behaving as though he is going to be in a competition. More specifically, he is roleplaying as Sammy. Continuing his Sammy impersonation, he heads to the McDonald's parking lot to the very spot where his son died. He then strips down and "started off with some basics, going through them slowly, trying to warm up. Then I went into some secret stuff that I'd been working on for years, shit I was going to show Sammy when he was good enough" (124). In this moment, Luther reenacts Sammy's life as he foresaw it. From beginner to pro, he moves his body in the ways he taught his son, and in the ways he planned to teach Sammy. For a moment, he is the reflection of Sammy and Sammy lives through him.

As he goes through his routine, Luther transcends himself. Even more than an avatar for Sammy, he becomes an avatar of nature. "My muscles ground against each other like ice floes in the cold silence," he claims: the imagery he uses propels him to being more than a man (124). In his moment of dedication to his son, Luther becomes primeval. This cannot last forever: "as morning approached, I lifted my frozen arms for one more shot and a loud crack shook the entire valley. A white light exploded in my head and my body shattered into a thousand tiny pieces. Then I blew like flakes of dirty snow down the gray, empty street" (125). The crack of his body breaking doesn't just affect him, it rocks the very landscape. The parking lot is witness to the birth, and death, of something visceral. Then, just as for an instant he was more than a man, he dissolves into less than. He comes to reality and presents himself as he sees it: dirty flakes of little significance. In a tick of dust-to-dust symmetry, Luther follows his boy to the grave and completes the cycle of trauma.

"Discipline" shows the middle and end of the cycle of trauma, but the first story of the series, "Real Life," shows the beginning. It is not only Sammy who finds himself following in his father's footsteps. Bobby, the narrator and protagonist of "Real Life," is traumatized by his father's approval, which can be won only through acts of violence.

"Real Life" shows the reader how Sammys are made. Dysfunction is achingly apparent in nearly every character, from a wife so desperate to entertain her husband that she'll fellate a hotdog in front of her son, to a man who takes swigs of alcohol out of a used ash tray because drinking from the bottle would make him an alcoholic (2–3). "Real Life" follows Bobby on the night when his parents take him to the drive-in theater. Bobby nips at his fingertips throughout the opening of the show, a nervous habit that comes out in full force around his father. By the time the main feature—*Godzilla*—begins to show, Bobby's father Vernon decides to take his son to the bathroom. While there, Vernon releases a string of obscenities that leads another man with his young son to demand that he watch his language. Vernon pretends to be cowed and then sucker punches the man, beating him viciously in front of his son. The other boy ends up attacking Bobby, much to Vernon's delight. At his father's prompting, Bobby beats the boy, breaking his nose. Vernon grabs his son, and they race back to the car, pulling out of the theater as sirens are heard in the distance. Vernon is pleased with Bobby, perhaps for the first time, and praises the boy for his violence. That night, Bobby lies in his bed, lapping the blood of the other boy off his knuckles, and reflects that he wants more. More of *what* is not entirely clear: more blood, more approval from his father? The two are inextricably linked.

Bobby does not disappoint his father; he proves that he had not been "ruined" by his mother—despite the fact that earlier in the story Vernon opines to Bobby that "you act more like your damn mother every day" (5). Bobby is the closest thing that Knockemstiff has to a George Willard. Appearing in three of the stories collected in the anthology, he is the only main character the reader sees grow into adulthood, and he represents the standard of normality, meaning the most common presentation of traits within a group. Therefore, it is telling that misogyny is so present in his stories as it reflects the cultural norm of the town—what passes for "normal" in Knockemstiff is violence, abuse, and the systematic devaluation of women and children.

Even the title of this first story, "Real Life," suggests the reality of Bobby's experience and breaks the audience away from any expectation of fairy tale happy endings Throughout *Knockemstiff*, multiple characters, including Bobby, attempt to break away from the town, only to find themselves inexplicably pulled back in. Even Agnes claims, "I'd be outta this hellhole in a minute if it wasn't for these kids" (3) when speaking to her sister on the phone. In many ways, Knockemstiff seems inescapable to the people who live there. But it is not some deep love of the land that keeps them trapped, but a learned and ingrained pattern of behavior that dates back to the early days of every resident in Knockemstiff, as is the case for Agnes.

As earlier established, Bobby is the closest character to an everyman within *Knockemstiff*. He is the character the reader sees grow and who appears more than tangentially in multiple stories. His will be our sample of childhood in Knockemstiff. "Real Life" begins with the line "my father showed me how to hurt a man one August night at the Torch Drive-in when I was seven years old. It was the only thing he was ever any good at" (1). This immediately sets up the dynamic of the father-and-son relationship the reader will glimpse during the story. Bobby learns from his father, but he does not respect him as a person, merely as a vehicle for violence. For his part, Vernon is even more dismissive of Bobby, referring to his teeth as "dick skinners" and telling him to get his head "out of [his] ass" (4–5). The disrespect becomes public humiliation when Vernon and Bobby enter the bathroom where "the smell of piss and popcorn hung in the hot dead air like insecticide" (5). Vernon encounters one of his friends and reports, "'I shit you not, Cappy,' my father was telling the man, 'This boy's scared of his own goddamn shadow. A bug's got more balls'" (5). He also announces to the bathroom full of strangers that "Bobby shoulda been a girl," the highest of insults from a man such as Vernon (6). This is a relationship of belittlement and emotional abuse.

There is one aspect of Vernon's personality that is hinted at but never explicitly stated: he cares far too much about what other people think. Of all the characters in *Knockemstiff*, Vernon is the one most consumed by the American Dream and outward shows of wealth. He is constantly buying new cars—the one they ride in in the story is his "third set of wheels in a year"—even though the family cannot pay their electricity bill (2). The American Dream is predicated on the idea that someone can "make it," that they can amass enough goods to show the world they are a success. Following the logic that wealth equals merit and poverty equals laziness, Vernon strives to show the world that he has merit according to the Dream. He craves the respect of those around him, which is why the way he chooses to punish Bobby most of the time is to degrade him in front of others, be it his mother or the men of the bathroom. He also drinks from the car's ashtray because he refuses to pull from the bottle in case people see him as a "goddamn wino" (3). In the bathroom, "the biggest sonofabitch I'd ever seen" brusquely confronts Vernon about his language, both figuratively and literally belittling Vernon in front of a crowd (6). Even worse, he calls Vernon "a damn drunk" in front of everyone, the very thing he was willing to take a mouthful of ash to avoid earlier in the night (7). Vernon cannot take the insult lying down and so attacks the man while his back is turned, and his retaliation is brutal:

> The room went quiet for a moment but when the man's son started screaming, my father exploded. He circled around the man, kicking the ribs with his work boots, stomping on the left hand until the gold wedding ring cut through to the bone of his finger. Dropping to his knees, he grabbed the man's glasses and snapped them in two, beat him in the face until a tooth popped through one meaty cheek. (8)

This is a personal assault taken to a degree that forces others to intervene and pull Vernon away. Vernon tries to make the man suffer beyond the physical, as seen when he breaks his glasses; he tries to break him down in any way he can.

While his father is confronted by a much bigger man over his language, Bobby instead focuses on the son of the other man—"a boy [his] size," noting "he looked happy, and I hated him instantly" (6). Bobby expresses a stronger feeling of loathing for the boy than for the father who has been abusing him since the start of the story, all because he is happy. The relationship he imagines the boy has with his father—a healthy one—fills him with such rage that he *hates* the boy. This hatred comes to a head when, after the larger man has been bru-talized, the young boy attacks Bobby. Vernon yells, "You back down, I'll blister your ass!" leaving his son with few alternatives (9). Nature and nurture come to a head in Bobby when he thinks, "I didn't want to fight, but the boy was nothing compared to the old man" and proceeds to fight back (9). He eventually gains ascendancy, breaking the other boy's nose before fleeing along with his father from the scene of the crime.

Following the fight is the first time any tenderness is shown between father and son. Vernon "stopped and knelt down in front of me. He was gasping for air. 'You did good, Bobby,' he said, wiping the sweat from his eyes. He gripped me by the shoulders and squeezed. 'You did real good'" (9). This is the only moment Vernon contacts another person without the express intent of doing them harm. Bobby has earned his father's respect, if only for the moment, by being just like him. Vernon cannot wait to share the news that his son is tough, first gushing to Agnes about the experience—claiming that the boy was twice the size of Bob-by—before yelling "This is the best night of my life!" out the window (10). It is interesting that even then he embellishes the story to impress his wife, as Bobby very specifically noted that he and the boy were the same size. She does not pro-vide the reaction he wants. Agnes is concerned for her son and calls Vernon a "sick bastard," and he responds in a familiar fashion: "I looked up just as he bashed my mother with his forearm. Her head bounced against the window. 'You sonofa-bitch!' she cried, covering her face with her hands" (10). Vernon will attack any-one who threatens his standing, no matter who is watching. In fact, he seems to prefer an audience so that others know how big and tough he is. Nurture wins out in Bobby when he "scooted across the seat and sat behind my father as we raced home" symbolically aligning himself with the violence that he helped perpetrate and relinquishing whatever softness his nature contained (10–11). Indeed, the boy who acts "more like [his] damn mother every day" abandons her and that behavior when he scooches over to his father's side. Notably, being on his father's side may bring him closer to the man, but it also shields him from Vernon's gaze, representing the protection he gains from appeasing and pleasing his father.

The cycle of abuse and trauma on display in this story takes on literal form in the mind of Bobby. On the ride home, he thinks, "*you did good*, I kept saying to myself, over and over. It was the only goddamn thing my old man said to me that I didn't try to forget" (11, italics in original). His thinking becomes a cycle in his own mind, repeating the lesson he had learned that night and cementing it in his brain—be like his father and life will be easier, his biggest abuser will approve of him. Bobby clings to the only positive reaction he has ever had from his father, burning the words into his mind and in doing so cementing the behavior. This idea is driven home when later that night, sitting alone in his room, Bobby licks the blood of the other boy off his hands and comments, "I wanted more. I would always want more" (12). As the title of the short story suggests, this is real life. Bobby is not saved from an abusive situation, nor is his mother. Instead, he leans into what it takes to survive: being who his father wants him to be. He inherits Vernon's bloodlust and is after more. Is blood the only thing that Bobby wants more of, though? Or is he after the thrill of a relationship formed and acceptance given. He gives up everything in the story to gain his father's approval: the movie he has been waiting all summer to see, the connection he has with his mother, his gentle nature, his sense of right and wrong. Everything about Bobby has been thrown to the wind, and all he is left with is wanting more because if his father's approval is not kept, he has lost all those things for nothing.

Throughout "Real Life," the reader is shown the way that a Knockemstiff resident is warped by his upbringing to eschew all the skills he needs to build meaningful relationships. The autodiegetic format of Pollock's writing—as opposed to the heterodiegetic nature of Anderson's—offers greater insight into what Robert Luscher calls "the personal degeneration and spiritual emptiness" of the townsfolk (199). We get an opportunity to know exactly how Bobby feels and what he is thinking in any given moment. We have front-row seats to the decisions he makes that will shape his future self. This mode of writing also takes the onus of the benefit of the doubt off the reader. Unlike *Winesburg*, Knockemstiff's inhabitants do not get an affable George Willard who simultaneously contrasts them with his normality while offering an often-generous look at their shortcomings. Instead, the reader knows there is no nobility behind their poverty, just desperation, substance abuse, and PTSD. Folks of the holler are meaner than their Winesburgian counterparts; they murder, rape, and steal on more than one occasion, all for the reader to see.

Layne Neeper compares Pollock to one of the most famous figures in American Gothicism: Flannery O'Connor. Neeper describes O'Connor's formula as "grotesque character X encounters violent act Y and is ironically redeemed by grace even in the moment of extreme circumstance" (48). Grotesques abound in both Knockemstiff and Winesburg, and in the case of the former, there is no shortage of violent acts, so all that is missing is a moment of purifying Christian grace. But grace has no place in Knockemstiff, for "even the church had fallen on tough times" and women threaten to kill each other in front of the pastor (Pollock 157). Rather than redemption, the order of the day in Knockemstiff is, according to Neeper, "deterministic degeneration, irrevocable decline into corruption and loss" (48). This degeneration does not stop with the individual but rather forms a cycle of trauma in which the present is stalked by the past. The meanness of the people of Knockemstiff is not born of a vacuum but rather a learned trait passed from, in this case, father to son. This reflects the Gothic trope of hauntings though they are psychological reiterations of the past rather than spiritual.

Cyclical trauma reveals a pattern on display in *Knockemstiff* that leads to the decay of the town—a lack of growth and an obsession with the past that leads to its resurgence. With no new perspectives and hearts resistant to change, the people of Knockemstiff molder in place.

All of this comes to be because of the American Dream. Both Luther and Vernon are obsessed with status and glory, with external shows of success that can be levied into social currency. One desires for his son to be an award-winning body builder, measuring his worth through his hard work and ability to achieve; the other craves respect from his community, which he attempts to earn through fancy cars and grandstanding, seeing his son as just another facet of life by which to find glory. Neither man views his child as a separate person, but rather as a reflection of himself and his success. In the same way, the American Dream works to convince people that outward signs of success are the only kind that truly count and that failing to attain those signs of success makes someone unworthy of the gentler things in life. When poverty and loss become moral failings—after all, only hard work is required for success, so anyone who has not "made it" is simply lazy—the path towards abuse is laid. This mind set is like a virus, replicating itself from father to son, one generation to the next, creating a cycle of abuse in which the present is constantly being molded into the shape of the past.

The folk of the holler are held captive by the mindset of the American Dream, which separates people and traps them in past-obsessed cycles. When the American Dream's promise of mobility proves impossible to achieve, the resulting shame and frustration must be displaced onto the next generation. Children become scapegoats for their parents' failures and vehicles for their parents' abandoned ambitions. The gothic elements of Pollock's work—the haunting of the present by the past—manifest not as supernatural phenomena but as psychological patterns that trap families in destructive cycles. Bobby's transformation from a gentle child to a violence-craving adolescent and Luther's obsessive projection of his failed dreams onto Sammy demonstrate how personal trauma becomes cyclical when parents view their children as extensions of themselves rather than as separate individuals. In this way, *Knockemstiff* serves as both a critique of the American Dream's false promises and a warning about what happens when a society offers no meaningful alternatives to the myth of self-made success. The cyclical trauma that defines Knockemstiff is not just a product of individual pathology but of a cultural mythology that demands success while making it impossible, creating endless cycles of disappointment, abuse, and death.

University of Denver

Works Cited

Bruhm, Steven. "Contemporary Gothic: Why We Need It." *The Cambridge Companion to Gothic Fiction*, edited by Jerrold E. Hogle, Cambridge UP, 2002, pp. 259–76.

Hogle, Jerrold E. "Introduction: The Gothic in Western Culture." *The Cambridge Companion to Gothic Fiction*, edited by Jerrold E. Hogle, Cambridge UP, 2002, pp. 1–20.

Kim, Eunji. "Entertaining Beliefs in Economic Mobility." *American Journal of Political Science*, vol. 67, no. 1, 2023, pp. 39–54. doi.org/10.1111/ajps.12702.

Luscher, Robert M. "Down the Road from Winesburg: The Spatiotemporal Aesthetics of the Short Story Sequence in Donald Ray Pollock's *Knockemstiff* and Laura Hendrie's *Stygo*." *Short Fiction in Theory and Practice*, vol. 3, no. 2, 2013, pp. 193–210.

Neeper, Layne. "Appalachian Apocalypse: Pollock's *Knockemstiff* and the Unredeemable Underclass." *Kentucky Philological Review*, no. 28, 2013, pp. 45–53.

Pollock, Donald Ray. *Knockemstiff*. Broadway Books, 2009.

Meridel Le Sueur and the Crafting of Proletarian Regionalism in the Midwest in the 1930s, 1940s, and Beyond

Michael C. Steiner

eridel Le Sueur had a complex relationship with the land and people of her native Midwest. Across nine and a half decades, from her birth in Murray, Iowa, in 1900 to her death in Hudson, Wisconsin, in 1996, she attained a deeply rooted, often fraught connection to her region. In a 1975 interview she told Patria Hampl, "As a child, I felt in my bones the immense contradictions of American midwestern life and also its hidden potential strength and beauty." The heartland, she continued, is "not just the sentimental place, but the place of massacres, a place of death as well. We have to look at our region as something we took from the Indians and that was taken from us" (Hampl 62). Le Sueur expressed forceful feelings about the Midwest throughout her life, describing, for example, in the 1937 short story "Our Fathers," the "hunters, trappers, killers, bitter women, along with stillborn babies and boys who tramped the prairies … pushing the margins back and back … preparing for a great destiny which never came to them" ("Our Fathers" 117).

Le Sueur's faith in proletarian regionalism grew from a deeply ingrained, often conflicted identity with the Midwest. Despite her keen awareness of the region's profound flaws—its shallow roots, class struggles, racial strife, and history of exploitation—she consistently professed a hard-earned, deeply rooted love of place. "I'm a passionate Midwesterner, my being springs from the Middle West, the landscape and the people that nourish me," she told another interviewer in 1982. "I have always felt that the region in which you live creates your body, creates your spirit, creates your whole being," she emphasized (Goldman).

Le Sueur knew the strengths and weaknesses of her fellow Midwesterners, feeling both joy and despair about their troubled relationship with the land and each other. Yet she held steadfast to her faith that the common folk would awake to forge a better world. "The people are a story that is long, incessant, coming alive from the earth in better wheat … persistent and inevitable," she memorably affirmed in 1945. "The people always know that some of the grain will be good, some of the crop will be saved," she declared, and "that from the bloodiest year some will survive to outfox the frost" (Le Sueur, *North Star Country* 321).

Her hope that Midwesterners would "outfox the frost" to build a truly equitable society free from the failings of capitalism may seem foolishly utopian in face of the capitalistic counter-progressive forces dominant in her era and ours. V. F. Calverton's 1931 condemnation of regionalists like Le Sueur as "modern day Don Quixotes tilting at steel windmills" (40) or Bernard DeVoto's 1936 lampoon of naïve Midwesterners spouting "coterie manifestos … reeking of the soil" exemplify wide-ranging criticisms in the 1930s (414). University of Iowa art historian H. W. Janson's attack on his colleague Grant Wood in 1946 and his accusation that "almost every one of the ideas of the regionalist credo could be matched more or less verbatim from the writings of Nazi experts on art" (Janson 186) echoed a common equation of regionalism with perilous right-wing politics that persists into the twenty-first century.[1]

How Le Sueur advocated a "proletarian regionalism" despite such condemnations and maintained a mythopoetic love of place is the basic theme of this essay. To trace the rise and fall and possible rebirth of her radical regional hope, this paper follows three steps. It begins with an overview of the first half of Le Sueur's vivid life, from her birth and itinerant upbring in the 1910s and '20s to her emergence as a feminist voice in the Communist Party in the 1930s and '40s. The essay then focuses on Le Sueur's rising faith in a midwestern-forged proletarian regionalism and struggle along with other regionalists to have their grass roots visions accepted by the Party hierarchy. Her efforts to forge a radical regionalism during these years are primarily traced through three early publications—her short story "Corn Village" (1931), her creative reportage "I Was Marching" (1934), and her speech "Proletarian Literature and the Middle West" (1935)—that paved the way for her regional masterpiece *North Star Country*, published in 1945. A brief final section summarizes how Le Sueur's work across these decades reflects the promise and pitfalls of building a radical, feminist-based regionalism in the Midwest and elsewhere from the 1930s to the present.

Midwestern Background and Early Life, 1900–1930

Meridel Le Sueur was born in February 1900 in Murray, Iowa, where her father, William Wharton, served as a Disciples of Christ minister. Her mother, Marian, who came from a long line of midwestern abolitionists, was a 19-year-old student at Drake University in Des Moines, Iowa, when she met and married the charismatic minister in the mid-1890s. Soon after their marriage the young couple moved to a series of small congregations across the Great Plains, eventually arriving in San Antonio, Texas, in 1910, where 10-year-old Meridel and two younger siblings experienced increasing conflict and eventual separation between their parents.[2]

William and Marian were a mismatched couple. The stressful relationship between a domineering husband, described by Meridel as a "Lothario preacher," and his idealistic wife, a vigorous advocate for birth control and women's rights, ended in 1910 when Marian fled with her children from Texas and began divorce proceedings. "Because the state of Texas made women and children chattel with no property or civil rights," Le Sueur wrote of this experience, "my mother kidnapped us in the middle of the night and fled north like a black slave woman" to Oklahoma, "where the laws were more liberal" ("Ancient People" 22).

Between the ages 10 and 17 Meridel grew up in a series of reform-minded, female-based households in Oklahoma, Minnesota, and Kansas, as her mother became increasingly active as a socialist advocate and orator for women's rights, temperance, and birth control. "She barnstormed the little towns," her daughter recalled, "to speak in tents with quartets, horn blowers and juggling acts, but always the farm and village women waited to speak to her and she saw their eyes, and the children at their skirts, and their weighted and torn bodies" (Le Sueur, *Crusaders* 42–43).[3] When Meridel was in her early teens in 1914, her mother joined the faculty at the small, newly founded People's College in Fort Scott, Kansas, a leftist institution of learning that Le Sueur recalled as "a radiant center, not only for the Midwest, but for travelers who came through from all over the world" (*Crusaders* xxi).

It was at the People's College that Le Sueur met Helen Keller, Eugene Debs, Lincoln Steffens, Ella (Mother) Bloor, Alexander Berkman, and other radical reformers who spoke there. It was here that 14-year-old Meridel also met shell-shocked survivors of the Ludlow massacre in Colorado who had come to Fort Scott to raise money, an experience that left a lasting impression. While teaching at the college, her mother met and married Arthur Le Sueur, a socialist lawyer who had recently lived in Minot, North Dakota, and who would have a positive impact on his stepdaughter's life. Meridel admired how her idealistic stepfather "stood on the soap box with the Industrial Workers of the World during the free speech fight and was arrested with them" and would remain a tireless advocate for justice who never lost faith in the wisdom of the masses ("Ancient People" 38).

Within weeks of the nation's entry into the First World War in November 1917 the People's College was ransacked and burned to the ground by right-wing vigilantes, and the Le Sueur family fled to Minneapolis, Minnesota. From their house on Harriet Avenue, Marian and Arthur continued to defend radicals and promote freedom of speech despite the repressive efforts of the Minnesota Commission of Public Safety, which, in Le Sueur's words, acted "like a fascist junta" to silence them (*Crusaders* xxiii). It was through her parents' organizing work until their deaths in the early 1950s that Meridel continued to meet left-wing luminaries, among them Big Bill Haywood, Emma Goldman, John Reed, Margaret Sanger, Theodore Dreiser, and Carl Sandberg (Coiner 75–76; Hedges 2–3).[4] Because of their politically radical home life, the Le Sueur children were ostracized at their public schools, and Meridel dropped out as a 17-year-old, ending her formal education.

Eager for alternative schooling and with her parents' encouragement, Le Sueur moved to Chicago to attend Bernarr MacFadden's alternative Physical Culture School in 1917. A year later she traveled to New York to live in a Greenwich Village anarchist commune with Emma Goldman and study acting at the

American Academy of Dramatic Arts. Of her challenging years of late adolescence in New York, Le Sueur remembered a visiting Edna St. Vincent Millay referring to her as "the corn virgin of the prairies" (Pratt 226). In 1920 she travelled to the West Coast, and after a deeply disillusioning stint as a stunt woman and silent movie extra in Hollywood in the early '20s, Le Sueur moved on to San Francisco, where she worked briefly as a left-wing radio host as well as the voice of Betty Crocker.

She joined the Communist Party in 1924 and began writing articles for the *Daily Worker*. With the literary guidance of Wisconsin writer Zona Gale, Le Sueur published her first short story, "Persephone," in *Dial* magazine in May 1927.[5] She was arrested in San Francisco for protesting the Sacco and Vanzetti executions in August 1927, gave birth to her first child after returning to St. Paul in 1928, and lived in the Upper Midwest until her death in 1996 (*Crusaders* xi–xxix).[6]

Le Sueur emerged as a prolific proletarian writer at the peak of her power during the 1930s. To support herself and her family in that decade, she produced over two dozen pieces of radical reportage; nearly thirty short stories; a book, *Worker Writers*, that served as a manual for the night classes she taught through the Minnesota branch of the WPA; a novella, "The Horse," published in 1934; and a series of poems and popular pieces appearing in *Vogue* and *Harper's Bazaar*. During the '30s, she also wrote a searing feminist novel, *The Girl*, that remained unpublished until 1978 (Hedges 8).[7]

Living a financially precarious life and raising two daughters—Rachel, born in 1928, and Deborah, born in 1931—as a single mother, Le Sueur poured her energy into writing about and promoting a wide range of left-wing causes. Much of her material came from direct experience, for example, several months spent "living in a Minneapolis community of women squatting in an abandoned warehouse" (Hennessy 18). The warehouse period became the inspiration for *The Girl* and was the site where she and a group of working-class women writers "met every night to raise our miserable circumstances to the level of sagas, poetry, cry outs" (*Girl* 183). She organized midwestern writers' conferences, helped edit and launch several radical regional magazines, held office in the John Reed Club, served as vice president of the League of American Writers, persisted as a feminist writer and journalist within the male-dominated Communist Party, and was one of the few women to speak at the American Writers' Congresses in 1935 and 1937.

She forged friendships with Richard Wright, Jack Conroy, Nelson Algren, Sanora Babb, Tillie Lerner Olsen, Josephine Herbst, and other radical heartland regionalists who opposed the dictates of the East Coast–centered Communist Party. With them she worked to create a grass roots aesthetic that drew directly upon the voices of working-class people. Although Le Sueur maintained her ties to the Communist Party throughout her life, her midwestern radicalism, determined feminism, and "intense lyricism regarding the land" bravely contradicted party orthodoxy throughout the 1930s, 1940s, and beyond (Denning 220).

Before being largely silenced during the "dark time" of 1950s and '60s for her political beliefs and constantly harassed by FBI agents, Le Sueur achieved at least two major creative breakthroughs. She worked to bring a much-needed female perspective to the male-dominated left, and she promoted a left-wing vision of regionalism. Affirming her feminist vision, she wrote in her journal in 1934, "There is no use building the communist party on dogmatism and leaving out the tenderness, the essential touch" (Coiner 96). Reaffirming this in a 1985 interview, she emphasized how "I never looked upon the Left as being something you just submitted to. I fought them. I kept my lyrical style" (Coiner 108).[8]

Her sensitivity to women's emotions also ran against mainstream canons in the 1930s and '40s. After a *Scribner's* editor in the early 1930s rejected her story about childbirth and urged her to write more like Hemingway, for example, she curtly noted that "fishin', fightin', and fuckin' were not my major experiences" (qtd. in Coiner 108). The deep female grounding of her work would be recovered and praised in the 1970s when, as a recent critic observed, "Le Sueur was hailed as an icon of feminism, celebrated for her devotion to working-class women and her ardent feelings for nature and Native American culture" (Wald, *Exiles* 99).

While striving to instill a more subjective, racially diverse female perspective to the left during the 1930s and early '40s, Le Sueur also promoted a forward-looking working-class regionalism, a significant contribution that deserves equal attention. Starting in the early 1930s, she created a revolutionary vision in opposition to the nostalgic and reactionary regionalisms on the right that filled much of the landscape. In doing so she "wed a feminist consciousness," in Douglas Wixson's words, "to progressive ideals in midwestern settings" (358). "Hers was a grass roots regionalism inflected by the progressive and populist socialism bred in the Midwest," Rosemary Hennessy astutely observed, and it was forged, she wrote, as Le Sueur "listened to the talk of the people of the prairie, especially the women of the prairie, and revealed their lives with profound tenderness" (159).

As she advocated regionalism from the left in the 1930s and early '40s, Le Sueur was keenly aware of the need to steer between both right-wing versions of regionalism and left-wing critics of regionalism. Looking back at her efforts to launch a proletarian regionalism, she scorned the local colorists, back to the land advocates, and Southern Agrarians on the right, and roundly indicted the contributors to *I'll Take My Stand* published in 1930 as members of "the Sludge School of Writing!" who "did a yeoman's service to capitalist culture" (qtd. in Schleuning, *America* 133). In place of what she described as the "old regionalism which breeds reaction" and "seeks impossible reversions to the past, returns to the soil," she endorsed a forward-looking grass roots ideology "united against fascist attacks" and serving as "a factor in national unity" (qtd. in Schleuning, *America* 132). Deeply critical of regionalism on the right, Le Sueur also had to fend off attacks from comrades on the left who condemned her for romanticizing the folk and accused her of promoting reactionary returns to the soil that played into the hands of the capitalist establishment. Looking back, Le Sueur bitterly recalled how beginning in 1934 Party functionaries censored "my midwesternism, my regionalism" as counter revolutionary (qtd. in Wixson 380–81).

How she journeyed between these extremes to create a radical proletarian regionalism across the 1930s and early '40s, a vision that may have promise for the present, is a primary theme of this essay. To map that trip, the following pages spotlight three pieces published in the early to mid-1930s before focusing on *North Star Country*, her most powerful regionalist declaration, published in 1945.

Foring Proletarian Regionalism in the Midwest, 1930–1945

Le Sueur's radical feminist regionalism emerged after her return to Minnesota from California in late 1927. She left soon after the executions of Sacco and Vanzetti in August of that year, and the birth of her daughters back home intensified her feelings about her native region. She had written a myth-based, midwestern-inflected story, "Persephone," that appeared in the *Dial* in May 1927 while she was living in California, but it was with the publication of "Corn Village" in *Scribner's Magazine* in August 1931 that she expressed a fully developed, feminist regional vision. This partially autobiographical story is filled with a sense of critical affection and unrequited love for her native region. "Like many Americans," she begins, "I will never recover from my sparse childhood in Kansas." "The blackness, weight and terror of childhood in mid-America strike deep into the stem of life," she continues. And stepping back, Le Sueur writes that "The Middle West is all so familiar to me and yet is always unfamiliar, a dream, an unreality" ("Corn Village" 7–8).[9]

Reminiscent of the mournful voices in Edgar Lee Masters's *Spoon River Anthology* (1915) and Sherwood Anderson's *Winesburg, Ohio* (1919), Le Sueur writes, "I am filled with terror when I think of the emptiness and ghostliness of mid-America" ("Corn Village" 8). Relating the "terrifying beauty" of the plains "where I was born ... while the land was lying low in this mid-winter solstice" ("Corn Village" 10), Le Sueur describes, in words echoing Hamlin Garland's *Main-Travelled Roads* (1891) and Ole Rølvaag's *Giants in the Earth* (1927), the grim loneliness of so many rural folk for whom "the land lies desolate like a loved woman who has been forgotten" ("Corn Village" 11). While part of her story describes rare moments when the lonely townspeople are briefly drawn together, Le Sueur's overriding theme concerns her personal, hard-won reconciliation with the Midwest.

Growing up in this vast mid-continent landscape, "with its sense of ruin and desolation," Le Sueur writes that she has devoted herself to "trying to get your meaning, making things up about you, trying to get you alive with significance and myth." "I have sensed your beauty and your terror and your evil. I have come from you mysteriously wounded," she confesses, yet her affection for the place is steadfast ("Corn Village" 24). Ending with a powerful regional paean, Le Sueur proclaims, "Not going to Paris or Morocco or Venice, instead staying with you, trying to be in love with you, bent upon understanding you, bringing you to life," has been her commitment and calling. "For your life is my life and your death is mine also," she concludes ("Corn Village" 25).

Soon after publishing "Corn Village," Le Sueur added an urgent political message to her hard-won sense of place. During the summer of 1934 she participated in the Minneapolis Teamsters' Strike. Occurring two years after the radical Iowa Farmers' Holiday strike led by Milo Reno in 1932, the nationally prominent Minnesota event foreshadowed the beginnings of a long-lasting, left-leaning farmer-labor alliance in the state. In one of her most powerful pieces of writing and a first-hand account, "I Was Marching," Le Sueur described how anti-union violence and the deaths of two of her fellow strikers at the hands of the Minneapolis police and deputized citizens galvanized her revolutionary commitment. "A terrible communal excitement ran through the hall like a fire through a forest," she wrote as her isolated ego joined a larger, revolutionary whole ("I Was Marching" 184). "I am one of them, yet I don't feel myself at all," she realized as she joined a mass protest. "I feel most alive and yet for the first time in my life I do not feel myself as separate," she realized ("I Was Marching" 187).[10]

"This is real movement issuing from the close reality of mass feeling," Le Sueur wrote as her ego merged with others in a massive funeral procession. "This is the first real rhythmic movement I have ever seen. My heart hammers terrifically" as we "are moving softly, rhythmically, terribly … I was marching with a million hands, movements, faces. I felt my feet join in that strange shuffle of thousands of bodies moving with direction," she recalled ("I Was Marching"

188). "It was as if an electric charge had passed through me, my hair stood on end, I was marching" are the last words of her essay published in the *New Masses*, which largely echoed Communist Party orthodoxy ("I Was Marching" 191).

A few months later, Le Sueur, redoubling her commitment to the working class and to writing wholeheartedly from their perspective, described this immersion "as stepping into a dark chaotic passional world of another class, the proletariat." This powerful foundation, "which is still perhaps unconscious of itself like a great body sleeping, stirring, strange" demanded the full devotion of all revolutionary writers, who must abandon "The Fetish of Being Outside," she concluded ("Fetish" 22–23).[11]

In October 1934, shortly after publishing her "Marching" and "Fetish" essays and hoping to build a regional movement within the East Coast–dominated Communist Party, Le Sueur and many of her midwestern colleagues attended the national conference of the John Reed Clubs held in Chicago. Members representing ten Reed Clubs across the nation were at the meeting. Here, in Wixson's words, "a division in the making between the Party cultural functionaries, located in the East, and the midwestern literary radicals" erupted (377). At this meeting Le Sueur, Herbst, Algren, Wright, Babb, and other midwestern and western members were accused of fostering dangerously reactionary regionalism that undermined the Communist cause.[12]

The hinterland radicals also learned at a party caucus in a Chicago hotel room that the central committee had dissolved their John Reed Clubs because of what were perceived to be their counterrevolutionary activities. As Le Sueur remembered, Manhattan party functionaries, represented by Alexander Trachtenberg, attacked the supposed regressive agrarianism emanating from the Midwest. *Partisan Review* editors Philip Rahv and William Phillips, she recalled in a 1980 interview, "made this awful speech about Jack's [Conroy's] writing and my writing" arguing that "there's no use writing about the farmer, that he didn't love the land—that was just romanticism." "They said … my writing was romantic and sentimental. They even brought up nativism," she recalled, and attacked "my regionalism" as reactionary (Wixson 380–81).

Missouri-born, ex-coal miner Conroy recalled that this East Coast assault came across as a confusing abstraction to Midwesterners who "had been raised on Sockless Jerry Simpson" (Wixson 381). "The ideological tempests raging in New York," Conroy recalled in 1965, "seemed unreal and remote out in the Midwest where C.I.O. organizers were getting their heads cracked while organizing factories" (Conroy 38). "Out in the Midwest of penny auctions and burning corn, we were far from abstract debates raging in New York City coffee pots. How many Marxian angels could dance on the point of a hammer and sickle?" the heartland radical sarcastically asked (qtd. in Wixson 533). Richard Wright, also at the meeting, was "stunned" and deeply disillusioned to learn that because the New York–directed "People's Front Policy was now the correct vision of life," the John Reed Clubs "would no longer exist," and that the Chicago branch's magazine, *Left Front*, would be terminated (Wright 136).[13]

Six months later, in the last week of April 1935, the Midwesterners, still chafing from the ideological class and East Coast condescension in Chicago, made their way to New York to attend a national gathering of radical writers, the inaugural meeting of the American Writers' Congress. Le Sueur joined forces there with a contingent of midwestern and Great Plains writers, among them her friends Conroy, Wright, Algren, Babb, Herbst, Lerner Olsen, and painter Joe Jones. They remained steadfast about adding regional voices to the East Coast–dominated Communist Party (Wright 68–70; Wixson 377–82).

The Congress convened on Friday, April 26, at the Mecca Temple in Manhattan, before an audience of four thousand facing a stage filled with dignitaries and a vast banner declaring "Fascism Is Death to Culture." The next morning, Le Sueur, Conroy, Wright, and Algren spoke before another sizable crowd at the nearby New School for Social Research. Conroy gave a bombastic talk on "The Worker as Writer" that was widely ridiculed, and Wright spoke briefly on the isolation of young Black writers, but only Le Sueur directly addressed regionalism. Her paper, "Proletarian Literature and the Middle West," was the sole voice directing attention to the nation's vast interior; she stood out as the only woman to deliver a published speech at the meeting.[14]

She opened with a bleak Dust Bowl image of the Middle West "blowing away because nothing has been rooted there to hold the soil into the earth." "The rooted things," she stressed, "have been torn up by greed for lumber, coal, iron, railroad, and wheat." "Nowhere in America are the ravages of *laissez faire* colonization so apparent as in the Middle West" she continued, where "the great wheat and railroad kings.... have driven the worker and the petty bourgeois over the prairies like sheep going from one town to another, going from industry to the farm, and from the farm to industry, and being milked dry" ("Proletarian Literature" 135). The drought and vast pine forests cut down stood as "awful testimony to one of the worst and swiftest exploitations that the world has ever known, when the Middle West, a rich fertile sleeping valley," was "laid waste" in "the space of fifty years" ("Proletarian Literature" 136).

Despite this harsh history, she found promise in the emergence of a true "mid-Western culture" from "the growing yeast of the revolutionary working class," where "a unity of action, and a communal expression, is being made between the farmer and the industrial worker on the militant front of struggle" ("Proletarian Literature" 136). From the iron range to the wheat and corn belts, from the coal fields of Illinois to the blown-out lands of the Dakotas, she detected a unifying labor movement and the rise of dynamic people's culture. "This is the slow beginning of a culture," Le Sueur argued, "the slow and wonderful accumulation of an experience that has hitherto been unspoken, that has been a gigantic movement of labor, the swingdown of the pick, the ax that has made no sound but now is being heard" ("Proletarian Literature" 136).

A vision of working-class people finally expressing themselves and their voices being heard as they transform the Midwest is at the heart of Le Sueur's essay. She listed her working-class colleagues, Algren and Conroy, who appreciated the "use and function of native language," and she praised the powerful heartland vernacular of the International Workers of the World, who "spoke an American language, not an English," spreading their lore like Johnny Appleseed across the land ("Proletarian Literature" 137). Most significantly, Le Sueur alluded to her recent work through the Minnesota Federal Writers' Project in which "a hundred and fifty women from factory and farm wrote down their great proletarian experience" and began "a communal relationship and revolutionary ideology" ("Proletarian Literature" 137).[15]

Her essay ends with the hope that having gained a voice and communal identity workers will know that "[r]evolution can spring up from the windy prairie as naturally as wheat." "Now we know where to put down our roots, that have never been put down, that have been waiting through a bad season," she declared ("Proletarian Literature" 138). "We, of the petty bourgeois and the working class, have been dissenters, individual madmen, anarchists against the machine; but now the Middle Western mind is finding a place, sensing a new and vigorous interaction between himself and others," she asserted. "In the Middle West," Le Sueur concluded, "it is only this united cultural front that can save us from falling into the last hypocrisy of the ruling classes—fascism" ("Proletarian Literature" 138).

Despite its powerful imagery and argument, this appeal for a midwestern working-class radical regionalism was essentially ignored at the Writers' Congress. In the nearly thirty published pages of "Discussion and Proceedings" summarizing the meeting, Le Sueur's paper was briefly noted by Waldo Frank as stressing "this great period of ferment, and the need for warmth" and "organic experience" (Frank 189–90), while other essays received paragraphs and pages of commentary. A culminating announcement, introduced by Michael Gold as "a very serious and historic moment in this Congress," revealed the Party's deep doubts about regionalism (184). As the spokesperson for the presiding committee, St. Louis native Orrick Johns presented a new "permanent framework" for their movement, strengthening "the central structure of the League of American Writers" and thus "eliminated the need for any local branch of the League" (185). Rejecting grass roots heresies from the hinterlands and condemning heartland radicalism, Johns pronounced that the "Executive Committee obviously must consist of writers of standing" who "must be permanently located in New York" (185).

Defying such East Coast dictates and power moves, Le Sueur and her midwestern allies continued to press for recognition of a radical voice from the hinterlands during the 1930s and beyond. In the process she became the most prominent proponent of a forward-looking grass roots history that invoked, in Michael Denning's words, "regional patterns of dissent" where "working people, proletarians" drew upon a proud tradition of protest (220). Looking back decades later Le Sueur recalled advocating a "progressive regionalism" that "would become a factor in national unity, it would build upon local traditions in which each region is rich, restoring them as national symbols—Haymarket, John Brown, the American dreams of freedom and creation which have moved against the money dreams of power" (qtd. in Schleuning, *America* 132).

Between 1936 and the publication of *North Star Country* in 1945, Le Sueur devoted much of her energy to planting seeds for a radical midwestern regionalism whose example would inspire similar efforts in regions across the nation. Rejecting party orthodoxy, she was the prime force behind a Midwest writers' conference in Chicago in June 1936 that paralleled similar conferences that year in Cleveland, Minneapolis, and San Francisco. In an article published in mid-November in the *Pacific Weekly*, she listed results of the Chicago meeting, stressing its formal resolution to "break off dependence upon the publishing East," and she urged her California colleagues organizing the San Francisco conference to nurture a forward-looking regionalism "of class roots, class history ... to create stronger and richer roots for the growth of creative personality, a rich and wide audience" ("Mid-western Writers' Conference" 324).[16]

In addition to promoting regional conferences, Le Sueur was a moving force behind the Midwest Federation of Arts and Professions, which "aimed to foster regional publication networks to build a local audience for Midwestern writers" (Mickenberg 33). Through this group, formed in 1936, she and Iowa writer Dale Kramer launched a journal, simply titled *Midwest*, to speak for progressive writers, thinkers, and workers and "resurrect a history of struggle" to help transform the region and the nation (Mickenberg 33).[17] Although their journal lasted only four issues between August 1936 and January 1937, it conveyed Le Sueur's faith that "the lumberjacks, the whistle punks, the gandy dancers who laid the railroads, the immigrant women" could write their own history and achieve a proletarian regionalism (qtd. in Mickenberg 38). And in 1936 as well, she issued a call "for the creation of a true historical and progressive regionalism, which can be a carrier of the vital traditions of Mid-American life and serve as a unifying factor against the old regionalism which breeds reaction." "This regionalism," she continued, "will be built upon the actual life patterns of each region, its industries and mines and markets, as well as its soil" ("Mid-Western Writers' Conference").

The 1940 publication of *Salute to Spring*, a collection of Le Sueur's journalism and short fiction written across the 1930s, brought her work to wider attention. With an invitation from Erskine Caldwell in 1941 to contribute a book on the Upper Midwest to his newly launched American Folkways series, and with the financial support of a Rockefeller research grant a year later, she researched, wrote, and published her sweeping folk history for a popular audience in 1945. While much of her earlier work had directly advocated, in Alan Wald's words, "revolutionary regionalism as an authentic people's culture," *North Star Country* achieved this historic survey in sweeping mythopoetic language (Wald, "Many Lives" 25).

Her highly eclectic book received mixed, if not negative reviews. Harvard professor Howard Mumford Jones, after describing it as "something more than mildly eclectic history," asked, "Why is the folkway writer exempt from the usual canons of historical scholarship? And … what is a 'folkway', anyhow?" (11). West Coast writer Stewart Holbrook, after praising her "fine feeling for the right word" and ability to "put drama into a scene," complained that "the effect of the entire book is misleading. From it a total stranger would get the impression that pretty much all of North Star Country is under mortgage to fat and grinning bankers; and that most of the farms had blown away on dust storms anyway." He concluded that much of her book "is erroneous to a degree bordering on fantasy" (3). Historian John T. Flanagan argued that although the book is "woefully inadequate" as standard history, it has value as "an impressionistic account," yet condescendingly concluded that "the same lack of continuity that has kept Miss Le Sueur from becoming a successful novelist is visible here" (4).

In a rare, largely positive review, midwestern historian Walter Havighurst praised *North Star Country* as "truly a folkways book ... written with an ear close to the earth and a heart close to the people" that "has a poetic truth despite factual error" (357–58). And in a praiseful essay in the *New Masses*, Howard Fast wrote that "only the Middle West of America produces this kind of book ... a folksay fabric blown like hot glass from the peoples' speech." "This is a rich, full book, not to be taken in one draught," he concluded (25).

Le Sueur began the wide-ranging prose poem that baffled so many contemporary critics by swiftly tracing the deep human history at the heart of the continent where Minnesota, Wisconsin, and their prairie edges now exist and then announcing her fundamental purpose in sweeping Whitmanesque prose. "A lion does not write a book," Le Sueur declared. "The broken trail of the people must be followed by signs of myriad folk expressions in story, myth, legend, reflecting the struggle to survive; in the spore of old newspapers, folkways marking the rituals of birth, death, harvest, planting, in the embroidery on the pillow, the democratic quilt." "Folkways are malleable," she continued. "They disappear as inland rivers do and reappear to flood a continent ... a new harvest coming with a new tool." "Folklore is the hieroglyphics of all man's communication, both obvious and subterranean," she crisply concluded (*North Star Country* 4).

Her narrative traces a deep history from the retreat of the glaciers to a complex sequence of cultures across the land, beginning with the first peoples and then uncovering the triumph as well as the tragedy of the frontier. Like Garland, Rølvaag, and Iowa-born historian Avery Craven, who described the pioneers who settled the state as "ruthless, destructive, wasteful, acquisitive" people whose "values were quite unfitted to live in the world they had created" (382), Le Sueur consistently expressed a tough-minded love-hate relationship with the land and folk of her native region.[18]

Consciously drawing upon Garland and Rølvaag, Le Sueur depicts "the bloodstains and marks of struggle: the desolation of shanties, windows gaping still like the eyes of mad women who could not stand the solitude; the fleeing man seen in the unshut doors he didn't close behind him as he fled from Wisconsin to Minnesota to the Dakotas, and then back again." Yet alluding directly to Emerson and Turner, she also celebrates the birth of "a new society, unique, set down green in the wilderness … rearing a new culture from the blend of diverse strands." "Without the haven of the middle border country, the opening of the West," she argues, democracy and belief in the dignity of each person "might have died at the Cumberland Gap. Here it was given time, cradled and sustained in the Mississippi Valley" (*North Star Country* 5–6).[19]

Le Sueur uncovers conflict as well as cooperation across the emerging region where "a grinding of the racial glaciers as fierce as that of the natural glaciers … made the topsoil of the North Star Country" (*North Star Country* 15). She depicts the arrival and interaction "of people of every nationality," beginning with French explorers and fur traders, followed by "Norwegians, Finns, Croatians, Germans, Irish, Danish, English, Italian, African, and the many and various migrations" across the burgeoning heartland (*North Star Country* 28). "America has not known how to evaluate the folk cultures," she writes. "They are an underground stream, enriching, revitalizing, strengthening the fiber of the human spirit in a way that has never been measured" (*North Star Country* 126).

Tracing the birth of a richly diverse region and its painful coming of age, Le Sueur emphasizes both the human and environmental costs of settlement. The depletion of the land, she notes, went hand in hand with the destruction of its native peoples. Her three-chapter section "Woe to My People!" is a groundbreaking treatment of the string of broken treaties culminating in the stark tragedy of the bloody Sioux Uprising in Minnesota followed by the mass execution of thirty-eight Sioux and Ojibway insurgents in December 1862. The broken treaty of 1862, an act of "Skullduggery" that resulted in mass starvation, she writes, "led to one of the bloodiest days of American history" and "reduced a great nation of over twenty-eight thousand people, representing an old and noble culture, to a few hundred … who were stoned as they were deported over the border" (*North Star Country* 84–85).

Remindful of the ecological concerns of fellow midwestern regionalists, John Wesley Powell, John Muir, and Aldo Leopold, Le Sueur catalogued the environmental havoc of the frontier while maintaining hope for the rise of a land ethic among its common folk. "The wood is felled, the land has blown away, ruined towns lie like slag on the prairie," she writes (*North Star Country* 23). "In a short space of time man has defaced and destroyed this earth," she continues. "The destruction of the prairie grass … has let the soil blow away" (Le Sueur, *North Star Country* 34). Drawn from her personal experience of Dust Bowl devastation in the 1930s, she concludes hopefully, "There is something about the American earth that is curiously loved. Even like this, with dark doom of ruin over it, everyone sees it as it originally was: lovely, green, Eldorado, with clear streams and broad pastures beside the still rivers" (*North Star Country* 262).

Deep currents of critical affection and utopian promise run throughout *North Star Country*. Le Sueur repeatedly asserts her faith that despite their blind mistakes and victimization by capitalist overlords, oppressed farmers and industrial workers, small town folk and city dwellers, will rise and forge a more just and balanced region serving as an example to the nation. She juxtaposes the rapaciousness of railroad, lumber, and iron barons James J. Hill, Friedrich Weyerhaeuser, and Andrew Carnegie, to the socialist seeds planted by German, Danish, and Finnish immigrants. And she praises the grass roots crusades of progressive leaders, among them radical Republican Carl Schurz, agrarian populist Ignatius Donnelly, and socialist governor Floyd B. Olson, who fought for a truly equitable society.[20]

Her final sections, "Struggle" (containing accounts of the 1932 Iowa Farm Holiday movement and the 1934 Minneapolis Teamsters' strike) and "Stride On, Democracy" (focusing on the profound changes wrought by the Second World War) bring *North Star Country* to a tentatively hopeful conclusion. Farm Holiday leader Reno's words, "If a man isn't radical today, he hasn't enough red blood in his veins to stain a handkerchief," precede her account of the proletarian solidarity in Minneapolis (*North Star Country* 272). The rise of working-class consciousness in midwestern strikes is redoubled by the experiences of young men fighting fascism overseas and forging new hope. "Restless we sense new frontiers, in vast and intricate combinations, using the democratic legacy in new extensions of old and barely realized forms," she writes. "Our hope is real, and we move forward to great ends, in new configurations of life" (*North Star Country* 302).

Foreseeing a rough road toward this better world, Le Sueur's book ends by affirming her faith in the essential wisdom and endurance of the folk. "The people are a story that never ends, a river that winds and falls and gleams erect in many dawns," she fearlessly asserts. "The people are a story that is long, incessant, coming alive from the earth in better wheat … persistent and inevitable. The people always know that some of the grain will be good, some of the crop will be saved, some will return and bear the strength of the kernel, that from the bloodiest year some will survive to outfox the frost," she vividly concludes her folk epic (*North Star Country* 321).

Looking Forward

Le Sueur maintained her faith in the resilience and ultimate triumph of the working class throughout her life. Amid Cold War repression in 1956 in the essay "The Dark of the Time," she affirmed her trust in "the great culture of the underground common to our people emerging in the night like rich herbal emanations" and her belief that "the source of American culture lies in the historic movement of our people" ("Dark of Time" 50, 58).[21] In a short story published in the late 1940s, "Song for My Time," Le Sueur described an interracial picnic and barbeque in Minnesota in late August 1945. Scandinavians, Greeks, Lithuanians, and "comrades from Haiti come to work in the beets," gathered to celebrate the war's end and to continue their fight against new forms of repression "until every man on earth had a space of dignity and stood in the light that included all others" ("Song" 12, 16).

In a vivid 1974 reminiscence, "The Ancient People and the Newly Come," Le Sueur professed, "The immigrants, the native people, the exiles from revolutions, were as militant and explosive as the soil or the landscape or the cyclonic weather" ("Ancient People" 42). She recalled hearing as a 13-year-old Eugene Debs proclaim, "All we want is the earth for the people." Such words reinforced her life-long faith that "these prairie agrarian prophets, these sagas of the people, still rise in the nitrogen of the roots" ("Ancient People" 45–46). Underscoring the role of women in regional renewal, Le Sueur declared in 1978 that "we as woman contained the real and only seed and were the granary of the people" and stressed that the writer's role is "to mirror back the beauty of the people, to urge and nourish their vital expression and their social vision" ("Afterwords" 199). At the end of her last book, *The Dread Road* (1991), an apocalyptic account of a bus ride through a future ruined landscape, Le Sueur described a sudden vision of "[t]he wheat fields and the corn fields burst into bread.… It is a love affair with my country. Always I have lived in her, as with a beloved body, mother child husband." "Father, lover, child taught me the wonderful earth of the middle country," she concluded (*Dread Road* 47).

More than any proletarian regionalist of her generation, Le Sueur persistently believed, as Wixson argued in 1994, that by drawing upon a "remarkable tradition of human dignity, protest, and hope" across the region, "the rhizomes of midwestern radical culture" would send "up new shoots through the soil of experience" (484). "With almost a religious fervor," Blanche Gelfant wrote in 1998, "Le Sueur was looking for the saving remnant—and she found it in her own Midwest" (333). More recently, in 2022, historian Joe Schiller stated, "Meridel Le Sueur's life and work remind us of the hopeful and radical potential of regionalism and place—that tradition and history, rather than being reactionary, can gird people for progressive struggle." In 2023, Rosemary Hennessy praised Le Sueur for uncovering "the sensibilities that bind people to the land" and for insisting "that women feel them distinctly" (150). Le Sueur's "grass roots feminism" was imbued with "the talk of the people of the prairie, especially the women, and revealed their lives with profound tenderness," Hennessy concluded (159).

Near the end of *North Star Country* Le Sueur praised "[t]he young men and women who have gone to far lands" to fight fascism. On their return, she believed, they would build upon their global experience as well as upon their region's past to restore the land to the laboring class. "Our past is usable today," she wrote of this "double fight." "Restless, we sense new frontiers, in vast and intricate combinations, using the democratic legacy in new extensions of old and barely realized forms," she confirmed (*North Star Country* 302).

"We of the north have agile practice and swift equilibrium in forever changing forms," Le Sueur affirmed in the last pages of *North Star Country*. She found hope in the voice of a common man who proclaimed, "We got in us the river, the hills, the real things past and present." "We have fought this wild boar of power, and escaped the scaffold, garrote, cannonball, and slavery many times and we will again" (*North Star Country* 321), the proud worker asserted echoing a radical regional faith that was tested throughout Meridel Le Sueur's life. Her persistent vision of left-wing regionalism waiting to "outfox the frost" in the Midwest and emerge in fresh forms to transform the nation is a brave hope whose viability remains uncertain amid the fraught conditions of the first decades of the twenty-first century.

California State University, Fullerton

Acknowledgments

In addition to two perceptive anonymous reviewers, I am indebted to many midwestern scholars and writers. They include Cory Haala, Jon Lauck, Joe Schiller, Jeff Wells, Becka Tilsen, Pamela Mittlefehldt, Peter Gildenhuys, Jim Dowd, and especially Jack Mearns, Rosemary Hennessy, and Lucy Lefren Steiner for their comments and help on versions of this essay given at the Midwestern History Association meeting in Des Moines, Iowa, May 15, 2025.

Notes

1. For a more detailed analysis of Grant Wood's position in the regional debates at the University of Iowa and elsewhere in the 1930s and early '40s and its relevance to Le Sueur, see Michael C. Steiner's "Grant Wood and the Politics of Regionalism." For a discussion of the range of regional ideologies in the 1930s, see Steiner, "Regionalism in the Great Depression," as well as Steiner, "The Midwest and the Rise of American Regionalism, 1890–1915," for an overview of the Midwest as the birthplace of American regional theo-

ry. Examples of continued condemnation of regionalism as the stepchild of fascism and totalitarianism include Roberto M. Dainotto, in *Place in Literature: Regions, Cultures, Communities*, who argues that regionalism with its vision of "imaginary communities, happy and beautiful in their orthodox and pristine purity" (17) is a menace in the postmodern world and that any effort to join Marxism and regionalism is "an untenable project" (27). Also see Wolfgang Schivelbusch, *Three New Deals: Reflections on Roosevelt's America, Mussolini's Italy, and Hitler's Germany, 1933–1939*, who perceives affinities between American regionalism in the 1930s and "the cult of the soil, land, and 'organic' society" (112) that flourished in fascist Europe, and who warns that "emphasis on soil in all its forms, from farmer's fields to the regional landscape" (115) fosters repressive regimes.

2. Much of this overview of Le Sueur's life, especially from her birth in 1900 to the publication of *North Star Country* in 1945, is indebted to five thoughtful biographies, written after the Red Scare of the 1950s and '60s. These include, in order of publication, Neala Schleuning, "Meridel Le Sueur: Toward a New Regionalism"; Schleuning, *America, Song We Sang Without Knowing: The Life and Ideas of Meridel Le Sueur*; Elaine Hedges, "Introduction," in *Ripening*; Constance Coiner, *Better Red: The Writing and Resistance of Tillie Olsen and Meridel Le Sueur*; and Rosemary Hennessy, *In the Company of Radical Women Writers*. Hennessy's chapter five, "The Radical Ecology of Meridel Le Sueur" (147–88), is an especially comprehensive treatment of her life and work.

3. *Crusaders* was originally published by Blue Heron Press, New York, in 1955.

4. See Coiner, *Better Red*, pages 75–76, and Hedges, "Introduction," pages 2–3, for reference to these and other prominent leftists who visited the Le Sueur household during Meridel's early years in Minnesota.

5. Regarding Zona Gale (1874–1938), Wisconsin-born writer and winner of the 1920 Pulitzer Prize, and her impact on Le Sueur, see Coiner, pages 78–79, and Alan Wald, "The Many Lives of Meridel Le Sueur (1990–1996)."

6. Much of this information comes from Le Sueur, *Crusaders*, pages xi–xxix, as well as from Schleuning, Hedges, Coiner, and Hennessy.

7. Hedges discusses the history of Le Sueur's novel *The Girl* on page 135. For a detailed though partial list of Le Sueur's publications, see Schleuning, "Selected Bibliography of Meridel Le Sueur," in Schleuning, *America, Song We Sang Without Knowing*, pages 165–71.

8. Coiner's chapter three, "Meridel Le Sueur: Biographical Sketch and Reportage," is an indispensable analysis of Le Sueur's personal life and literary effort to bring a lyrical, female-based perspective to left-wing writing.

9. "Corn Village" was originally published in *Scribner's Magazine* (Aug. 1931, pp. 133–40).

10. "I Was Marching" first appeared under the same title in *New Masses* (vol. 12, 18 Sept. 1934, pp. 16–18).

11. "The Fetish of Being Outside" first appeared under the same title in *New Masses* (vol. 14, 26 Feb. 1935, pp. 22–23).

12. Wixson's discussion of the divisive 1934 Chicago meeting, pages 171–72, 376–82, is the most thorough account in print. Also see Daniel Aaron, "The Demise of the John Reed Clubs," in his *Writers on the Left*, pages 297–300, for an earlier useful treatment.

13. For further details about Wright's role as a regionalist and deep dismay with the centralized Communist Party's distrust of midwestern leftists, see Steiner, "Richard Wright, the Warmth of Other Suns, and Chicago's Impact on a Southern Migrant to the Black Metropolis, 1927–1937."

14. Regarding the nearly all-male 1935 Writers' Congress, Coiner notes, "[O]n the opening night of the Congress, organizers recruited Josephine Herbst at the last minute when they realized they needed a token woman on the program" (35). Of Le Sueur's presence, Coiner notes, "Le Sueur was the lone female member of the 1935 Congresses' sixteen member Presiding Committee" (81).

15. Le Sueur's original handbook for the Minnesota Works Project Administration has been revised and reprinted as *Worker Writers*. For a thoughtful study of her efforts to nurture a people's history through the WPA-sponsored Labor School in Minneapolis, see Christopher Kempf, "'A Vast Uni-

versity of the Common People': Meridel Le Sueur and the Crafting of the Nineteen-Thirties Literary Left," especially pages 233–37. As Blanche Gelfant writes in another context, "She considered herself their scribe, someone who continued the tradition of writing down words that otherwise might be evanescent and unheard" (327).

16. "Such conferences," she vividly concluded, "create an exciting body of communal thought and growth … existing in the warmth of comradeship instead of enmity and jealousy.… the living glowing nuclei of a new life within the maggoty body of a social corpse" (324).

17. I am indebted to Mickenberg's definitive discussion of Le Sueur's efforts through her short-lived journal and conference organizing in the mid- to late 1930s.

18. In their treatment of the land, Craven (1885–1980) continued, such settlers were "able only to destroy its air, its water, and its resources—people who would measure success largely in terms of wealth accumulated … and progress in terms of more things, more leisure, and more power" (382).

19. Le Sueur quotes Turner's passage, "Western democracy was no theorist's dream. It came stark and strong and full of life, from the American forest," from his "Contributions of the West to American Democracy," published in 1903, on page 136 of *North Star Country*.

20. See chapters "Refugee Seed" (125–35) and "Hayseeds Like Me" (199–216). Governor Olson's forecast of a workers' revolution is cited, page 289 of *North Star Country*.

21. "The Dark of the Time" was originally published in *Masses and Mainstream* (vol. 9, Aug. 1956, pp. 12–21).

Works Cited

Aaron, Daniel. "The Demise of the John Reed Clubs." *Writers on the Left*, Avon Books, 1961, pp. 297–300.

Calverton, V. F. *American Literature at the Crossroads*. University of Washington Book Store, 1931. University of Washington Chapbook No. 48.

Coiner, Constance. *Better Red: The Writing and Resistance of Tillie Olsen and Meridel Le Sueur.* U of Illinois P, 1998.

Conroy, Jack. "The Contemporary Fact," in "The Thirties, a Symposium." *Carleton Miscellany*, vol. 6, winter 1965, pp. 36–39.

Craven, Avery. "A History Still Unwritten." *Western Historical Quarterly*, vol. 2, no. 4, Oct. 1971, pp. 377–83.

Dainotto, Roberto M. *Place in Literature: Regions, Cultures, Communities.* Cornell UP, 2000.

Denning, Michael. *The Cultural Front: The Laboring of American Culture in the Twentieth Century.* Verso Press, 1997.

DeVoto, Bernard. "Regionalism, or the Coterie Manifest." *Saturday Review of Literature*, vol. 15, 1937, pp. 413–15.

Fast, Howard. "Of Giant Stride." Review of *North Star Country*, by Meridel Le Seuer. *New Masses*, vol. 58, 8 Jan. 1946, pp. 23–24.

Flanagan, John T. "Book Week." *New York Herald Tribune Books*, 23 Dec. 1945.

Frank, Waldo. "Discussion and Proceedings." Hart, pp. 189–90.

Gelfant, Blanche. Afterword. *North Star Country*, by Meridel Le Seuer, U of Minnesota P, 1998, pp. 323–33.

Gold, Michael. "Discussion and Proceedings." Hart, pp. 184.

Goldman, Connie. "Faces: Meridel Le Sueur." Interview with Meridel Le Sueur. *Minnesota Public Radio*, 1 Aug. 1982, archive.mpr.org/profiles/connie-goldman.

Hampl, Patricia. "Meridel Le Sueur—Voice of the Prairie." *Ms. Magazine*, vol. 4, Aug. 1975, pp. 62–66, 96.

Hart, Henry, editor. *American Writers' Congress.* International Publishers, 1935.

Havighurst, Walter. Review of *North Star Country*, by Meridel Le Seuer. *Wisconsin Magazine of History*, vol. 29, Mar. 1946, pp. 357–58.

Hedges, Elaine. Introduction. *Ripening: Selected Work*, by Meridel Le Sueur, edited by Elaine Hedges, The Feminist Press, 1990, pp. 1–28.

Hennessy, Rosemary. *In the Company of Radical Women Writers.* U of Minnesota P, 2023.

Holbrook, Stewart. Review of *North Star Country*, by Meridel Le Seuer. *Weekly Book Review*, vol. 16, Dec. 1945, p. 3.

Janson, H. W. "Benton and Wood: Champions of Regionalism." *Magazine of Art*, vol. 39, May 1946, pp. 184–86, 198–200.

Johns, Orrick. "Discussion and Proceedings." Hart, pp. 184–86.

Jones, Howard Mumford. "Folklore and the Upper Midwest." Review of *North Star Country*, by Meridel Le Sueur. *Saturday Review of Literature*, vol. 29, 5 Jan. 1946, p. 11.

Kempf, Christopher. "'A Vast University of the Common People': Meridel Le Sueur and the Crafting of the Nineteen-Thirties Literary Left." *ELH*, vol. 88, spring 2021, pp. 225–50.

Le Sueur, Meridel. "Afterwords." *The Girl*, 2nd ed., Midwest Villages & Voices, 2022, pp. 199–200.

———. "The Ancient People and the Newly Come." *Growing Up in Minnesota: Ten Writers Remember Their Childhoods*, edited by Chester G. Anderson, U of Minnesota P, 1976, pp. 17–46.

———. "Corn Village." *Salute to Spring*, International Publishers, 1940, pp. 7–25.

———. *Crusaders: The Radical Legacy of Marian and Arthur Le Sueur*. Blue Heron Press, 1955.

———. "The Dark of Time." *Song for My Time: Stories of the Period of Repression*, West End Press, 1977, pp. 49–58.

———. *The Dread Road*. West End Press, 1991.

———. "The Fetish of Being Outside." *New Masses*, vol. 14, 26 Feb. 1935, pp. 22–23.

———. *The Girl*. West End Press, 1978.

———. *I Hear Men Talking and Other Stories*. Edited by Linda Ray Pratt, West End Press, 1984, pp. 237–43.

———. "I Was Marching." *Salute to Spring*, International Publishers, 1940, pp. 177–91.

———. "Mid-Western Writers' Conference." 13 June 1936. Meridel Le Sueur Papers, Minnesota State Historical Society, Box 17.

———. *North Star Country*. Book Find Club, 1945.

———. "Our Fathers." *Ripening: Selected Work*, edited by Elaine Hedges, Feminist Press, 1990, pp. 114–23.

———. "Persephone." *Dial*, vol. 82, May 1927, pp. 371–78.

———. "Proletarian Literature and the Middle West." *American Writers' Congress*, edited by Henry Hart, International Publishers, 1935, pp. 135–38.

———. "Song for My Time." *Song for My Time*, West End Press, 1977, pp. 9–18.

———. *Worker Writers*. West End Press, 1982.

Mickenberg, Julia. "'Revolution Can Spring Up from the Windy Prairie As Naturally As Wheat': Meridel Le Sueur and the Making of a Radical Regional Tradition." Steiner, *Regionalists on the Left*, pp. 25–46.

Pratt, Linda Ray. Afterword. *I Hear Men Talking and Other Stories*, by Meridel Le Sueur, West End Press, 1984, pp. 225–36.

Schiller, Joe. "Literary Landscape: Meridel Le Sueur: Miner's Shack, Picher, Oklahoma." *New Territory Magazine*, newterritorymag.com/literary-landscapes/meridel-le-sueur-picher-oklahoma/.

Schivelbusch, Wolfgang. *Three New Deals: Reflections on Roosevelt's America, Mussolini's Italy, and Hitler's Germany, 1933–1939*. Henry Holt, 2004.

Schleuning, Neala. *America, Song We Sang Without Knowing: The Life and Ideas of Meridel Le Sueur*. Little Red Hen Press, 1983.

———. "Meridel Le Sueur: Toward a New Regionalism." *Books at Iowa*, vol. 33, no. 1, 1980, pp. 22–41.

Steiner, Michael C. "Grant Wood and the Politics of Regionalism." *Middle West Review*, vol. 3, no. 1, fall 2016, pp. 71–95.

———. "The Midwest and the Rise of American Regionalism, 1890–1915." *Middle West Review*, vol. 7, no. 1, fall 2020, pp. 9–30.

———. "Regionalism in the Great Depression." *Geographical Review*, vol. 73, no. 4, Oct. 1983, pp. 430–46.

———, editor. *Regionalists on the Left: Radical Voices from the American West*. U of Oklahoma P, 2013.

———. "Richard Wright, the Warmth of Other Suns, and Chicago's Impact on a Southern Migrant to the Black Metropolis, 1927–1937." *MidAmerica*, vol. 50, 2023, pp. 60–78.

Wald, Alan M. *Exiles from a Future Time: The Forging of the Mid-Twentieth-Century Literary Left*. U of North Carolina P, 2002.

———. "The Many Lives of Meridel Le Sueur (1990–1996)." *Monthly Review*, vol. 49, Sept. 1997, pp. 23–31.

Wixson, Douglas. *Worker/Writer in America: Jack Conroy and the Tradition of Midwestern Literary Radicalism, 1898–1990*. U of Illinois P, 1994.

Wright, Richard. "I Tried to Be a Communist." *Atlantic*, vol. 174, Aug. 1944, pp. 61–70.

Review Essay

The Liberal Heartland

Wesley R. Bishop

The Liberal Heartland: A Political History of the Postwar American Midwest, edited
by Jon K. Lauck and Catherine McNicol Stock. University Press of Kansas,
2025. 440 pp.

I n the American political imagination, few regions are as misunderstood or
as contested as the Midwest. Cast too often as a monolith—white, rural,
conservative, "real"—the heartland of American life has long been both
idealized and caricatured in national discourse. That is what makes *The Liberal
Heartland: A Political History of the Postwar American Midwest*, edited by Jon K.
Lauck and Catherine McNicol Stock, not only timely but essential. The volume,
a companion to the 2020 edited collection *The Conservative Heartland*, seeks
to rebalance the historical narrative, recovering the long, rich, and frequently
overlooked traditions of liberal, progressive, and even radical politics that have
shaped the Midwest from the end of the New Deal through the rise of Trumpian
populism.

Over twenty deeply researched chapters, the collection focuses on stories
of forgotten reformers, coalition builders, and local activists. It reveals how the
region was a crucible for not only conservatism but also labor militancy, environmental stewardship, queer organizing, feminist activism, and Indigenous
self-determination. From the prairie states to industrial cities, the Midwest
emerges here as a site of political contestation and innovation—not simply a
passive bystander to East and West Coast developments but an engine of democratic experimentation in its own right.

This is not merely an act of historiographical recovery, though it is that. It is
also a rejoinder to the widespread belief that the Midwest was, and is, politically

homogenous. The strength of the book lies in its insistence that the Midwest contains multitudes—and that any serious understanding of American political history must account for this complexity.

One of the major interventions of *The Liberal Heartland* is its insistence that postwar liberalism was not confined to coastal enclaves. Contributors map out a broad regional topography of progressive action, covering everything from Richard Hatcher's historic mayoral victory in Gary, Indiana, to Paul Wellstone's insurgent Senate campaign in Minnesota. We meet Lydia Cady Langer, a fierce advocate for social justice in North Dakota, and Mary Jean Collins, who brought feminist organizing to Chicago's labor movement. These figures, often omitted from national political narratives, form the beating heart of this collection.

What distinguishes many of these case studies is their local rootedness. Rather than portraying liberalism as a top-down force imposed by elites, the essays highlight grassroots movements that engaged deeply with the specific social, racial, and economic contexts of midwestern communities. The chapter on Jim Jontz, for instance, shows how the environmentalist movement in Indiana could be built upon local land-use concerns. Similarly, the essays on Indigenous rights activists in the Upper Midwest situate their work within longer histories of settler colonialism, treaty violations, and resistance.

Multiple chapters explore the overlaps between queer, labor, feminist, and racial justice movements, showing that the Midwest was a space where coalition politics could and did thrive. James McQuaid illustrates this with his chapter, "That Other Minority: The UAW, Midwestern Politics, and Pre-Stonewall Queer-Labor Solidarity." It is a good essay in its discussion of queer-labor alliances before Stonewall—an example that challenges both regional stereotypes and national chronologies—and challenges researchers to think about more discreet ways pro-queer politics were practiced in often hostile environments.

While this book is historical in scope, its significance is clearly felt in the present. In recent years, the Midwest has once again become a stage for political transformation. The uprisings following the police killings of George Floyd in Minneapolis, Tamir Rice in Cleveland, John Crawford III in Beavercreek, Breonna Taylor in Louisville, and Patrick Lyoya in Grand Rapids were not isolated events. They reflected both deep systemic injustices and long-simmering frustrations with how midwestern communities—especially Black, Indigenous, and working-class communities—have been misrepresented and marginalized in national politics.

The Liberal Heartland helps us understand these uprisings not simply as spontaneous reactions to injustice, but as the latest expressions of a longer tradition of midwestern dissent. These protests, like those led by Fred Hampton or Oscar López Rivera in earlier decades, belong to a regional legacy of agitation and organizing. When commentators or political elites invoke the "heartland" as shorthand for conservative values, they erase the lived realities and political commitments of millions. This book challenges that erasure head-on.

Indeed, one of the collection's implicit arguments is that the very idea of the "Midwest" has often been a rhetorical tool used to discipline national political discourse. By resuscitating the region's liberal histories, the editors and contributors complicate this narrative and offer new tools for interpreting both past and present movements. The collection is meticulously edited, and the range of contributors is impressive. Lauck and Stock deserve praise for assembling a volume that is not only comprehensive in scope but intellectually coherent.

The scholarly push to rethink midwestern history has in recent years found one of its most persistent champions in Jon K. Lauck. His call for a new regional historiography—one that takes the Midwest seriously as a site of intellectual and political innovation—has yielded a robust body of work, and *The Liberal Heartland* represents a continuation of sorts in that ongoing project. Similarly, Catherine McNicol Stock has long sought to recover the overlooked and often misunderstood radicalism embedded in rural and midwestern communities. Across works such as *Rural Radicals* and *Nisei Soldiers Break Their Silence*, Stock has insisted that the countryside is not a political void but a site of insurgent traditions, class conflict, and democratic experimentation. This edited collection continues both editors' scholarly projects by foregrounding the Midwest as a region with its own heterogeneous political past—one that cannot be reduced to the familiar binaries of conservative heartland or agrarian nostalgia.

Lauck and Stock allow this volume to speak in many voices, and some of the best chapters here implicitly challenge any temptation toward midwestern moralism. Essays that foreground urban Black radicalism, queer rural organizing, or Indigenous critiques of settler land regimes reveal a region as fractured and contradictory as the nation itself. This is where the book is at its best—when it abandons nostalgia and listens closely to the conflicts and coalitions that actually shaped the political terrain.

In its totality, *The Liberal Heartland* represents a major contribution to the fields of regional history, political history, and American studies. It is a model for how to do regional scholarship without falling into parochialism. By foregrounding voices from across the political and cultural spectrum of midwestern liberalism, the editors present a more textured account of the region—one that resists both conservative caricature and liberal abandonment.

The collection also speaks to a broader scholarly need: the recovery of regional nuance in an era of national generalization. As political scientists and pundits increasingly reduce the American electorate to red and blue zones, books like this remind us that political identities are always mediated by place, history, and memory. That the Midwest has been a site of liberal and leftist imagination, not merely reactionary retrenchment, should inform how we teach, write, and organize today.

Moreover, as universities and cultural institutions across the Midwest continue to reckon with their roles in reproducing dominant national narratives, *The Liberal Heartland* offers a valuable resource. Its chapters can serve as entry points for rethinking curricula, museum exhibits, public history projects, and activist genealogies. It also invites scholars working in other regions to undertake similar projects of historical recovery and political reevaluation.

If there is one message to take from this book, it is that regional history matters—not because regions are static containers of identity, but because they are dynamic arenas of struggle and change. The liberal heartland of this collection is not a nostalgic utopia nor a corrective myth. It is a space of political creativity and contradiction, a region where battles over the meaning of justice, democracy, and freedom have always been waged.

As scholars, we owe it to the communities we study—and to those we belong to—to tell fuller stories. That includes the story of a Midwest that has long harbored visions of a more just and inclusive nation. In times of backlash and authoritarian drift, these stories are not luxuries. They are necessities.

The Liberal Heartland gives us those stories. And for that, it deserves our close attention, our critical engagement, and our sincere gratitude.

Jacksonville State University and North Meridian Press

Review Essay

ARS POETICA VIVENDI?
The Art of Living in Midwestern Poetry

Ali Beheler

Harper, Mary Catherine. *The Found Object Imagines a Life: New and Selected Poems.* Cornerstone Press, 2022. 153 pp.

Rozga, Margaret. *Holding My Selves Together: New and Selected Poems.* Cornerstone Press, 2021. 145 pp.

As both a reader and a writer, I'm often struck by how poems about anything *but* writing can shift, hologram-like, into *ars poetica* when viewed from the right slant. Two recent collections from longtime midwestern poets—Mary Catherine Harper's *The Found Object Imagines a Life* and Margaret Rozga's *Holding My Selves Together*—had me wondering whether collections of poems from across a writer's lifetime might be read, with a similar shift of perspective, as *ars vivendi*. Unlike other books drawn from one period of a writer's life, these collections dramatize, across their length and distinct sections, the work of rendering unity from disparate experiences and selves, composing the "I" from its scattered fragments, as each of us must do in living. Both collections are engaged in finding linkages between remembered and present selves at the same time as they struggle to articulate the role that poetry plays in the construction and mediation of these selves across time. And in both, what it means to live a life with and through poetry is seen, by the end, to be one of a poet's more persistent and animating questions, often driving them, for respite and fodder, into the natural world.

Both collections begin with poems recollecting the speaker's family of origin. In Harper's first full-length collection, *The Found Object Imagines a Life*, the poems of this opening foray haunt the remainder. Via sparing personal detail, rendered with lyrical restraint and precise metaphors drawn from the physicality of the Midwest, the speaker mines layers of memory to trace the subtle movement of intergenerational trauma, whereby violence born of violence is "cradled down in the gut / of generations" (5), held "just under / the leathered skin / ready to erupt" (25). These eruptions are figured as the result of so many quietly brewing tornados, like the speaker's mother's "once-upon-a-pressure-cooking / body / that spiraled us all" (24). A brother's hinted mental illness in such a home is depicted as a "stormy mind rotating / not low enough to lift the roof, / just close enough to prime a vacuum[,]" the effect of his love in these conditions likened to "wind loving loose shingles just before / it sends the hail pelting down" (19).

In the midst of such storms of family dysfunction, Harper explores the survival strategy of forgetting as well as the first of many tensions animating her work—the tension between memory and forgetting in the poet's craft. Calling to mind Nietzsche's claim that forgetting can be necessary for flourishing, the speaker of the eponymous poem of the first section, "Stories to Misremember," instructs that "[t]here are events to be told / exactly as they happened, / bare facts … to be … re-tasted / once, twice, but on the third / time to be misremembered … intentionally," so as to "deflect poison" (18). The opening poem renders such truth-deviating memory in an unforgettable image, calling it "as hollow as an egg with its insides blown out / and painted painstakingly with … precisely rendered scenes never quite / true" (2). While the paint "conspire[s] with its / artist against veracity," the motivation is a desire on the part of such a fragile being for a sense of wholeness, "to be glued / together" (2).

Here we run up against another animating tension of Harper's collection—the tension between the poet's perception and desire. On one hand, the speaker notes that family members "look" more intensely at each other than at strangers, recalling how their mother's complaint "about the cost of mothering, / something broken loose as I fell / from her body, / something about a ruined pelvis" gave birth to the speaker's need to "interrogate [their mother's] eye" even as they longed for "an honestly averted gaze" (22). This averting is achieved better with strangers, the speaker finds—for instance, during train travel, when fellow travelers easily "resize / our lives" in the "incidental communit[ies]" of conversation wherein "[e]ach story of what was never quite / true" deviates from the facts of the past for the sake of this momentary bond, its "warm[th]" (13). However, the intensity of gaze reserved for family does not itself deliver true perception. While both art and love may be fueled by a longing to depict their subjects with accuracy and beauty, "The Art of Love" suggests that something in the "messy manners of living" makes such "limn[ing]" far easier in the case of "dead things" and renders our attempts at really seeing the living "disproportion[ate] ... misshapen ... a blur" (21). One saving grace from within this looking-longing tension can be, the speaker hints, the oblique, indirect gaze in which we find ourselves when attending to and writing about the other animal species populating the natural world, as the "story I write now to soften / the edges of the past, / the story of the squirrel I stopped to watch / just yesterday" allows the speaker to finally, self-reflexively, find at least the image of herself "looking back at [the squirrel] / directly" (23).

Life beyond humanity is the site of another tension that Harper's collection explores in the section "Earning Apocalypse"—the individual's alienation from, and belonging within, the natural world. Heeding its etymological thread connoting *un-covering*, the speaker finds "apocalypse" built into the shared "grammar" of all living metamorphoses, her young self having learned to read both the transition of tadpole to frog and "the quake / of change in my own small / body" as the "apocalypse / of each live thing" (89), of "one life meandering to its end, another beginning there" (88). Despite such continuity linking all the living, "apocalypse"—in its broader sense as destruction of life and its conditions—is read by the speaker as a particularly human-caused phenomenon that, "unlike resurrection, is an earned thing / coming at a cost" (86). As to the origin of this earning, the speaker observes a persistent alienation of human from other animals that "begins" in the former's attempt to "defy / the ice" through sacrificing the lives of animals beyond its own species for its own preservation, wrapping itself warm inside "the sheep's cold body" (76). Beside such cataclysmic physical brutalities the speaker places the more aesthetic, "romantic" errors of humans projecting themselves onto other beings within nature as either their likenesses or their ends, "[a]s if nuthatches were designed … for the express purpose of / providing atmosphere for me," as if birdsong were the same as "[m]y human cry" (80).

Even as other animals inspire wonder and poetry, this inspiration so often comes at the cost of their anthropomorphization, dashing any hope of true perception of them. The speaker of "Earning Apocalypse" notes that "I philosophize ant biomass / citing its parallel to human mass … I poeticize bee colonies / making of them a metonymy for the hive of humans," and the speaker laments that in doing so, "I fail, I fail, I fail / to see the fact of insects having their own eyes / … their own somatic moods / … their own smell / beyond all philosophy" (86). Torn between the dual anthropocentric perceptions of "thrill" and threat in the face of other animals, the speaker locates a desire to transcend both narrow routes, "to be a snake shedding its skin[,]" to rediscover a forgotten continuity with these other animals (93). Such a dispensation is granted, once again, in certain quiet moments of looking at the natural world and its non-human inhabitants. In some of these moments, the speaker contends that "my cornea's gaze" can surrender and open itself for the entry of "dragonfly," "hummingbird moth," "praying manti[s]," "earwi[g]," and "spider," each transforming "from the inside" the speaker's perceptive powers, helping them to "[s]e[e] beyond" artificial species barriers, "reminding me that we hummed together once" (94–95).

In its eponymous final section, Harper's collection reaches its apex of craft and depth in poems that weave a direct consideration of the poet's vocation into the themes and tensions already at work. Here, it is almost exclusively trees, rather than other animals, that serve as the dominant images, metaphors, and interlocutors in a series of *ars poetica* poems exploring the tension within poetic craft between creation and revelation, opacity and transparency. In one poem, the speaker describes their tendency toward abstraction in writing as a protective practice that helps them work toward a readiness for self-revelation, much like the sycamore tree is only ready to shed its leaves and bark in winter, "stripped down to the bone" in this one "[u]nashamed [s]eason" (126). Elsewhere, the speaker nearly laments their sober, restrained approach to craft—its "[l]ow [d]rama … never / scripted into three-dimensional / space but ironed flat to suit this / sheet of paper" (136)—as well as their preference for "clean-sliced words" in "neat rows" (138). The writer's worry here is that lyric abstraction tilts toward a distance and irreality that the beauty of metaphors help to content us with rather than to correct. For, as poets, we "wedg[e] word into word" to make a "buffer" composed of the "wretched ecstasy" of the bend of metaphors as they approach so closely, but never really capture, the truth of the things written about, just as the "glass-burdened limbs" of "an ice-stormed tree" may "bend to near-breaking" without tipping into the break (125). Yet, the break of the limb, its "finality," is just what our love of it fears most—a plain truth that metaphor can never *say* (125). Poets, who "love from afar," are caught up in the pleasure of this almostness of metaphor, kept from a deeper, more direct confrontation with the truth of their loves, always "euphemizing" but never "daring to say simply" (125), perhaps "ever fearing … the moment the sentence / ends" (135). Thus, it is not only self-preservation that causes our misperceptions, but our own thrall to the beauty of nature—beauty which we long to project over ourselves via metaphor, stealing it at the cost of truth.

Toward the end of the collection, as it continues exploring the poetic inspiration of nature and the tension between true perception and the poet's craft, bodies of water and found objects replace trees as the poet's interlocutors. In one poem, the speaker faces Lake Erie, its heavy crashes in a storm overwhelming their body and felt competence: "[m]e as vulnerable / as this soaked journal on someone's lap / … artless," while the Lake, personified, "overpower[s] … / … any words I might conjure up / to match … your fury[,]" making words seem "nothing compared to you" (147). For these "words … can never contain … / never encompass you" (146). Despite such a failure of the poet's tools to capture their object (or because of it?), the speaker is driven to use words not to contain but simply to "[r]eply to" the Lake, christening themselves, in contrast to the Lake's "Tempest," as "Drowning Words"—a name to honor the understanding that the poet's productions will "becom[e] as nothing" (147). Relevance shifts to the action of response, the attempt—"I must try"—that issues in words, not to the question of those words' permanence or grandeur (147). In the collection's final, and eponymous, poem, it is a found object that is personified, that "[i]magines a [l]ife" (146) made possible by the mysterious force by which they capture and command the imagination and body of a poet "to compose / poems about me / to recite me over and over," the force of obsession rendering the object as "crawling script / just under the parchment / of [the poet's] skin" (149). Looking back to an earlier poem addressed "To the Untethered Word," whom the poet calls "[y]ou, my tornado … stirring the tide" (131), a reader might easily imagine that words are also found objects upon which we stumble, toward which we are drawn obsessively, and which we position in space as art—poetry being that art of repurposing mere communication tools, transforming them into works, on the page, whose lives may seem longer than but are just as finite as ours.

The poems in Harper's collection tend to align along the left margin, their free verse typically rendered in complete sentences parcelled into mid-length lines and stanzas of usually six lines or fewer, with frequent enjambment and end punctuation. Infrequently, Harper's poems may experiment with the space of the page via indentation of some lines, stanzas, or, sometimes, a pattern of one-word monostitches indented far to the right, toward the end of the previous line, not quite a contrapuntal, like a leaf just detached from a branch and falling.

Also taking its title from its final section, Margaret (Peggy) Rozga's *Holding My Selves Together* reads and even names itself as the work of looking back on many chapters of a life and attempting to find the throughlines with which they might be interwoven.

The first section of *Holding My Selves Together*, "Alice Marathons," is animated by a number of quasi-persona poems in which the speaker explores her "girlhood story" through self-identification with Alice of *Alice's Adventures in Wonderland*, introducing threads of the speaker's burgeoning desires—for beauty, action, and poetry—that continue to plait the remainder of the collection

(2). Not quite a persona but more of a mask, "Alice" in these poems functions as a thinly veiled metaphor for the speaker as a girl, and "running" is used, throughout, as a metaphor for seeking beauty in worldly action, for "... beauty / is what she was running after" (17). Speaker-Alice discovers reading, writing, and poetry—the path through which she'll ultimately pursue beauty—during this period when, from her sister's books, including a volume of Keats, she "tucks scarcely realized words / into her pocket[,] ... [r]uns[,] / trips[,] falls" (3). She is drawn to poetry with hesitation, finding "challenge after challenge" there and wondering, for instance, at its arrangement into stanzas—"[w]hat reason ... for skipping so?/ [i]t makes her jumpy" (4).

The young speaker-Alice, like her literary namesake, is also rudely awakened to all that's "wrong with this world" in the adults around her (18); she finds "all quarrel so dreadfully" (6) in this "inverted world where people / shallow as playing cards rule" (31) and the "times are ... rude, rough, incomprehensible" (16). The young poet senses that poetry can provide a dispensation in such cases, for "poets ... [, l]ike Alice, ... match words to what /... we've seen[,]" and, further, "know how to invent rules" that, like the magic mushroom of Wonderland-Alice, can right-size the poet to the situation and "shelter Alice in words" (31). The "Alices" who need shelter are all such young girls who dream of creating beauty through externally focused action, whether it's "living / abroad," "turn[ing] a rubbish-strewn vacant lot into a flourishing / community space," "organiz[ing] ... to protest the / war," or "go[ing] door to door to get a read on / racial issues, get[ting] out the vote" (28). Speaker-Alice learns to "marathon" in the sense of seeing the long game here, which is making of the search for beauty and the actions that create it a lifelong affair—a lifetime of acting and writing and entwining the two to encourage other Alices—for "[o]ne does not win. / The race is bigger than that" (17). Toward the end of the section, the speaker wonders if "maybe, pen in hand or sitting at a computer, chasing / words that ... bid me fetch / their gloves and fans ... / ... I still am / Alice" (29).

Recalling Faulkner's suggestive assertion that the past is never dead, the second section of Rozga's collection, "The Last Six Miles Are the Hardest," confronts the tendency of history's broad sweep to "rememb[er] the dream" but overlook the individual experiences—sometimes "nightmares"—of those who animated it on the ground (44). Rozga shows that such details are still accessible via the individual voice raised in memory. Drawing from Rozga's experience in the civil rights movement of the late 1960s in Alabama and Milwaukee, this section finds the speaker returning to these sites to discover "ghosts riding shotgun" (41), still "unpurged from my mind" (66). The struggle is in how to make the lived experience of that individually haunting history accessible to the "young audience[s]" of new generations (64), to "keep the movement moving" (69). The speaker finds that, while the present of a community's surface memory may have lost much of the past—individuals, monuments, even unwritten records—in fact, "[t]he moment folds into eternity," each moment of individual struggle existing "forever," from "the contorted faces" to "the opening at the end of the gun barrel" (72). It is the poet's memory and work that is able to access that eternal moment and send it to the "heart" of listeners, where it might become "song" (70).

While Rozga's style tends toward plain-spoken narrative and includes sparing lyrical flourishes, there is a lyric sensibility on view in this idea that the individual poet has a role to play in history's spiritual continuity. One way to take up this role is via a "poetry of fact," exemplified by the docu-poetics at the heart of this section, where a number of poems pull from newspaper articles, a Supreme Court decision, and the simple eyewitness memory of a particular date to resurrect basic facts that might re-animate the intensity of the participants' lived experience. One poem draws mere numbers from a newspaper article to render the asymmetry of support and resistance, recalling that on August 29, 1967, there were "235 marchers" on the 16th Street Viaduct in Milwaukee, facing "125 policemen / in riot helmets / [and] 5000 counter-demonstrators" (53). Likewise, the fact of local resistance and indifference is recaptured by the specific recollection that multiple protests of "over a hundred" picketers at the homes of local aldermen and alderwomen resulted in no change to "[t]he number voting for fair housing" in Milwaukee at this time, which remained just "One. Alderwoman" (47). The poet's song might also begin as a "night-written poem," emerging from the snatches of memory awake at those hours—fragile, "evaporat[ing]," but leaving sometimes "a line" of memory (69). The speaker urges us to "say" these lines recollecting what we have seen, and when the poem "stalls," to "[r]e-write it," circulate it so that receptive hearts can "turn it into song" (70).

The poems in Rozga's third section, "Even in Beauty," had me recalling Aristotle's claim that a poet needs to have an eye for resemblances. Rozga finds many of the metaphors for more personal, human matters—especially the matter of poetic creation—in the natural world, just as Harper does; for Rozga, it is most often vegetal life displaying such resemblances. The section's first poem links, by proximity on the page, the literal human production of "the woman [...] in labor / ... at the foot of a tree / ... gather[ing] in push" to the earth's push as it "flowers around her" (76). The image of the garden forms a throughline from the first section, in which Alice's garden haunts her as a dream of her future access to beauty, to this one, in which the garden becomes a metaphor for both body and mind. In one poem, the idea of the speaker's partner's fast-growing disease "takes root" and drives the speaker toward the action of "upend[ing] the earth as if / the other could be rooted out" (78). The title of the shortest poem of the collection metaphorically links "An Onion, a Clove of Garlic, the Heart," suggesting in animal and vegetal images how, in time, the first two of the titular referents "sweeten, grow pungent, and harden," the final word of the title suggesting, in lyric resonance, that the human heart follows a similar path. In the next poem, "an oak seedling" is taken as a metaphor for "what I could with such fierce will [do]," providing its "lesson in how to burl," turning time underground and the shedding of its "tough outer shell ... / [that] protects the heart" into "oak-spun stories / ... [that] rise ... in a web to the sky," seeming to chart a path for the speaker to follow (81). In two later poems, vegetal beings become metaphorical prayers. In "If Ever a Prayer," the speaker's vision of small green ovals of eventual peaches up the length of a peach tree reveals that the branches are "bowing slightly toward center / arcing toward infinite sky" like human arms opening in the imagined direction of the divine (103). In "On the Vertical," cutting open an onion at this angle reveals the resemblance of its insides to layers of "[h]ands cupped, touching / at fingertips, at bottom of palms," which the speaker names "layers of prayer / ... cradling the slim green / center" (104).

This entwinement of organic nature and human concern and action is repeated in the strongest of a few explicit *ars poetica* poems of the third section. "Rising at Dawn" depicts the poet not as conscious creator of words—since "you cannot force the word" (100)—but as distracted receiver, one who waits on words to rise up when they will, this rising aided by turning the poet's body and mind to a captivation in the physical universe. The "maples budding / birds in motion" help to erase the "sense of time" so that, the speaker claims, "I'm always watching, listening, / unseeing, unhearing until [the word] arrives" (100). It is easy, by the end of the section, to interpret so many of these vegetally populated poems as *ars poetica* poems, such as "The Plot," in which the reader is instructed to "[s]catter seeds freely" into the implied garden, though "[s]ome won't take root ... / ... will be pulled, mistaken for weeds, / some arrested in a sudden late freeze / or washed away ... or starved" (77).

The strongest poems in the collection's eponymous final section continue to grow more lyrical, less literal and narrative, and continue to twist into *ars poetica* poems inflected by vegetal and animal metaphors. They return to a concern of the collection's beginning—the young girl's struggle to find her way into poetry—depicting with honesty the liminal moments of solitude in which these past worries reveal their continuity with the present. The speaker writes, alone at her kitchen island, of the subtle disintegration that aging's wisdom provides, of the felt mutual permeability between herself and her mother and between her younger and older selves: "Myself still a child. Even as a woman at an island. A mother. A grandmother" (132). These connections between selves across time are often felt at the precipice between night and morning light. In "Light Rising," the speaker recalls such a moment when "[through] fog, I sensed / growth I could not yet see / rising like the split of a seed / on a slender leaf, against all odds" (135). In another poem, at dawn, "somewhere through the haze an artist / emerges in the still dark hush" (134). Through all of her multiple selves, the speaker is still doing the work of a poet, which is not to *be* a poet, or to *have become* one, but still to be in the midst of becoming one through the ongoing acts of writing, which birth both disappointment and hope, as the speaker claims to "carry a sack full of failures. / It is the way I pray. I draw letters / freed from words … pull them back / into words … a line … a poem" (133). The "Ode to Hope" ends with a reminder about the discipline of writing and its precarious beginnings: "First the words of others. / First a seedling.… / First a fence around the tender stem. / First protection against bark being stripped away / by hungry deer.… / First a single word, single sound. / … First silence without hope." (116–17). By the collection's end, across decades of the life of the poetic "I," writing has not become an effortless outpouring—for such first unknowing steps as these remain requisite. This same beginning, in hesitation or hopelessness or a judgment of momentary failure, we have seen elsewhere in this collection, describing the young Alice's first forays into poetry and the young adult speaker's first forays into social justice work. All meaningful action, the collection seems to say and show, is a long game, not one step but a continual stepping, not one swallow but the endless summer of a lifetime.

Formally, Rozga's free verse poems tend to align along the left margin and to unfold in enjambed and punctuated stanzas. In a few poems, contrapuntal form suggests multivocity and allows a more capacious inhabiting of the page. Since Rozga's poems tend toward literal description and the narrative mode, often focusing on setting, action, and direct "telling," there is not a great amount of formal experimentation or lyric variation within the poems. However, one of the more interesting craft aspects of the collection is found in how the structure mirrors, or literally performs, the work at the heart of the themes of the collection, that of weaving together multiple selves. The penultimate poem of each section acts as a summative gathering of strands (topics, words, images) from within the current section, and the final poem plaits them with themes from the next section, while also providing the latter's title. These elements of structure perform the complex interplay of closing, continuation, and opening of various chapters of a life, each one emerging from and in continuity with the previous one.

Hastings College

Works Cited

Aristotle. "Poetics." *The Basic Works of Aristotle*, edited by Richard McKeon, Random House, 1941, pp. 1455–57.

Faulkner, William. *Requiem for a Nun*. Chatto and Windus, 1919.

Nietzsche, Friedrich. *On the Advantage and Disadvantage of History for Life*. Hackett, 1980.

ANNUAL BIBLIOGRAPHY OF
MIDWESTERN LITERATURE, 2023

Robert Beasecker, Editor
Grand Valley State University

This bibliography includes primary and secondary sources of midwestern literary genres published, for the most part, during 2023. Criteria for inclusion of authors are birth or residence within the twelve-state area that defines the Midwest. Fiction and poetry using midwestern locales are included irrespective of their authors' ties with this region. Primary sources are listed alphabetically by author, including (if applicable) designations of locale within square brackets at the end of each citation. However, because of space constraints, primary source materials are limited to separately published works; those appearing in literary journals and magazines are generally not included. Secondary sources, usually journal articles, books, or doctoral dissertations, are listed by subject; critical editions of midwestern authors will be found here as well.

Not included in this bibliography are the following types of material: works only published in electronic format; reprints or reissues of earlier works, except for some new or revised editions; baccalaureate or masters theses; entries in reference books; separate contents of collected essays or *Festschriften*; audio or video recordings; electronic databases; and internet websites, which have the tendency to be unstable or ephemeral.

Abbreviations used in the citations denoting genre and publication types are as follows:

A	Anthology	jrnl	Journalism
bibl	Bibliography	juv	Juvenile fiction
biog	Biography	lang	Language; linguistics
corr	Correspondence	M	Memoir
crit	Criticism	N	Novel

D	Drama	P	Poetry
gen	General studies	pub	Publishing; printing
hist	History	rev	Review essay
I	Interview(s)	S	Short fiction

Citations for novels, poetry, short stories, memoirs, and other types of literature about the Midwest, as well as those written by midwestern authors, are continually sought by the editor for inclusion in this annual bibliography. Please send them to Robert Beasecker via email: beaseckr@gvsu.edu.

Primary Sources

Aaronovitch, Ben. *Winter's Gifts* (N). Burton, Mich.: Subterranean Press, 2023. [Wis.]

Abbott, Megan. *Beware the Woman* (N). NY: G.P. Putnam's Sons, 2023. [Mich.]

Adamczyk, Laura. *Island City* (N). NY: FSG Originals, 2023. [Midwest]

Adams, Beth. *Fools Rush In* (N). Danbury, Conn.: Guideposts, 2023. [Dennison, Ohio]

Agatep, Renée. *Ohio Radio* (P). South Bend, Ind.: Wolfson Press, 2023. [Ohio]

AJ the Grinda. *That's the Way It Goes* (S). S.l.: Mind-Grind Publishing, 2023. [Milwaukee, Wis.]

Akers, Saundra Crum. *Dead or Alive?* (N). S.l.: Badgeley Publishing, 2023. [Cincinnati, Ohio]

Alexander, Johnnie and Dana Lynn. *Love's a Mystery in Crooksville OH* (N). Danbury, Conn.: Guideposts, 2023. [Crooksville, Ohio]

———. *Love's a Mystery in Gnaw Bone IN* (N). Danbury, Conn.: Guideposts, 2023. [Gnaw Bone, Ind.]

Alexander, Kwame. *Why Fathers Cry at Night* (M; P). NY: Little, Brown, 2023. [Chicago, Ill.]

Alicia, Kristen. *You've Been Served* (N). Shrewsbury, Pa.: Amara, 2023. [Mich.]

Allan, Barbara. *Antiques Foe* (N). Edinburgh: Severn House, 2023. [Iowa]

Allan, Lewis. *Mouse in the Box* (N). S.l.: Stretched Studio, 2023. [Milwaukee, Wis.]

Allbaugh, K.D. *Borgia Rose* (N). S.l.: Battle Ridge Rising Sun Press, 2023. [Wis.]

Amis, Fedora. *See President McKinley or Die Trying* (N). S.l.: M Books, 2023. [St. Louis, Mo.]

Amodeo, John. *Leaving Gary* (N). Herndon, Va.: Mascot Books, 2023. [Gary, Ind.]

Anderson, June Gossler. *The Other Side of Anoka* (N). Andover, Minn.: Grannygirl Press, 2023. [Anoka, Minn.]

Anderson, William J., et al., eds. *Rewilding Hope* (P). S.l.: League of Minnesota Poets, 2023. [Minn.]

Anselmo, Anthony. *The Spirit of the North Wind* (juv). Duluth, Minn.: Black Bears & Blueberries Publishing, 2023. [Minn.]

Armstrong, Douglas D. *Sun Dog Memory* (N). Whitefish Bay, Wis.: Lexington House Press, 2023. [Kan.]

Armstrong, Kelley. *Hemlock Island* (N). NY: St. Martin's, 2023. [Lake Superior]

Ashberg, Anne. *The Target* (N). S.l.: Williams and Charles Publishing, 2023. [Mich.]

Ashe, Gregory. *The Face in the Water* (N). S.l.: Hodgkin & Blount, 2023. [Mo.]

———. *The Spoil of Beasts* (N). S.l.: Hodgkin & Blount, 2023. [Mo.]

Atkinson, Rita Williams. *Of the Embers* (N). Meadville, Pa.: Fulton Books, 2023. [Milwaukee, Wis.]

Austin, Winter. *Straight for the Kill* (N). Toronto: Tule Publishing Group, 2023. [Iowa]

Avery, Laura. *The Year of Second Chances* (N). NY: William Morrow, 2023. [Minn.]

Axelrood, Larry. *Stealing Justice* (N). NY: Post Hill Press, 2023. [Chicago, Ill.]

B., Tina. *A Naptown Hitta Saved Me* (N). S.l.: Grand Penz Publications, 2023. [Indianapolis, Ind.]

Baart, Nicole. *The Long Way Back* (N). NY: Atria Paperback, 2023. [Minn.]

Bailey, Jen. *Unexpecting* (juv). NY: Wednesday Books, 2023. [Milwaukee, Wis.]

Baldwin, Kate. *The Formations* (N). Madison, Wis.: Streamwood Press, 2023. [Wis.]

Balzo, Sandra. *Any Pot in a Storm* (N). Edinburgh: Severn House, 2023. [Wis.]

Bang, Mary Jo. *A Film in Which I Play Everyone* (P). Minneapolis: Graywolf Press, 2023.

Barile, Paul. *Hope Rises* (juv). Chicago: Lexigraphic Press, 2023. [Chicago, Ill.]

Barnhill, Kelly. *The Crane Husband* (N). NY: Tordotcom Books, 2023. [Midwest]

Bartels, Erin. *Everything Is Just Beginning* (N). Grand Rapids, Mich.: Revell, 2023. [Detroit, Mich.]

Bartone, M.T. *Payne Avenue* (N). St. Paul, Minn.: Modern Prose Press, 2023. [St. Paul, Minn.]

Bastian, James. *Willa's Pursuit* (N). Denver, Colo.: Conundrum Press, 2023. [Wis.]

Baumann, Joe. *Hot Lips* (S). Monroe, Ill.: Curious Curls Publishing, 2023. [Mo.]

———. *The Plagues* (S). Stevens Point, Wis.: Cornerstone Press, 2023. [St. Louis, Mo.]

Bautz, Daniel. *Aristotle James and the Phantom Funeral Coach* (juv). S.l.: Anatolian Press, 2023. [Ohio]

———. *Life Is in the Blood* (N). S.l.: Anatolian Press, 2023. [Millersburg, Ohio]

Bayer, John. *Lead a Norse to Water* (N). S.l.: Melicrate Press, 2023. [N.D.]

Bayer, Lucy. *A Convenient Amish Bride* (N). Toronto: Love Inspired, 2023. [Ohio]

Bayless, Sally. *Donors, Deception & Death* (N). Rolla, Mo.: Kimberlin Belle Publishing, 2023. [Mo.]

———. *Home Tours, History & Homicide* (N). Rolla, Mo.: Kimberlin Belle Publishing, 2023. [Mo.]

———. *Sales, Secrets & Suspects* (N). Rolla, Mo.: Kimberlin Belle Publishing, 2022. [Mo.]

Beartrack-Algeo, Alfreda. *Father Eagle and the Hunter* (juv). Summertown, Tenn.: 7th Generation, 2023. [S.D.]

Beck, Hazel. *Big Little Spells* (N). Toronto: Graydon House, 2023. [Mo.]

Beckstrand, Jennifer. *Happily Ever After on Huckleberry Hill* (N). NY: Zebra Books, 2023. [Wis.]

Begleiter, Steven H. *Leaving Cleveland* (N). S.l.: Boulder Point Publishing, 2023. [Cleveland, Ohio]

Bentley, Terri Neunaber. *For Love of Family* (N). Greenville, S.C.: Ambassador International, 2023. [Ill.]

Berg, Elizabeth. *Earth's the Right Place for Love* (N). NY: Random House, 2023. [Mo.]

Berg, Steve. *Lost Colony* (N). NY: Evets Publishing, 2023. [Minneapolis, Minn.]

Berg, Sue. *Driftless Desperation* (N). Mineral Point, Wis.: Little Creek Press, 2023. [La Crosse, Wis.]

Bernstein, David. *Island Medicine* (N). Grand Rapids, Mich.: Buddha of the Valley Press, 2023. [Beaver Island, Mich]

Berry, Lucinda. *Off the Deep End* (N). Seattle: Thomas & Mercer, 2023. [Minn.]

Bertucci, John. *Conspiracy Unveiled* (N). Burnsville, Minn.: FuzionPress, 2023. [Mich.]

Biebel, Brett. *Winter Dance Party* (N). Boulder, Colo.: Alternating Current Press, 2023. [Iowa]

Bill, Frank. *Back to the Dirt* (N). NY: Farrar, Straus and Giroux, 2023. [Ind.]

Bill, J. Brent. *Amity: Stories from the Heartland* (S). Winchester: Roundfire Books, 2023. [Midwest]

Bills, Clare. *Stay out of That Room!* (N). Polk City, Iowa: Midwestern Books, 2023. [Minn.]

Bird, Charles G. *The Straits of Detroit* (N). Clinton Twp., Mich.: Read-a-Book Publishing, 2023. [Detroit, Mich.]

Bishop, Jenn. *Free Throws, Friendship, and Other Things We Fouled Up* (juv). San Francisco: Chronicle Books, 2023. [Cincinnati, Ohio]

Bishop, Wesley R., ed. *To Write the World* (A). S.l.: North Meridian Books, 2023. [Ohio]

Bithell, Rachel. *Brave Bird at Wounded Knee* (juv). Mendota Heights, Minn.: Jolly Fish Press, 2023. [S.D.]

Blakemore, K.T. *The Good Time Girls* (N). Mesa, Ariz.: Sycamore Creek Press, 2023. [Kan.]

———. *The Good Time Girls Get Famous* (N). Mesa, Ariz.: Sycamore Creek Press, 2023. [Kan.]

Blankenship, Debbie S. *Gone: Year Two* (N). Eugene, Or.: Resource Publications, 2023. [Midwest]

Bolina, Jaswinder. *English as a Second Language* (P). Port Townsend, Wash.: Copper Canyon, 2023.

Bolton, Ginger. *Cinnamon Twisted* (N). NY: Kensington Books, 2023. [Wis.]

Bongiovanni, Archie. *Mimosa* (N). NY: Abrams ComicArts Surely, 2023. [Minneapolis, Minn.]

Booher, David. *Specs* (N). Los Angeles: Boom! Studios, 2023. [Ohio]

Borin, Fran. *Orion O'Brien and the Spirit of Quindaro* (juv). Traverse City, Mich.: Mission Point Press, 2023. [Kansas City, Kan.]

———. *The Phantoms of Wakarusa* (juv). Traverse City, Mich.: Mission Point Press, 2023. [Lawrence, Kan.]

Boswell, Bettie, et al. *Christmas in Ohio* (S). Georgetown, Tenn.: Mt. Zion Ridge Press, 2023. [Ohio]

Boulley, Angeline. *Warrior Girl Unearthed* (juv). NY: Holt, 2023. [Mich.]

Bow, Erin. *Simon Sort of Says* (juv). Los Angeles: Disney Hyperion, 2023. [Neb.]

Boyd, Dannie. *Fractured Oak* (N). Fairlawn, Ohio: Indigo Dot Press, 2023. [Ohio]

Boyer, Clyde. *Girl out of Time* (juv). Seattle: Girl Friday Books, 2023. [Ind.]

Bracero, Lesley. *Love Is a Sacrifice* (juv). NY: Morgan James Publishing, 2023. [Chicago, Ill.]

Bradford, Laura see Quinn, Emily

Bradley, Lauren. *Deathly Alive* (N). Pittsburgh: Dorrance Publishing, 2023. [Mo.]

Brady, Ali. *The Comeback Summer* (N). NY: Berkley Books, 2023. [Chicago, Ill.]

Breen, Paul. *A Sudden Interest in Shakespeare* (N). S.l.: Dutch Hollow Press, 2023. [Madison, Wis.]

Brennan, Matthew. *The End of the Road* (P). American Fork, Utah: Kelsay Books, 2023.

Brice, Morgan. *Peacemaker* (N). Tallahassee, Fla.: Darkwind Press, 2023. [St. Louis, Mo.]

Brinkman, William. *A Fire in the Shadows* (N). S.l.: Anti-Psychic Kitty Press, 2023. [Bolingbrook, Ill.]

Brogan, Tracy. *Art of the Chase* (N). Suttons Bay, Mich.: Oliver-Heber Books, 2023. [Mich.]

Broidy, Steve, ed. *Rhyme & Rune* (P). Charlotte, N.C.: Main Street Rag Publishing, 2023. [Ohio]

Bronski, Sally Nelson. *Running Uphill: A Minnesota Theater Memoir* (M). Minneapolis: Afton Press, 2023. [Minn.]

Browder, Catherine. *The Manning Girl* (N). Raleigh, N.C.: Regal House Publishing, 2023. [Kan.]

Brown, Adrienne, Maree. *Maroons* (N). Chico, Calif.: AK Press, 2023. [Detroit, Mich.]

Brown, Alan and Brian Brown. *Lake Honor* (N). Pensacola, Fla.: World Castle Publishing, 2023. [Branson, Mo.]

Brown, Brian see Brown, Alan

Brown, Frank London. *This Is Life* (S). Chicago: From Beyond Press, 2023. [Chicago, Ill.]

Brown, H.M.S. *Wayward Guilt* (N). Columbus, Ohio: Leaux Cay Press, 2023. [Ohio]

Brown, Irene Bennett. *Miss Royal's Mules* (N). Las Vegas, Nev.: Wolfpack Publishing, 2023. [Kan.]

———. *One True Deed* (N). Las Vegas, Nev.: Wolfpack Publishing, 2023. [Kan.]

———. *Somebody's Business* (N). Las Vegas, Nev.: Wolfpack Publishing, 2023. [Kan.]

———. *Tangled Times* (N). Las Vegas, Nev.: Wolfpack Publishing, 2023. [Kan.]

Brown, Lynn MacKaben. Furs and Fevers (N). NY: Austin Macauley Publishers, 2023. [Ind.]

Brown, Teri M. *An Enemy Like Me* (N). Austin, Tex.: Atmosphere Press, 2023. [Ohio]

Brunstetter, Wanda E. *Letters of Comfort* (N). Uhrichsville, Ohio: Barbour Publishing, 2023. [Ind.]

———. *Letters of Trust* (N). Uhrichsville, Ohio: Barbour Publishing, 2023. [Ind.]

Buhr, Thomas A. *The Outgoing* (N). Traverse City, Mich.: Mission Point Press, 2022. [Mich.]

Bujold, Lois McMaster. *Knot of Shadows* (N). Burton, Mich.: Subterranean Press, 2023.

Bull, Barbara E. *Checkered Pasts* (N). Shelby, Mich.: Cherry Point Publishing, 2023. [Mich.]

Burkhart, Monika L. *If Love Be Lost* (N). S.l.: Luminescent Paintbox, 2023. [St. Louis, Mo.]

Burns, Debbie. *You're My Home* (N). Naperville, Ill.: Sourcebooks Casablanca, 2023. [St. Louis, Mo.]

Burns, Heidi Wall see MacBride, Michael

Burns, V.M. *Bookclubbed to Death* (N). NY: Kensington Books, 2023. [Mich.]

———. *Murder on Tour* (N). NY: Kensington Books 2023. [Mich.]

Burns, Valerie. *Murder Is a Piece of Cake* (N). NY: Kensington Books, 2023. [Mich.]

Burt, Anne. *The Dig* (N). Berkeley, Calif.: Counterpoint, 2023. [Minn.]

Burton, Sherry A. *Spirit of Deadwood* (N). S.l.: Dorry Press, 2023. [Deadwood, S.D.]

Busha, Gary C. *Turtles—Nose to Nose* (P). Sturtevant, Wis.: Wolfsong Publications, 2023. [Wis.]

Byas, Taylor. *I Done Clicked My Heels Three Times* (P). NY: Soft Skull Press, 2023.

Bynum, James. *Lake Street Jimmy* (juv). Minneapolis: Cutz Too Publishing, 2023. [Minneapolis, Minn.]

Cai, Delia. *Central Places* (N). NY: Ballantine Books, 2023. [Ill.]

Cain, Steven. *Bets & Breakfasts* (N). S.l.: Upon the Moment Publishing, 2023. [Ind.]

Caine, Danny. *Picture Window* (P). Orlando, Fla.: Autofocus Books, 2023. [Kan.]

Cameron, W. Bruce. *Love, Clancy* (N). NY: Forge Books, 2023. [Kansas City, Mo.]

Campanella, J.J. *Summon the Angels* (N). Bloomfield, N.J.: Uvula Publishing, 2023. [Cleveland, Ohio]

Caña, Natalie. *A Dish Best Served Hot* (N). Toronto: MIRA, 2023. [Chicago, Ill.]

Cancelmo, Joseph A. *Detroit Unrequited* (N). NY: Heliotrope Books, 2023. [Detroit, Mich.]

Canter, Robert. *The South Bend Dart Frog Murders* (N). Parker, Colo.: Outskirts Press, 2023. [South Bend, Ind.]

Cárdenas, Brenda. *Trace* (P). Pasadena, Calif.: Red Hen Press, 2023.

Carlson, David. *Suffer the Children* (N). Kenmore, Wash.: Coffee Town Press, 2023. [Detroit, Mich.]

Carlson-Voiles, Polly. *Star Party* (juv). St. Paul: Minnesota Historical Society Press, 2023. [Minn.]

Carter, Sarah Anne. *The Cookie Connection* (N). S.l.: SAC Publishing, 2023. [Springfield, Ohio]

Case, Doug Paul, ed. *A Flame Called Indiana: An Anthology of Contemporary Hoosier Writing* (A). Bloomington, Ind.: Indiana U P, 2023. [Ind.]

Cass, Laurie. *A Troubling Tail* (N). NY: Berkley Prime Crime, 2023. [Mich.]

Castillo, Linda. *An Evil Heart*. NY: Minotaur Books, 2023. [Ohio]

Cates, Anna, ed. *Little Black Box* (P). Eugene, Or.: Resource Publications, 2023. [Ohio]

Catherwood, Michael. *Near Misses* (P). Wayne, Neb.: WSC Press, 2023. [Neb.]

Chao, Gloria. *When You Wish upon a Lantern* (juv). NY: Viking, 2023. [Chicago, Ill.]

Chapin, Malissa. *Murder Goes Glamping* (N). Oshkosh, Wis.: Ivory Keys Press, 2023. [Wis.]

Chapman, Vannetta. *Her Amish Adversary* (N). Toronto: Love Inspired, 2023. [Ind.]

———. *An Unusual Amish Winter Match* (N). Toronto: Love Inspired, 2023. [Ind.]

Cheeseman, Timothy and Jeannine Jordan, eds. *River & Rust* (P). Lima, Ohio: Meandering Bard, 2023. [Ohio]

Chenault-Kilgore, Monica. *Long Gone, Come Home* (N). Toronto: Graydon House, 2023. [Cincinnati, Ohio]

Cheng, Jack. *The Many Masks of Andy Zhou* (juv). NY: Dial Books, 2023. [Detroit, Mich.]

Chern, Lina. *Play the Fool* (N). NY: Bantam Books, 2023. [Chicago, Ill.]

Cherry, Bryon. *Death Moan* (P). Detroit: Willow Books. 2023. [Milwaukee, Wis.]

Chmielarz, Sharon. *Duet in the Little Blue Church* (P). Minneapolis: Nodin Press, 2023.

Christen, Julie. *Nokota Voices* (juv). Drayton Valley, Alb.: BWL Publishing, 2023. [N.D.]

Christenson, Andrea. *How Sweet It Is* (N). S.l.: Sunrise Publishing, 2023. [Minn.]

Chronister, Jan. *Duluth: Zenith City & Beyond* (P). S.l.: Poetry Harbor, 2023. [Duluth, Minn.]

Claire, Dana. *Hunterland* (N). Brentwood, Tenn.: CamCat Books, 2023. [Wis.]

Clark, Shane. *The Devil Won't Keep Us Apart* (N). North Hampton, N.H.: Mindstir Media, 2023. [Ohio]

Clark, Tracy. *Fall* (N). Seattle: Thomas & Mercer, 2023. [Chicago, Ill.]

———. *Hide* (N). Seattle: Thomas & Mercer, 2023. [Chicago, Ill.]

Clarke, Amy Suiter. *Lay Your Body Down* (N). NY: William Morrow, 2023. [Minn.]

Clay, Dan. *Becoming a Queen* (juv). NY: Roaring Brook Press, 2023. [Mich.]

Clements, Sandy. *Kaleidoscope of Secrets* (N). Chicago: Story Tell Publishing, 2023. [Chicago, Ill.]

Coble, Colleen. *Break of Day* (N). Nashville, Tenn.: Thomas Nelson, 2023. [Mich.]

———. *Dark of Night* (N). Nashville, Tenn.: Thomas Nelson, 2023. [Mich.]

Cochran, Peg. *Berried Grievances* (N). S.l.: Beyond the Page Publishing, 2023. [Mich.]

Coco, Nancy. *Give Fudge a Chance* (N). NY: Kensington Books, 2023. [Mich.]

Cohen, Joshua. *Past Imperfect* (N). St. Paul, Minn.: Kasva Press, 2023. [Cleveland, Ohio]

Coleman, R.K. *The Great Get-Together* (juv). St. Paul: Minnesota Historical Society Press, 2023. [Minn.]

Coleman, Stephanie. *Life in the Middle* (N). Carol Stream, Ill.: Focus on the Family, 2023. [Ind.]

Collard, Andrew. *Sprawl* (P). Athens: Ohio U P, 2023. [Detroit, Mich.]

Collins, Kate. *Gone But Not for Garden* (N). NY: Kensington Books, 2023. [Mich.]

Connor, Chase. *Head for Murder* (N). Dallas, Tex.: Lion Fish Press, 2023. [Iowa]

Conway, Tove. *Northern Sights* (juv). St. Paul, Minn.: Beaver's Pond Press, 2023. [Minn.]

Cooper, Shantiana. *Fallin for a Chi-Town Savage* (N). S.l.: Cole Hart Signature, 2023. [Chicago, Ill.]

———. *Fallin for a Chi-Town Savage 2* (N). S.l.: Cole Hart Signature, 2023. [Chicago, Ill.]

Copa, Libby. *A Low Diving Bird* (N). S.l.: Desert Animal, 2023. [Mo.]

Corley, Kevin. *The Begotten* (N). S.l.: Sixteen Tons Publication, 2023. [Ill.]

Costa, Shelley. *No Mistaking Death* (N). S.l.: Level Best Books, 2023. [Ohio]

Costagliola, Brunella. *The Dinosaur Woman* (juv). Nashville, Tenn.: Wee B. Books, 2023. [N.D.]

Coster, Mélanie de. *Lettres du Kansas* (N). Toulouse: Éditions Milan, 2023. [Kan.]

Cottingham, Dale. *Midwest Hymns* (P). American Fork, Utah: Kelsay Books, 2023. [Midwest]

Couch, Robbie. *If I See You Again Tomorrow* (juv). NY: Simon & Schuster, 2023. [Ill.]

Cowdrey, Richard. *You've Got This, Fiona* (juv). Grand Rapids, Mich.: Zonderkidz, 2023. [Cincinnati, Ohio]

Cox, Michelle. *A Haunting at Linley* (N). Berkeley, Calif.: She Writes Press, 2023. [Omaha, Neb.]

Craig, Patrick E. *The Boy in Blue Denim* (N). Huston, Id.: P&J Publishing, 2023. [Ohio]

Crane, Ben. *A Man of Lies* (N). NY: Pegasus Crime, 2023. [Chicago, Ill.; Omaha, Neb.]

Cravens, Claudia. *Lucky Red* (N). NY: Dial Press, 2023. [Dodge City, Kan.]

Crisler, Curtis L. *Doing Drive-Bys on How to Love in the Midwest* (P). S.l.: C&R Press, 2023. [Midwest]

Crowder, Tracy Occomy. *Montgomery and the Case of the Golden Key* (juv). NY: Tu Books, 2023. [Chicago, Ill.]

Crown, Zaire. *Silence* (N). NY: Dafina Books, 2023. [Detroit, Mich.]

Crusie, Jennifer and Bob Mayer. *Lavender's Blue* (N). S.l.: Cool Gus Publishing, 2023. [Ohio]

———. *One in Vermillion* (N). S.l.: Cool Gus Publishing, 2023. [Ohio]

———. *Rest in Pink* (N). S.l.: Cool Gus Publishing, 2023. [Ohio]

Currie, Lindsay. *It Found Us* (juv). Naperville, Ill.: Sourcebooks Young Readers, 2023. [Forest Park, Ill.]

Curtis, Jane. *Reach Her in This Light* (S). Stevens Point, Wis.: Cornerstone Press, 2023. [Madison, Wis.]

Cushing, Nicole. *The Plastic Priest*. Forest Hill, Md.: Cemetery Dance Publishing, 2023. [Ind.]

Cutter, Charles. *Under the Ashes* (N). Traverse City, Mich.: Mission Point Press, 2023. [Mich.]

D'Angelo, Florence. *Niglíču: She Comes Out Alive* (N). Port Jervis, N.Y.: Independent Thinking Press, 2023. [S.D.]

Dams, Jeanne M. *Music and Murder* (N). Edinburgh: Severn House, 2023. [Chicago, Ill.]

Daniel, N. *An Outcome As Perfect As Morning* (N). S.l.: Black Coffee Press, 2023. [Minneapolis, Minn.]

Daniels, Jim Ray. *The Luck of the Fall* (S). East Lansing: Michigan State U P, 2023. [Detroit, Mich.]

Danvers, Holly. *Read to Death at the Lakeside Library* (N). NY: Crooked Lane, 2023. [Wis.]

Dargan, Cherie. *The Legacy* (N). Cody, Wyo.: WordCrafts Press, 2023. [Iowa]

Darlington, C.J. *Heart of Belonging* (N). Carol Stream, Ill.: Focus on the Family, 2023. [Ind.]

Davies, Diane. *Willy: The Covid Rescue Pup* (juv). S.l.: Writers' Branding, 2023. [Minn.]

Davis, Dana L. *Don't Stop the Music* (juv). Paris: Auzou, 2023. [Iowa]

———. *Fake Famous* (juv). NY: Skyscape, 2023. [Iowa]

Dawson, J.R. *The First Bright Thing* (N). NY: Tor Books, 2023. [Midwest]

Day, Maddie. *Four Leaf Cleaver* (N). NY: Kensington Books, 2023. [Ind.]

Deal, Janice. *Strange Attractors* (S). Philadelphia: New Door Books, 2023. [Ill.]

Dean, Audrey. *And Two Makes Four* (N). Garibaldi Highlands, B.C.: Extasy Books, 2023. [Wis.]

Dean, Daren. *Roads* (N). S.l.: Cowboy Jamboree Press, 2023. [Mo.]

Dean, Lou. *Autumn of the Big Snow* (N). Dinosaur, Colo.: Clinescot Publishing, 2023. [Kan.]

Deeren, R.S. *Enough to Lose* (S). Detroit: Wayne State U P, 2023. [Mich.]

DeKeyser, Stacy. *How to Catch a Polar Bear* (juv). NY: Margaret K. McElderry Books, 2023. [Milwaukee, Wis.]

DeLaurentis, Karin. *Tomorrow, after Christmas* (N). Columbus, Ohio: Biblio Publishing, 2023. [Ohio]

Dempsey, Diana. *The Unstoppable Eliza Haycraft* (N). S.l.: Bramerton Press, 2023. [St. Louis, Mo.]

DeNiro, Anya Johanna. *OKPsyche* (N). Easthampton, Mass.: Small Beer Press, 2023. [Minn.]

Denman, Amie. *Last Summer on Christmas Island* (N). Toronto: Harlequin, 2023. [Mich.]

———. *A Merry Little Christmas* (N). Toronto: Harlequin, 2023. [Mich.]

———. *Under the Mistletoe* (N). Toronto: Harlequin, 2023. [Mich.]

Desai, Sara. *To Have and to Heist* (N). NY: Berkley Books, 2023. [Evanston, Ill.]

DeSmet, Christine. *Holly Jolly Fudge Folly* (N). Atherton, Qld.: Writers Exchange E-Publishing, 2023. [Wis.]

———. *Undercover Fudge* (N). Atherton, Qld.: Writers Exchange E-Publishing, 2023. [Wis.]

Deveraux, Jude. *My Heart Will Find You* (N). Toronto: Mira, 2023. [Kansas City, Mo.]

Diede, Kimberly. *Five Golden Friends* (N). S.l.: Endless Ripple Press, 2023. [Minn.]

Dieker, Nicole. *Like, Subscribe, and Murder* (N). Sandy, Or.: Shortwave Media, 2023. [Iowa]

———. *Shakespeare in the Park with Murder* (N). Sandy, Or.: Shortwave Media, 2023. [Iowa]

Dietrich, Milana. *The Crow Won't Tell* (N). Encino, Calif.: Putnam & Smith, 2023. [Neb.]

Dill, Mark. *Spirit of Speedway* (juv). Bloomington, Ind.: Xlibris, 2023. [Speedway, Ind.]

Dilworth, Sharon. *To Be Marquette* (N). Pittsburgh: Bridge & Tunnel Books, 2023. [Marquette, Mich.]

Dobrinska, Leah. *Mayhem in Circulation* (N). S.l.: Level Best Books, 2023. [Wis.]

Dominique, J. *First Come Thugs, Then Come Marriage* (N). S.l.: Cole Hart Signature, 2023. [Chicago, Ill.]

———. *First Come Thugs, Then Come Marriage 2* (N). S.l.: Cole Hart Signature, 2023. [Chicago, Ill.]

———. *First Come Thugs, Then Come Marriage 3* (N). S.l.: Cole Hart Signature, 2023. [Chicago, Ill.]

Donaldson, Monique L. *Deceived 2* (N). S.l.: Major Key Publishing, 2023. [Cleveland, Ohio]

Dorch, Edwina Louise. *The Alford Plea* (N). Bloomington, Ind.: Xlibris, 2023. [Kansas City, Mo.]

Dorf, Marilyn. *Friday's House and Other Stories* (S). London: Austin Macauley Publishers, 2023. [Midwest]

Dornbush, Jennifer. *Last One Alive* (N). Ashland, Or.: Blackstone Publishing, 2023. [Chicago, Ill.; Mich]

Dougherty, Mike. *Como Flats* (N). Charleston, S.C.: Palmetto Publishing, 2023. [St. Paul, Minn.]

Doyle, Kevin R. *Clean Win* (N). Kenmore, Wash.: Camel Press, 2023. [Mo.]

Dranfield, Wendy. *The Night She Vanished* (N). London: Bookouture, 2023. [Midwest]

Dreesen, Robert J. *I Don't Smoke Enough to Quit* (M; P). Philadelphia: Paul Dry Books, 2023. [Neb.]

Dufer, Brett. *Endless River* (P). Rockeport, Mo.: Pebble Publishing, 2023. [Mo.]

Dulka, Trish. *Chances Are* (N). Leschenault, W. Aus.: Book Reality Experience, 2023. [Ohio]

Dunbar, Carol. *A Winter's Rime* (N). NY: Forge Books, 2023. [Wis.]

Dundee, Wayne D. *Devil's Tower* (N). Las Vegas, Nev.: Wolfpack Publishing, 2023. [Neb.]

———. *The Gun Wolves* (N). Las Vegas, Nev.: Wolfpack Publishing, 2022. [Neb.]

———. *Wildcat Hills* (N). Las Vegas, Nev.: Wolfpack Publishing, 2023. [Neb.]

Dunn, Chelsea Burton. *By Moonlight* (N). Dunedin, Fla.: 4 Horsemen Publications, 2023. [Kansas City, Mo.]

———. *Moon Bound* (N). Dunedin, Fla.: 4 Horsemen Publications, 2023. [Kansas City, Mo.]

Dykema, Alesha. *Everything She Has* (N). S.l.: Brandywine Publishing, 2023. [Indianapolis, Ind.]

Dziedzic, Grzegorz. *Gangway* (N). Warsaw: Wydawnictwo Agora, 2023. [Chicago, Ill.]

Dzikowski, Barbara. *The Fireweed Moon* (N). S.l.: Wiara Books, 2023. [Ohio]

Ebenstein, Alex. *Melon Head Mayhem* (N). Sandy, Or.: Shortwave Media, 2023. [Mich.]

Eden, Sarah M., ed. *The General* (S). S.l.: Maple Lane Publishing, 2023. [Galena, Ill.]

Edwards, Malon. *If Wishes Were Obfuscation Codes* (S). Boston: Fireside Fiction, 2023. [Chicago, Ill.]

Elizabeth, Francis. *Drugs and Other Things to Do in Cleveland* (N). S.l.: Pressed Pulp, 2023. [Cleveland, Ohio]

Engel, Amy. *I Did It for You* (N). NY: Dutton, 2023. [Kan.]

Erebia, Federico. *Pedro & Daniel* (juv). Montclair, N.J.: Levine Querido, 2023. [Ohio]

Erickson, Alex. *Death by Iced Coffee* (N). NY: Kensington Books, 2023. [Ohio]

Ernst, Kathleen. *The Solace of Stars* (N). S.l.: Level Best Books, 2023. [Wis.]

Eskens, Allen. *Saving Emma* (N). NY: Mulholland Books, 2023. [Minn.]

Estleman, Loren D. *City Walls* (N). NY: Forge Books, 2023. [Cleveland, Ohio]

———. *Vamp* (N). NY: Forge Books, 2023.

Evans, Allan. *Killer Smile* (N). Salt Lake City: Immortal Works, 2023. [Minn.]

Evans, Lillie and Tony Perona, eds. *Amber Waves of Graves* (S). S.l.: Speed City Press, 2023. [Ind.]

Fairchild, B.H. *An Ordinary Life* (P). NY: W.W. Norton, 2023. [Midwest]

Fakih, Kimberly Olson. *Little Miseries* (N). Encino, Calif.: Delphinium Books, 2023. [Iowa; Minn.]

Fick, D.M.S. *Lewis Sinclair and the Gentlemen Cowboys* (N). Brentwood, Tenn.: CamCat, 2023. [Midwest]

Finkbeiner, Susie. *The All-American* (N). Grand Rapids, Mich.: Revell, 2023. [Detroit, Mich.]

Flanagan, Erin. *Come with Me* (N). Seattle: Thomas & Mercer, 2023. [Ohio]

Flower, Amanda. *Blueberry Blunder* (N). NY: Kensington Books, 2023. [Ohio]

———. *Dating Can Be Deadly* (N). NY: Kensington Books, 2023. [Ohio]

———. *Honeymoons Can Be Hazardous* (N). NY: Kensington Books, 2023. [Ohio]

———. *In Farm's Way* (N). Naperville, Ill.: Poisoned Pen Press, 2023. [Mich.]

Fluke, Joanne. *Pink Lemonade Cake Murder* (N). NY: Kensington Books, 2023. [Minn.]

Flynn, Matthew J. *China Code* (N). Naples, Fla.: Speaking Volumes, 2023. [Milwaukee, Wis.]

Foley, John. *Ghost of a Chance* (N). NY: Austin Macauley Publishers, 2023. [St. Paul, Minn.]

Ford, Richard. *Be Mine* (N). NY: Ecco Press, 2023. [S.D.]

Forrest, Claire. *Where You See Yourself* (juv). NY: Scholastic Press, 2023. [Minneapolis, Minn.]

Foster, Linda Nemec. *Bone Country* (P). Stevens Point, Wis.: Cornerstone Press, 2023.

Foster, Lori. *The Little Flower Shop* (N). NY: Canary Street Press, 2023. [Ind.]

Frailey, Fred W. *Seldom Willing* (N). Edwards, Colo.: Flanged Wheel Books, 2023. [Kan.]

Frasier, Anne. *The Night I Died* (N). Seattle: Thomas & Mercer, 2023. [Kan.]

Freligh, Sarah. *A Brief Natural History of Women* (S). S.l.: Harbor Editions, 2023. [Detroit, Mich.]

Friedl, Amy. AJ's *Adventures at Indiana Dunes* (juv). S.l.: Ingram Spark Publishing, 2023. [Ind.]

Fuller, Kathleen. *The Courtship Plan* (N). Grand Rapids, Mich.: Zondervan, 2023. [Ohio]

Fullerton, P.J.A. *Red Road Redemption* (S). Hillsboro, Wis.: Wisconsin Writers Association Press, 2023. [Wis.]

Gaiman, Neil. *What You Need to Be Warm* (juv). NY: Quill Tree Books, 2023.

Gard, Julie. *I Think I Know You* (P). Athens, Ga.: FutureCycle Press, 2023. [Duluth, Minn.]

Garland, Max. *Into the Good World Again* (P). Duluth, Minn.: Holy Cow! Press, 2023. [Wis.]

Garrett, RaeChell. *Promposal* (juv). NY: Little, Brown, 2023. [Mich.]

Gernon, Rebecca Willman. *The Sunflower Letters* (N). Covington, La.: HRH Dolland Press, 2023. [Kan.]

Gibson, Lena. *The Edge of Life* (N). Castroville, Tex.: Black Rose Writing, 2023. [S.D.]

Giesler, Andy. *Three Grams of Elsewhere* (N). Madison, Wis.: Humble Quill, 2023. [Wis.]

Ginsberg, Maggie. *Still True* (N). Madison: U Wisconsin P, 2022. [Wis.]

Girondi, Patrick. *New City* (N). NY: Skyhorse Publishing, 2023. [Chicago, Ill.]

Glenn, Dale. *Mystic Nights of the Wabash* (N). Toms River, N.J.: Paper House Publishing, 2023. [Ind.]

Goble, Steve. *Go Find Daddy* (N). Sarasota, Fla.: Oceanview Publishing, 2023. [Ohio]

Gold, Maxwell I. *Bleeding Rainbows and Other Broken Spectrums* (P). Erie, Colo.: Hex Publishers, 2023. [Ohio]

Goldman, Joel. *Bennie Moten's Blues* (N). S.l.: Character Flaw Press, 2023. [Kansas City, Mo.]

Goldman, Matt. *A Good Family* (N). NY: Forge Books, 2023. [Edina, Minn.]

Golodner, Lynne. *Woman of Valor* (N). S.l.: Scotia Road Books, 2023. [Skokie, Ill.]

Gould, Leslie. *I'll Be Seeing You* (N). Danbury, Conn.: Guideposts, 2023. [Dennison, Ohio]

Gourlay, Candy. *Wild Song* (juv). Oxford: David Fickling Books, 2023. [St. Louis, Mo.]

Goyer, Tricia. *The Buggy before the Horse* (N). Danbury, Conn.: Guideposts, 2023. [Ohio]

Graff, Keir see Patterson, James

Grandinetti, Danielle. *Confessions to a Stranger* (N). S.l.: Hearth Spot Press, 2023. [Wis.]

———. *Refuge for the Archaeologist* (N). S.l.: Hearth Spot Press, 2023. [Wis.]

Graves, Byron. *Rez Ball* (N). NY: Heartdrum, 2023. [Minn.]

Graves, T. Patrick. *A Menace to the Community* (N). London: Austin Macauley Publishers, 2023. [S.D.]

Gray, Anissa. *Life and Other Love Songs* (N). NY: Berkley Books, 2023. [Detroit, Mich.]

Gray, Shelley Shepard. *An Amish Cinderella* (N). NY: Kensington Books, 2023. [Ohio]

———. *Once upon a Buggy* (N). NY: Kensington Books, 2023. [Ohio]

———. *Sycamore Circle* (N). Ashland, Or.: Blackstone Publishing, 2023. [Ohio]

Grecian, Alex. *Red Rabbit* (N). NY: Nightfire, 2023. [Kan.]

Greeley, Brendan. *Secret Pizza* (N). S.l.: Party Cut Press, 2023. [Midwest]

Green, Stacy. *Bone Lake* (N). London: Bookouture, 2023. [Minn.]

———. *Her Last Tear* (N). London: Bookouture, 2023. [Stillwater, Minn.]

Greene, Jennifer. *Hideaway at Silver Lake* (N). NY: Avon, 2023. [Wis.]

Greer, Cindy. *Suzanna's Journey* (N). Maitland, Fla.: Xulon Press, 2023. [Neb.]

Greer, Heather. *Window of Opportunity* (N). Morrilton, Ark.: Scrivenings Press, 2023. [Harrisburg, Ill.]

Grey, Andrew. *Dragged to the Wedding* (N). Toronto: Carina Press, 2023. [Chicago, Ill.]

Griffith, Cary J. *Killing Monarchs* (N). Cambridge, Minn.: Adventure Publications, 2023. [Minn.]

Grover, Linda LeGarde. *A Song over Miskwaa Rapids* (N). Minneapolis: U Minnesota P, 2023. [Minn.]

Gunter, Rick J. *The Legend of Mad Howard* (N). S.l.: MoOzark Publishing, 2023. [Mo.]

Hackett, Tasha. *Wildflower on the Prairie* (N). Stromsburg, Neb.: Electric Moon Publishing, 2023. [Neb.]

Halperin, Hanna. *I Could Live Here Forever* (N). NY: Viking Books, 2023. [Madison, Wis.]

Hamilton, Laurell K. *Smolder* (N). NY: Berkley Books, 2023. [St. Louis, Mo.]

Hamilton, Victoria. *Sieve and Let Die* (N). S.l.: Beyond the Page Publishing, 2023. [Mich.]

Hammack, Bruce. *Murder on the Wichita* (N). S.l.: Jubilee Publishing, 2023. [Wichita, Kan.]

Handberg, Ron. *On Nowhere Street* (N). St. Paul, Minn.: Hawk Hill Literary, 2023. [Minn.]

Hannah, Andrea. *Where Darkness Blooms* (juv). NY: Wednesday Books, 2023. [Kan.]

Hannah, Darci. *Murder at the Pumkin Pageant* (N). NY: Kensington Books, 2023. [Mich.]

Hannon, Irene. *Into the Fire* (N). Grand Rapids, Mich.: Revell, 2023. [St. Louis, Mo.]

Hanscome, Jeanette. *Accentuate the Positive* (N). Danbury, Conn.: Guideposts, 2023. [Dennison, Ohio]

Hansel, Patrick Cabello. *Breathing in Minneapolis* (P). Georgetown, Ky.: Finishing Line Press, 2023. [Minneapolis, Minn.]

Hansen, Annie. *Get a Grip* (N). S.l.: HF Publishing, 2023. [Ill.]

Hardy, Joanne. *Abandoned* (N). Cathedral City, Calif.: AquaZebra Book Publishing, 2023. [Ill.]

Harrison, Kim. *Demons of Good and Evil* (N). NY: Ace, 2023. [Cincinnati, Ohio]

Hart, Sandra Merville. *A Not So Persistent Suitor* (N). S.l.: Wild Heart Books, 2023. [Ohio]

Hart, Tashia. *Native Love Jams* (N). Duluth, Minn.: Not Too Far Removed Press, 2023. [Minn.]

Hartman, Ruth J. *Dial M for Meow* (N). S.l.: Gemma Halliday Publishing, 2023. [Ind.]

Hauser, Robert. *Blood Summer 1862* (N). London: Austin Macauley Publishers, 2023. [Minn.]

Hawthorne, Geri. *Time Quest* (N). Conneaut Lake, Pa.: Page Publishing, 2023. [N.D.]

Haydon, Kathryn P. *Unsalted Blue Sunrise* (P). Chicago: Prairie Cloud Press, 2023. [Lake Michigan]

Haynes, Stan. *And Union No More* (N). S.l.: SMH Publishing, 2023. [Kan.]

Hazard, John. *Interrupt the Sky* (P). Nacogdoches, Tex.: Stephen F. Austin State U P, 2023. [Midwest]

Headen, Miesha Wilson see Ruhlman, Michael

Hechtman, Betty. *Sentenced to Death* (N). London: Severn House, 2023. [Chicago, Ill.]

Hedlund, Jody. *Calling on the Matchmaker* (N). Minneapolis: Bethany House, 2023. [St. Louis, Mo.]

Heinz, Rick. *Dawn* (N). Dunedin, Fla.: 4 Horsemen Publishers, 2023. [Chicago, Ill.]

Heitland, Bill. *Next Stop Chicago* (N). Bloomington, Ind.: Archway Publishing, 2023. [Ill.]

Helgerson, Joseph. *The Lost Galumpus* (juv). Boston: Clarion Books, 2023. [Minneapolis, Minn.]

Herne, Ruth Logan. *As Time Goes By* (N). Danbury, Conn.: Guideposts, 2023. [Dennison, Ohio]

Herrera, Jennifer. *The Hunter* (N). NY: G.P. Putnam's Sons, 2023. [Ohio]

Herron, Cynthia. *His Heart Renewed* (N). White Salmon, Wash.: Mountain Brook Ink, 2023. [Mo.]

Heyse, Ann. *The Light Is Ours* (N). Baileys Harbor, Wis.: Sand Beach Press, 2023. [Wis.]

Hickman, Demoris B. *Changed: Faceoff* (N). Florence, S.C.: Legacy Ink, 2022. [Detroit, Mich.]

Hill, Drew. *Crossing the Tracks* (N). Butler, Wis.: Evolved Publishing, 2023. [Kansas City, Mo.]

Hill, Nathan. *Wellness* (N). NY: Alfred A. Knopf, 2023. [Chicago, Ill.]

Hinsdale, Emily L. Hay. *Duck Hunt* (juv). Minneapolis: Magic Wagon, 2023. [Minn.]

Hirt, Douglas. *The Gold Chip* (N). Las Vegas, Nev.: Wolfpack Publishing, 2023. [Kan.]

Hockett, Jericho M. and Dennis Etzel, Jr., eds. *Kansas Speaks Out* (P). Topeka, Kan.: Actual Kansas Press, 2022. [Kan.]

Hollowell, Sarah. *What Stalks among Us* (juv). NY: Clarion Books, 2023. [Ind.]

Horan, Nancy. *The House of Lincoln* (N). Naperville, Ill.: Sourcebooks Landmark, 2023. [Springfield, Ill.]

House, Alexandra. *Goal* (N). S.l.: Pink Cashmere Publishing, 2023. [St. Louis, Mo.]

———. *Holding* (N). S.l.: Pink Cashmere Publishing, 2023. [St. Louis, Mo.]

Housewright, David. *In a Hard Wind* (N). NY: Minotaur Books, 2023. [Minn.]

Houston, Victoria. *Hidden in the Pines* (N). NY: Crooked Lane Books, 2023. [Wis.]

Hovde, Jenelle. *We'll Meet Again* (N). Danbury, Conn.: Guideposts, 2023. [Dennison, Ohio]

Hovey, Dean L. *The Last Rodeo* (N). Calgary, Alb.: BWL Publishing, 2023. [S.D.]

———. *Taxed to Death* (N). Calgary, Alb.: BWL Publishing, 2023. [Minn.]

———. *Whistling Fireman* (N). Calgary, Alb.: BWL Publishing, 2023. [Minn.]

Howerton, Phillip. *Gods of Four Mile Creek* (P). Kirksville, Mo.: Golden Antelope Press, 2023.

Hubbard, Charlotte. *Family Gatherings at Promise Lodge* (N). NY: Zebra Books, 2023. [Mo.]

———. *Hidden Away at Promise Lodge* (N). NY: Zebra Books, 2023. [Mo.]

Hugo, Lynne. *The Language of Kin* (N). St. Louis, Mo.: Blank Slate Press, 2023. [Dayton, Ohio]

Hunter, Dianna. *Clouded Waters* (N). Duluth, Minn.: Holy Cow! Press, 2023. [Minn.]

Hunter, Susan. *Dangerous Choices* (N). Leesburg, Va.: Severn River Publishing, 2023. [Wis.]

———. *Dangerous Deception* (N). Leesburg, Va.: Severn River Publishing, 2022. [Wis.]

Huntoon, Caroline. *Skating on Mars* (juv). NY: Feiwel and Friends, 2023. [Mich.]

Hurtubise, Charleen. *The Polite Act of Drowning* (N). London: Eriu, 2023. [Mich.]

Husom, Christine. *Deputy #714 Is Down* (N). Buffalo, Minn.: The wRight Press, 2023. [Minn.]

Irvin, Kelly. *Every Good Gift* (N). Grand Rapids, Mich.: Zondervan, 2023. [Kan.]

Ivy, Alexandra. *Desperate Acts* (N). NY: Zebra Books, 2023. [Wis.]

Izzi, Edward. *Dinner at Tony Napoli's* (N). S.l.: Cassino Publishing, 2023. [Chicago, Ill.]

Jackson, Danielle. *Accidentally in Love* (N). NY: Berkley Romance, 2023. [Chicago, Ill.]

Jacobs, James V. *Growing Season* (juv). Tallahassee: Father & Son Publishing, 2023. [Ind.]

Jacobson, Ellen. *Murder at the Library* (N). S.l.: Under Wraps Publishing, 2023. [N.D.]

Janae, Olivia. *The Loudest Silence* (N). S.l.: Ylva Publishing, 2022. [Chicago, Ill.]

Jebber, Molly. *Rachael's Decision* (N). NY: Zebra Books, 2023. [Ohio]

Jenkins, Beverly. *A Christmas to Remember* (N). NY: Avon Books, 2023. [Kan.]

Jenkins, Louis. *Collected Poems* (P). Bloomington, Minn: Will o' the Wisp Books, 2023. [Duluth, Minn.]

Jensen, Van. *Godfall* (N). Lincoln: U Nebraska P, 2023. [Neb.]

Jenski, Laura. *The South Dakota Beech Diet* (N). Boise: Snowbound Stories, 2023. [S.D.]

Jensvold, John. *Until the Big Water Takes Them* (N). Burnsville, Minn.: Kirk House Publishers, 2023. [Minn.]

Jeppesen, K.W. *Sweet, Lovely, Attentive* (N). Altona, Man.: Friesen Press, 2023. [Minn.]

Joern, Pamela Carter. *Toby's Last Resort* (N). Lincoln: U Nebraska P, 2023. [Neb.]

Johanson, Lynn-Steven. *One of Ours* (N). S.l.: Level Best Books, 2023. [Chicago, Ill.]

Johns, Patricia and Sandra Orchard. *Love's a Mystery in Last Chance IA* (N). Guideposts, 2023. [Last Chance, Iowa]

Johns, Robert. *O'Brien's Broken Play* (N). Austin, Tex.: River Grove Books, 2023. [Kent, Ohio]

Johnson, Debra S. *The Marshall Crain Story* (N). Ft. Myers, Fla.: Borasue Press, 2023. [Ill.]

Johnson, Judith. *Death upon the Wicked Stage* (N). S.l.: Kismet Mysteries, 2023. [St. Paul, Minn.]

Johnson, Leah. *Ellie Engle Saves Herself* (juv). Glendale, Calif.: Disney Hyperion, 2023. [Ind.]

Johnson, Wayne. *The Witch Tree* (N). London: Agora Books, 2023. [Minn.]

Johnston, Devin. *Dragons* (P). NY: Farrar, Straus and Giroux, 2023.

Johnston, Tim. *Distant Sons* (N). Chapel Hill, N.C.: Algonquin Books, 2023. [Wis.]

Johnstone, J.A. see Johnstone, William W.

Johnstone, William W. and J.A. *Johnstone. Preacher's Purge* (N). NY: Pinnacle Books, 2023. [Dak.]

Jollymore, Tim. *The Nothing That Is Not There* (N). Oakland, Calif.: Finns Way Books, 2023. [Minn.]

Jones, Gary F. *Stalking Throckmorton* (N). Waynesville, N.C.: BQB Publishing, 2023. [Wis.]

Jones, Stephen Mack. *Deus X* (N). NY: Soho Crime, 2023. [Detroit, Mich.]

Jones, Zachariah. *Convocation* (N). Stillwater, Minn.: Water Sign Books, 2023. [Deadwood, S.D.]

Jungkunz, Mariel. *Dreams of Green* (juv). NY: Astra Young Readers, 2023. [Ohio]

Kachuba, John B. *Haycorn Smith and the Castle Ghost* (juv). S.l.: Paper Angel Press, 2023. [Ohio]

Katz, Rachel Runya. *Thank You for Sharing* (N). NY: St. Martin's Griffin, 2023. [Chicago, Ill.]

Kay, Libby. *Faking the Fall* (N). Murrells Inlet, S.C.: Inkspell Publishing, 2023. [Ohio]

———. *Falling Again* (N). Murrells Inlet, S.C.: Inkspell Publishing, 2023. [Ohio]

———. *Falling for You* (N). Murrells Inlet, S.C.: Inkspell Publishing, 2023. [Ohio]

Kearney, Christine Gallagher. *What We Leave Behind* (N). Berkeley, Calif.: She Writes Press, 2023. [Minneapolis, Minn.]

Keeling, Cindy. *Dream City Dreaming* (N). Villa Park, Ill.: Petite Parasol Press, 2023. [Chicago, Ill.]

Kelkar, Supriya. *The Cobra's Song* (juv). NY: Simon & Schuster, 2023. [Mich.]

Keller, Rebecca A. *You Should Have Known* (N). NY: Crooked Lane Books, 2023. [Ill.]

Kennedy, James. *Bride of the Tornado* (N). Philadelphia: Quirk Books, 2023. [Midwest]

Kennedy, Sharon M. *A Summer of Discovery* (juv). Ann Arbor, Mich.: Modern History Press, 2023. [Mich.]

Kennis, Lois. *Rise on Eagles' Wings* (N). Plymouth, Mass.: Elk Lake Publishing, 2023. [Iowa]

Kiefer, Christian. *The Heart of It All* (N). Hoboken, N.J.: Melville House, 2023. [Ohio]

Kilmer, Maureen. *Suburban Hell* (N). London: Headline Accent, 2023. [Chicago, Ill.]

Kincaid, Sadie. *Dante* (N). S.l.: Red House Press, 2023. [Chicago, Ill.]

———. *Lorenzo* (N). S.l.: Red House Press, 2023. [Chicago, Ill.]

King, Bart. *Time Travel Inn 2* (juv). Waitsfield, Vt.: Chooseco, 2023. [Wis.]

Kingsbury, Karen. *Just Once* (N). NY: Atria Books, 2023. [Bloomington, Ind.]

——— and Tyler Russell. *Being Baxters* (juv). NY: Simon & Schuster, 2023. [Bloomington, Ind.]

Kinsinger, Lucinda J. *Rosanna in the Middle* (N). Harrisonburg, Va.: Christian Light Publications, 2023. [Wis.]

Kinzer, Becca. *Dear Henry, Love Edith* (N). Carol Stream, Ill.: Tyndale House, 2023. [Ill.]

Kitchen, Jeremy. *Mr. Crabby You Have Died* (N). Michigan City, Ind.: First to Know, 2023. [Chicago, Ill.; Detroit, Mich.]

Klavan, Andrew. *The House of Love and Death* (N). NY: Mysterious Press, 2023. [Ill.]

Klise, James. *I'll Take Everything You Have* (juv). NY: Algonquin Young Readers, 2023. [Chicago, Ill.]

Klise, Kate. *How Mr. Silver Stole the Show* (juv). NY: Feiwel and Friends, 2023. [St. Louis, Mo.]

Kluesner, Kevin. *Killer Speech* (N). S.l.: Level Best Books, 2023. [Wis.]

Knight, Samsun. *The Diver* (N). Iowa City: U Iowa P, 2023. [Great Lakes]

Knudson, D.R. *Twelve Beds* (N). St. Paul, Minn.: Beaver's Pond Press, 2023. [Minn.]

Koranda, Anthony. *Broken Bottles* (N). Chicago: Tortoise Books, 2023. [Chicago, Ill.]

Kotz, Ann Hanigan. *The Journey of Karoline Olsen* (N). Des Moines: Book Press Publishing, 2023. [Iowa]

Krapf, Norbert. *Homecomings: A Writer's Memoir* (M). Indianapolis: Indiana Historical Society Press, 2023. [Ind.]

Krause, Autumn. *Before the Devil Knows You're Here* (juv). Atlanta, Ga.: Peachtree Teen, 2023. [Wis.]

Kreigh, Gary L. *Circle of Chesterfield* (N). Foxground, Aus.: Alkira Publishing, 2023. [Chesterfield, Ind.]

Kronzer, Nicole. *The Roof over Our Heads* (juv). NY: Amulet Books, 2023. [Minn.]

Krueger, Avonlea Q. *The House on Cherry Street* (N). S.l.: Happy Little Sigh Publishing, 2023. [Grand Rapids, Mich.]

Krueger, William Kent. *The River We Remember* (N). NY: Atria Books, 2023. [Minn.]

Kubica, Mary. *Just the Nicest Couple* (N). NY: Park Row Books, 2023. [Chicago, Ill.]

Kyles, Cedric. *Flipping Boxcars* (N). NY: Amistad Press, 2023. [Mo.]

Lageschulte, Melanie. *The Lane That Leads to Christmas* (N). S.l.: Fremont Creek Press, 2023. [Iowa]

———. *The Road to Golden Days* (N). S.l.: Fremont Creek Press, 2023. [Iowa]

———. *The Route That Takes You Home* (N). S.l.: Fremont Creek Press, 2023. [Iowa]

Landis, Laurel J. *Gunshots in Grudgeville* (S). Waukesha, Wis.: Ten16 Press, 2023. [Wis.]

Langtry, Leslie. *Marked for Murder* (N). S.l.: Gemma Halliday Publishing, 2023. [Iowa]

———. *Method Actor Murder* (N). S.l.: Gemma Halliday Publishing, 2023. [Iowa]

———. *Monster Mash Murder* (N). S.l.: Gemma Halliday Publishing, 2023. [Iowa]

———. *Mythic Melee Murder* (N). S.l.: Gemma Halliday Publishing, 2023. [Iowa]

LaPres, Marie. *Beyond the Light* (N). S.l.: Sukey Publishing, 2023. [Mackinac Island, Mich.]

Lark, Sophie. *Bloody Heart* (N). Naperville, Ill.: Bloom Books, 2023. [Chicago, Ill.]

———. *Brutal Prince* (N). Naperville, Ill.: Bloom Books, 2023. [Chicago, Ill.]

———. *Savage Lover* (N). Naperville, Ill.: Bloom Books, 2023. [Chicago, Ill.]

———. *Stolen Heir* (N). Naperville, Ill.: Bloom Books, 2023. [Chicago, Ill.]

Lawson, Sonya. *The Shadow of the Dark* (N). S.l.: SauceBox Press, 2023. [Columbus, Ohio]

Leahy, Elisa Stone. *Tethered to Other Stars* (juv). NY: Quill Tree Books, 2023. [Columbus, Ohio]

LeClair, Jenifer. *Death in the Wolf Moon* (N). St. Paul, Minn.: Fog Harbor Press, 2023. [Grand Marais, Minn.]

Legg, John. *Final Justice* (N). Las Vegas, Nev.: Wolfpack Publishing, 2023. [Kan.]

Leonard, Julie. *Sheltering in Place* (P). Iowa City: Piping Plover Books, 2023.

Leoson, Mary Carroll. *The Butterfly Circle* (N). S.l.: Manta Press, 2023. [Cleveland, Ohio]

Leroux, Catherine. *The Future* (N). Windsor, Ont.: Biblioasis, 2023. [Detroit, Mich.]

Lesmeister, Keith Pilapil. *Mississippi River Museum* (N). Santa Rosa, Calif.: WTAW Press, 2023. [Iowa]

Levin, Donald. *The Arsenal of Deceit*. Ferndale, Mich.: Poison Toe Press, 2023. [Detroit, Mich.]

Levine, Jenna. *My Roommate Is a Vampire*. NY: Berkley Books, 2023. [Chicago, Ill.]

Lewis, Britney S. *The Dark Place* (juv). Glendale, Calif.: Disney-Hyperion, 2023. [Mo.]

Lewis, Patrice. *The Quilter's Scandalous Past* (N). Toronto: Love Inspired, 2023. [Ind.]

Lillard, Amy. *A Murder of Aspic Proportions* (N). Kensington Books, 2023. [Kan.]

———. *One More Time for Joy* (N). NY: Zebra Books, 2023. [Mo.]

———. *When Hattie Finds Love*. NY: Zebra Books, 2023. [Mo.]

Littles, T.C. *The Laws of Loyalty* (N). Farmingdale, N.Y.: Urban Renaissance, 2023. [Detroit, Mich.]

———. *Starving for Love* (N). Farmingdale, N.Y.: Urban Renaissance, 2023. [Detroit, Mich.]

Litton, Melvin. *Skin for Skin* (N). Hertford, N.C.: Gordian Knot Books, 2023. [Kan.]

Lodge-Rigal, Susannah. *Where the Light Feeds* (P). Gilbert, Ariz.: Gasher Press, 2023. [Ind.; Midwest]

Lopez, Angelina M. *Full Moon over Freedom* (N). Toronto: Harlequin, 2023. [Kan.]

Lopez, Joseph M. *Gas Station Stories* (P). S.l.: Writer Heights Publishing, 2023. [Wis.]

Lourey, Jess. *The Taken Ones* (N). Seattle: Thomas & Mercer, 2023. [Minn.]

Love, Tameka. *Lil Project Chick from the Chi 3* (N). S.l.: Cole Hart Signature, 2023. [Chicago, Ill.]

———. *My Thug Bae from the Chi* (N). S.l.: Cole Hart Signature, 2023. [Chicago, Ill.]

Lovelace, Robin Lee. *A Wild Region* (S). Indianapolis: Etching Press, 2023. [Ind.]

Lowery, Scott. *Mutual Life* (P). Georgetown, Ky.: Finishing Line Press, 2023.

Luczak, Raymond. *Far from Atlantis* (P). Washington, D.C.: Gallaudet U P, 2023. [Mich.]

Ludwig, Elizabeth. *Where Hope Dwells* (N). Danbury, Conn.: Guideposts, 2023. [Ohio]

Lukasik, Gail. *The Darkness Surrounds Us* (N). Brentwood, Tenn.: CamCat Publishing, 2023. [Mich.]

Lupton, E.H. *Dionysus in Wisconsin* (N). Madison, Wis.: Winnowing Fan Press, 2023. [Madison, Wis.]

Lynch, Molly. *The Forbidden Territory of a Terrifying Woman* (N). NY: Catapult Books, 2023. [Ann Arbor, Mich.]

Lynden, Audrey. *The Artful Bargain* (N). S.l.: Penske Publishing, 2023. [Wis.]

Lynn, Dana R. *Crime Scene Witness* (N). Toronto: Love Inspired Suspense, 2023. [Ohio]

———. *Her Secret Amish Past* (N). Toronto: Love Inspired Suspense, 2023. [Ohio]

———. *Hidden Amish Target* (N). Toronto: Love Inspired Suspense, 2023. [Ohio]

———. *Hunted at Christmas* (N). Toronto: Love Inspired Suspense, 2023. [Ohio]

——— see also Alexander, Johnnie

Lyons, Meredith R. *Ghost Tamer* (N). Ft. Collins, Colo.: CamCat Books, 2023. [Chicago, Ill.]

MacBride, Michael and Heidi Wall Burns. *The Thompson Twins: The Minnesota Mysteries* (juv). S.l.: Salty Books Publishing, 2023. [Minn.]

McCarthy, Kevin. *The Wintering Place* (N). NY: W.W. Norton, 2023. [Dak.]

McClay, Jocelyn. *The Amish Spinster's Dilemma* (N). Toronto: Love Inspired, 2023. [Wis.]

———. *Her Scandalous Amish Secret* (N). Toronto: Love Inspired, 2023. [Wis.]

McCoy, Ron. *Your Cowboy Is Gone* (N). Meas, Ariz.: Many Seasons Press, 2023. [Neb.]

McCurdy, Bob. *Until It's Over* (N). Baileys Harbor, Wis.: Range Light Press, 2023. [Wis.]

McDaniel, Tiffany. *On the Savage Side* (N). NY: Alfred A. Knopf, 2023. [Chillicothe, Ohio]

McGinley, Jerry. *.410 Avenger* (N). S.l.: Lake City Lights Books, 2023. [Madison, Wis.]

———. *Ghosts of Dharma Hills* (N). S.l.: Lake City Lights Books, 2022. [Wis.]

———. *Governor's Island Murders* (N). S.l.: Lake City Lights Books, 2023. [Wis.]

McGinnis, Mindy. *A Long Stretch of Bad Days* (juv). NY: Katherine Tegen Books, 2023. [Ohio]

McGonegal, Richard F. *The Forget-Me-Knot* (N). Warrensburg, Mo.: Cave Hollow Press, 2023. [Mo.]

McIntyre, Katherine. *Twilight Heist* (N). S.l.: Hot Tree Publishing, 2023. [Chicago, Ill.]

McKay, Tom. *Lost in the Black Hologram* (N). Dubuque, Iowa: River Lights Publishing, 2023. [Iowa]

McKee, Freesia. *Hummingbird Vows* (P). Los Angeles: Bottlecap Press, 2023.

McKee, Kittredge. *Homestead* (N). Red Bank, N.J.: Newman Springs Publishing, 2023. [Neb.]

Macmillan, Katie J. *Running Home* (N). S.l.: Beneath the Cottonwood, 2023. [Minn.]

Maddox, Jake. *Curling Crunch* (juv). North Mankato, Minn.: Stone Arch Books, 2023. [Minn.]

———. *Roster Rebound* (juv). North Mankato, Minn.: Stone Arch Books, 2023. [Ill.]

Magliuilo, Mike. *A Reason to Run* (N). Montpelier, Vt.: Rootstock Publishing, 2023. [Chicago, Ill.]

Maher, Kerri. *All You Have to Do Is Call* (N). NY: Berkley Books, 2023. [Chicago, Ill.]

Maillard, Keith. *In the Defense of Liberty* (N). Calgary, Alb.: Freehand Books, 2023. [Ohio]

Makkai, Rebecca. *I Have Some Questions for You* (N). NY: Viking Press, 2023.

Malone, Dave. *Bypass* (P). American Fork, Utah: Kelsay Press, 2023. [Midwest]

Mamet, David. *Everywhere an Oink Oink* (M). NY: Simon and Schuster, 2023.

Manfred, Freya. *When I Was Young and Old* (M; P). Minneapolis: Nodin Press, 2023.

Marie, Hazel. *Like Salt and Ash* (N). S.l.: Lake Country Press & Reviews, 2023. [Chicago, Ill.]

Marks, David. *Boomsters: An Unexpected Adventure* (N). Tucson, Ariz.: Wheatmark, 2023. [Chicago, Ill.]

Marquis, Krystal. *The Davenports* (juv). NY: Dial Books, 2023. [Chicago, Ill.]

Marston, Edward. *Homicide in Chicago* (N). London: Allison & Busby, 2023. [Chicago, Ill.]

Martin, Alexa. *Next-Door Nemesis* (N). NY: Berkley Books, 2023. [Ohio]

Martin, Cate. *The Teashop Terror* (N). Rogers, Minn.: Rotatoskr Press, 2023. [Minneapolis, Minn.]

Martin, Imogen. *Under a Gilded Sky* (N). S.l.: Storm Publishing, 2023. [Mo.]

Martin, Terri. *Voodoo Shack* (juv). Ann Arbor, Mich.: Modern History Press, 2023. [Mich.]

May, Scott Mitchel. *Breakneck* (N). S.l.: Anxiety Press, 2023. [Madison, Wis.]

Mayer, Bob see Crusie, Jennifer

Meehan, Jana. *Where the Lights Are Shining* (N). St. Louis, Mo.: Marquee Publishing, 2023. [St. Louis, Mo.]

Mehl, Nancy. *Blessings in Disguise* (N). Danbury, Conn.: Guideposts, 2023. [Ohio]

———. *Cold Pursuit* (N). Minneapolis: Bethany House, 2023. [St. Louis, Mo.]

Meier, Edward Gordon. *Appassionata for Mary Shelley* (P). Oshkosh, Wis.: UM Media, 2023. [Oshkosh, Wis.]

Mejia, Mindy. *To Catch a Storm* (N). NY: Atlantic Monthly Press, 2023. [Iowa]

Melby, Becky. *Let It Snow* (N). Danbury, Conn.: Guideposts, 2023. [Dennison, Ohio]

——— and Cynthia Ruchti. *Love's a Mystery in Embarrass WI* (N). Danbury, Conn.: Guideposts, 2023. [Embarrass, Wis.]

Menapace, Jeff. *Caleb: Return to Noodle* (N). S.l.: Mind Mess Press, 2023. [Ind.]

Mendez, Joel. *Forty Poems for City Living* (P). Chicago: LACASA Chicago Books, 2023. [Chicago, Ill.]

Metoui, Meriam. *A Guide to the Dark* (juv). NY: Henry Holt, 2023. [Ind.]

Meyer, Archie. *It Gets Easier in Minneapolis* (N). Minneapolis: Central and Lowry Presse, 2023. [Minneapolis, Minn.]

Meyer, Gabrielle. *For Sentimental Reasons* (N). Danbury, Conn.: Guideposts, 2023. [Dennison, Ohio]

———. *Under the Apple Tree* (N). Danbury, Conn.: Guideposts, 2023. [Dennison, Ohio]

Meyer, Susan Lynn. *A Sky Full of Song* (juv). NY: Union Square Kids, 2023. [N.D.]

Mierzejewski, William. *The Local Legend of Iron River* (N). Schaumburg, Ill.: eBooks2go, 2023. [Iron River, Mich.]

Millen, C.M. *Hinges* (juv). Toledo, Ohio: U Toledo P, 2023. [Ohio]

Miller, Jenna. *Out of Character* (juv). NY: Quill Tree, 2023. [Minneapolis, Minn.]

Miller, Julia. *The Inheritance* (N). S.l.: Five Feline Farm Press, 2023. [Mo.]

Miller, Julie. *The Evidence Next Door* (N). Toronto: Harlequin, 2023. [Kansas City, Mo.]

Miller, Kalena. *Shannon in the Spotlight* (juv). NY: Delacorte Books, 2023. [Minneapolis, Minn.]

Miller, Latisha. *Chaos in Da Chi 2* (N). S.l.: New Book Authors, 2023. [Chicago, Ill.]

Miller, Mary Ann. *Bones under the Ice* (N). Sarasota, Fla.: Oceanview Publishing, 2023. [Ind.]

Miller, Rowenna. *The Fairy Bargains of Prospect Hill* (N). NY: Redhook Books, 2023. [Midwest]

Milligan, A. Roy. *Fifty Shades of Snow* (N). Stockbridge, Ga.: Lock Down Publications, 2023. [Detroit, Mich; Pontiac, Mich.]

Million, Wendy. *Miss Matched* (N). Toronto: W by Wattpad Books, 2023. [Mich.]

Mindel, Jenna. *The Nanny Next Door* (N). Toronto: Love Inspired, 2023. [Mich.]

Mitchell, Caroline. *The Bone House* (N). Orlando, Fla.: Embla Books, 2023. [Slayton, Minn.]

Mitchell, Matthew. *Chaindevils* (N). S.l.: Weirdpunk Books, 2023. [Mo.]

Moehling, Joshua. *Where the Dead Sleep* (N). Naperville, Ill.: Poisoned Pen Press, 2023. [Minn.]

Molotti. *Opps in the Air* (N). Stockbridge, Ga.: Lock Down Publications, 2023. [Chicago, Ill.]

———. *Still Risky* (N). Stockbridge, Ga.: Lock Down Publications, 2023. [Chicago, Ill.]

Montag, Kassandra. *Those Who Return* (N). London: Quercus Publishing, 2023. [Neb.]

Montgomery, Robert U. *They're Back!* (N). Bonne Terre, Mo.: RUM Publishing, 2023. [Mo.]

Moore, Hilton Everett. *North of Nelson 2* (S). Covington, Mich.: Silver Mountain Press, 2023. [Mich.]

Moore, Lorrie. *I Am Homeless If This Is Not My Home* (N). NY: Alfred A. Knopf, 2023. [Midwest]

Moore, Susanna. *The Lost Wife* (N). NY: Alfred A. Knopf, 2023. [Minn.]

Moranville, Sharelle Byars. *Forget-Me-Not Blue* (juv). NY: Holiday House, 2023. [Des Moines, Iowa]

Moreland, Brian. *They Stalk the Night* (N). NY: Flame Tree Publishing, 2023. [Minn.]

Moreland, Miel. *Something Like Possible* (juv). NY: Feiwel and Friends, 2023. [Minn.]

Morgan, Sophie H. The *Witch Is Back* (N). Toronto: Harlequin, 2023. [Chicago, Ill.]

Morris, Kathleen. *Golddigger* (N). S.l.: Dunraven Press, 2023. [N.D.]

Morrissey, Hannah. *When I'm Dead* (N). NY: Minotaur Books, 2023. [Wis.]

Moulton, Rachel Eve. *The Insatiable Volt Sisters* (N). NY: Farrar, Straus and Giroux, 2023. [Ohio]

Moyer, Larissa C. *In Our Hands* (N). S.l.: Booklogix, 2023. [Chicago, Ill.]

Mozina, Andrew. *Tandem* (N). Chicago: Tortoise Books, 2023. [Mich.]

Muhlstock, Dan. *Domestic Beasts* (N). NY: Austin Macauley Publishers, 2023. [Detroit, Mich.]

Mulhern, Julie. *Back Stabbers* (N). Toronto: J & M Press, 2023. [Kansas City, Mo.]

———. *Fire and Rain* (N). Toronto: J & M Press, 2023. [Kansas City, Mo.]

———. *Shadow Dancing* (N). Toronto: J & M Press, 2023. [Kansas City, Mo.]

Mullins, Kimberly. *Suspicions* (N). Houston, Tex.: JKJ Books, 2023. [Chicago, Ill.]

Munroe, Fatima. *Weak for a Coldhearted Goon 2* (N). S.l.: Monreaux Publications, 223. [Milwaukee, Wis.]

Mustful, Colin. *Reclaiming Mni Sota* (N). Roseville, Minn.: History Through Fiction, 2023. [Minn.]

Nailor, Bob. *The Englische Voice* (N). S.l.: Shadow Street Press, 2023. [Shipshewana, Ind.]

———. *The Vietnam Voice* (N). S.l.: Shadow Street Press, 2023. [Ohio]

Nania, Jeff. *Musky Run* (N). Portage, Wis.: Feet Wet Writing, 2023. [Wis.]

Napolitano, Ann. *Hello Beautiful* (N). NY: Dial Press, 2023. [Chicago, Ill.]

Nash, Elle. *Deliver Me* (N). Los Angeles: Unnamed Press, 2023. [Mo.]

Neill, Chloe. *Cold Curses* (N). NY: Berkley Books, 2023. [Chicago, Ill.]

Neville, Paul. *The Garbage Brothers* (N). Eugene, Or.: IFD Publishing, 2023. [Chicago, Ill.]

Nguyen, Bich Minh (Beth). *Owner of a Lonely Heart* (M). NY: Scribner, 2023.

Nicholas, Dor'y. *Cottonwood Farm* (N). Pittsburgh: Dorrance Publishing Co., 2023. [Minn.]

Nickless, Barbara. *Play of Shadows* (N). Seattle: Thomas & Mercer, 2023. [Chicago, Ill.]

Norbury, Chris. *Little Mountain, Big Trouble* (N). Owatonna, Minn.: CSN Press, 2023. [Minn.]

Norris, Stephanie Nicole. *The Clarks of Northshire Bend* (N). S.l.: Love Is a Drug, 2022. [Chicago, Ill.]

Noyes, Dennis. *Yonders, Illinois* (N). S.l.: Trebol Editions, 2023. [Ill.]

Oates, Joyce Carol. *Zero Sum* (S). NY: Alfred A. Knopf, 2023.

O'Brien, Tim. *America Fantastica* (N). NY: Mariner Books, 2023.

Ogundimu, Alexandrine. *The Longest Summer* (N). Troy, N.Y.: CLASH Books, 2023. [Ind.]

Oh, Ellen, ed. *You Are Here: Connecting Flights* (juv). NY: Allida, 2023. [Chicago, Ill.]

Oldre, Bonnie. *Flood of Memories* (N). Tampa, Fla.: Gatekeeper Press, 2023. [Minn.]

O'Leary, Terence. *Fallen Timbers* (N). S.l.: Swan Creek Press, 2023. [Mich.]

Olson, Richard A. *Peoria Nights* (N). S.l.: Bold Venture Press, 2023. [Peoria, Ill.]

Omer, Mike. *Please Tell Me* (N). Seattle: Thomas & Mercer, 2023. [Ind.]

Orchard, Sandra see Johns, Patricia

Orlinsky, Lori. *The Windy City* (juv). Herndon, Va.: Mascot Kids, 2023. [Chicago, Ill.]

Osborne, Cayce. *I Know What You Did* (N). NY: Crooked Lane, 2023. [Madison, Wis.]

Oslund, Christy. *Dead before the End of the Road* (N). S.l.: Agora Books, 2023. [Mich.]

Owings, Frank N., Jr. *Thoughts in Rhyme* (P). Pittsburgh: Dorrance Publishing, 2023.

Painter, Lynn. *Betting on You* (juv). NY: Simon & Schuster, 2023. [Omaha, Neb.]

Parker, Carl A. *The Next Level* (N). S.l.: Another Chance Global Media, 2023. [St. Louis, Mo.]

———. *Unfinished Business* (N). S.l.: Another Chance Global Media, 2023. [St. Louis, Mo.]

Parris, Wendy. *Field of Screams* (juv). NY: Delacorte Press, 2023. [Iowa]

Patchett, Ann. *Tom Lake* (N). NY: Harper, 2023. [Mich.]

Paton, Priscilla. *When the House Burns* (N). Kenmore, Wash.: Coffeetown Press, 2023. [Minneapolis, Minn.]

Patterson, James and Keir Graff. *Minerva Keen's Detective Club* (juv). NY: Little, Brown, 2023. [Chicago, Ill.]

Paul, Robin. *Write Christmas* (N). Lakewood Ranch, Fla.: These Three Publishing, 2023. [Kansas City, Mo.]

Pelayo, Cynthia. *The Shoemaker's Magician* (N). Aberdeen, N.J.: Agora Books, 2023. [Chicago, Ill.]

Pensoneau, Taylor. *Corruption Incorporated* (N). New Berlin, Ill.: Downstate Publications, 2023. [Ill.]

Perry, Thomas. *Murder Book* (N). NY: Mysterious Press, 2023. [Chicago, Ill.; Ind.]

Phegley, Kiel. *Strikers* (juv). Minneapolis: Graphic Universe, 2023. [Flint, Mich.]

Philo, Jolene. *See Jane Dance!* (N). Polk City, Iowa: Midwestern Books, 2023. [S.D.]

Pillow, Michelle M. *A Streak of Lightning* (N). S.l.: Raven Books, 2022. [Wis.]

Pine, A.J. *The Second Chance Garden* (N). Naperville, Ill.: Sourcebooks Casablanca, 2023. [Ill.]

Pinkerton, Brian. *The Intruders* (N). NY: Flame Tree Publishing, 2023. [Ind.]

Pinkus, Harry. *Justified Malice* (N). Waynesville, N.C.: BQB Publishing, 2023. [Wis.]

Polacco, Patricia. *Palace of Books* (juv). NY: Simon & Schuster, 2023. [Battle Creek, Mich.]

Polito, Frank Anthony. *Rehearsed to Death* (N). NY: Kensington Books, 2023. [Detroit, Mich.]

Polk, Xavier. *The Hunter* (N). Detroit: Xray Universe, 2023. [Detroit, Mich.]

Powell, Syndi. *The Teacher's Unexpected Gift* (N). Toronto: Harlequin, 2023. [Mich.]

Power, Helen. *Phantom* (N). Ft. Collins, Colo.: CamCat Books, 2023. [Chicago, Ill.]

Power, Mona Susan. *A Council of Dolls* (N). NY: Mariner Books, 2023. [Chicago, Ill.; N.D.]

Prosch, Richard. *Cast a Wide Loop* (N). Waterville, Me.: Thorndike Press, 2023. [Neb.]

Qualio, Aaron. *The Heir* (N). Pittsburgh: Dorrance Publishing, 2023. [Wis.]

Quigley, Mindy. *Ashes to Ashes, Crust to Crust* (N). NY: St. Martin's Paperbacks, 2023. [Wis.]

Quinn, Emily and Laura Bradford. *Love's a Mystery in Peculiar, MO* (N). Danbury, Conn.: Guideposts, 2023. [Peculiar, Mo.]

Raffel, Dawn. *Boundless as the Sky* (N). Montclair, N.J.: Sagging Meniscus Press, 2023. [Chicago, Ill.]

Rainbow, Douglas. *Anoka Stories* (S). London: Austin Macauley Publishers, 2023. [Anoka, Minn.]

Raleigh, Michael. *Poe Street* (N). S.l.: Level Best/Historia, 2023. [Chicago, Ill.]

Ramirez, Pablo E. *Pocho Love* (P). Chicago: LACASA Chicago Books, 2023. [Chicago, Ill.]

Ramsay, Blaise. *Bloodlaw* (N). Dunedin, Fla.: 4 Horsemen Publications, 2023. [Chicago, Ill.]

Ratzlaff, Tara. *The Moth Came Back* (N). Kenmore, Wash.: Camel Press, 2023. [Minn.]

Razor, Peter. *Wiijiwaaganag* (juv). East Lansing, Mich.: Makwa Enewed, 2023. [Wis.]

Reed, Dwayne. *Simon B. Rhymin' Gets in the Game* (juv). NY: Little, Brown, 2023. [Chicago, Ill.]

Reed, J. Daniel. *Whispers in a Phone Booth* (N). Mt. Prospect, Ill.: Terra3, 2023. [Chicago, Ill.]

Rein, Arthur Kevin. *A Flame Worth the Candle* (N). S.l.: Open Books, 2023. [Wis.]

Reis, Patricia. *Unsettled* (N). Grass Valley, Calif.: Sibylline Press, 2023. [Iowa]

Reynolds, Eric T. *The Lost Town of Garrison* (N). Kansas City, Kan.: Hadley Rille Books, 2023. [Kan.]

Reynolds, Justin A., ed. *House Party* (juv). NY: Joy Revolution, 2023. [Chicago, Ill.]

Richards, Dusty. *Westbound* (N). NY: Pinnacle Books, 2023. [Ohio]

Richards, Lloyd Devereux. *Maidens of the Cave* (N). NY: William Morrow, 2023. [Ill.; Ind.]

Richards, Natalie D. *Four Found Dead* (juv). Naperville, Ill: Sourcebooks Fire, 2023. [Ohio]

Richey, Sheri. *Cat in Control* (N). S.l.: Cagelink, 2023. [Ohio]

Rivers, Krystina. *Last New Beginning* (N). Valley Falls, N.Y.: Bold Strokes Books, 2023. [Chicago, Ill.]

Roberts, J.R. *To Steal from the Dead* (N). Naples, Fla.: Speaking Volumes, 2023. [Kan.]

Roberts, Les. *The C.I.* (N). Lutz, Fla.: Down & Out Books, 2023. [Cleveland, Ohio]

Roberts, Lori. *Sing a Song of Murder* (N). Bedford, Ind.: Crecelius Haus Publishing, 2023. [Bedford, Ind.]

Roberts, Sherry. *Up There* (N). Apple Valley, Minn.: Osmyrrah Publishing, 2023. [Minn.]

Robertson, Jenny. *Hoist House* (S). Stevens Point, Wis.: Cornerstone Press, 2023. [Minn.]

Robinson, C.C. *Upheaval* (N). Cincinnati: Manifold Publishing, 2023. [Cincinnati, Ohio]

Rogers, Pattiann. *Flickering* (P). NY: Penguin Books, 2023.

Rose, Renee. *The Gatekeeper* (N). S.l.: Wilrose Dream Ventures, 2023. [Chicago, Ill.]

Rosenberg, Aaron. *Yeti Left Home* (N). Pennsville, N.J.: NeoParadoxa, 2023. [Minn.]

Rouser, Kathleen. *Rumors and Promises* (N). S.l.: Wild Heart Books, 2023. [Mich.]

Ruchti, Cynthia see Melby, Becky

Ruhlman, Michael and Miesha Wilson Headen, eds. *Cleveland Noir* (S). Brooklyn, NY: Akashic Books, 2023. [Cleveland, Ohio]

Russell, Rachel D. *It's Your Love* (N). S.l.: Sunrise Publishing, 2023. [Minn.]

Russell, Tyler see Kingsbury, Karen

Ryan, Annelise. *Death in the Dark Woods* (N). NY: Berkley Books, 2023. [Wis.]

Ryan, Suzy. *Saving Summer* (N). Surfside, Fla.: Warrior Publishing, 2023. [Kan.]

Ryberg, Jason, ed. *Out Here We Say "Mizzoura"* (P). Kansas City, Mo.: Spartan Press, 2023. [Mo.]

Ryker, Celia. *Augusta* (N). Montpelier, Vt.: Rootstock Publishing, 2023. [Detroit, Mich.]

Rzezotarski, Darlene Wesenberg. *Tannenbaum Arms* (N). S.l.: Wecker Press, 2023. [Milwaukee, Wis.]

Sage, Susan E. *Dancing in the Ring* (N). Castroville, Tex.: Black Rose Writing, 2023. [Detroit, Mich.]

Sales, Leila. *The Museum of Lost and Found* (juv). NY: Amulet Books, 2023. [Ohio]

Sampson, Bill. *Wheat Fields* (N). Topeka, Kan.: Flint Hills Publishing, 2023. [Lawrence, Kan.]

Sandford, John. *Judgment Prey* (N). NY: G.P. Putnam's Sons, 2023. [St. Paul, Minn.]

Sandvig, S.K. *The Girl in the Thistles* (N). Indianapolis: Paper Raven Books, 2023. [Dak.; Minn.]

Savage, Nick. *Us of Legendary Gods* (N). Dunedin, Fla.: 4 Horsemen Publications, 2023. [Chicago, Ill.]

Savit, Gavriel. *Come See the Fair* (juv). NY: Alfred A. Knopf, 2023. [Chicago, Ill.]

Sawyer, Kim Vogel. *The Tapestry of Grace* (N). Colorado Springs, Colo.: WaterBrook, 2023. [Kan.]

Scalzi, John. *The Dispatcher: Travel by Bullet* (N). Burton, Mich.: Subterranean Press, 2023. [Chicago, Ill.]

Schaffhausen, Joanna. *Dead and Gone* (N). NY: Minotaur Books, 2023. [Chicago, Ill.]

Schiffer, Kiersten. *Play My Meant to Be* (N). S.l.: Sweet Light Press, 2023. [Ind.]

Schneiderhan, Caitlin. *Flight of Icarus* (N). NY: Random House Worlds, 2023. [Ind.]

Schrack, Debbie. *Over the Fence* (juv). White Bear Lake, Minn.: Fire & Ice, 2023. [Minn.]

Schroeder, Anne. *The Bundling Year* (N). Las Vegas, Nev.: CKN Christian Publishing, 2023. [Ohio]

Score, Lucy. *Forever Never* (N). Naperville, Ill.: Bloom Books, 2023. [Mackinac Island, Mich.]

Scott, Anika. *Sinners of Starlight City* (N). NY: William Morrow, 2023. [Chicago, Ill.]

Scott, Thomas. *State of Qualms* (N). S.l.: High Road Press, 2023. [Ind.]

———. *State of Remains* (N). S.l.: High Road Press, 2023. [Ind.]

———. *State of Suspense* (N). S.l.: High Road Press, 2023. [Ind.]

Sealey, Nicole. *The Ferguson Report* (P). NY: Alfred A. Knopf, 2023. [Ferguson, Mo.]

Seifert, Mary. *Diamonds, Diesel & Doom* (N). Angel Fire, N.M.: Secret Staircase Books, 2023. [Minn.]

———. *Fishing, Festivities & Fatalities* (N). Angel Fire, N.M.: Secret Staircase Books, 2023. [Minn.]

Seim, Chloe Chun. *Churn* (N). Huntsville: Texas Review Press, 2023. [Kan.]

Sereno, Annie. *Leave It to the March Sisters* (N). NY: Forever, 2023. [Ill.]

Setnicker, David. *Lost on the Fourth of July* (juv). St. Paul, Minn.: Beaver's Pond Press, 2023. [Minn.]

Severance, Melissa B. *Anna* (N). Lake Elmo, Minn.: Blink Books, 2023. [Minn.]

Shanahan, Charif. *Trace Evidence* (P). Portland, Or.: Tin House, 2023.

Shawl, Nisi. *Speculation* (N). NY: Tu Books, 2023. [Mich.]

Shawver, Thomas. *Dirty Book Murder* (N). Las Vegas: Rough Edges Press, 2023. [Kansas City, Mo.]

———. *Left Turn at Paradise* (N). Las Vegas: Rough Edges Press, 2023. [Kansas City, Mo.]

———. *Widow's Son* (N). Las Vegas: Rough Edges Press, 2023. [Kansas City, Mo.]

Sheffield, T.K. *Model Suspect* (N). Mukwonago, Wis.: Making Hay Press, 2023. [Wis.]

Shertok, Heidi. *Unorthodox Love* (N). NY: Alcove Press, 2023. [Minneapolis, Minn.]

Shipman, Viola. *Famous in a Small Town* (N). Toronto: Graydon House, 2023. [Good Hart, Mich.]

———. *The Wishing Bridge* (N). Toronto: Graydon House, 2023. [Frankenmuth, Mich.]

Shoaf, Linda. *All I Want for Christmas Is an Alibi* (N). S.l.: White Feather Press, 2023. [Mich.]

Simon, L.C. *Bridge over Troubled Water* (N). Murrells Inlet, S.C.: Covenant Books, 2023. [Minn.]

Sims, Laura. *How Can I Help You* (N). NY: G.P. Putnam's Sons, 2023. [Midwest?]

Skubal, Mike. *The Outhouse Papers* (N). Savage, Minn.: Hodag Press, 2023. [Rhinelander, Wis.]

Slan, Joanna Campbell. *Mask or Raid* (N). Hobe Sound, Fla.: Spot On Publishing, 2023. St. Louis, Mo.]

Slor, Zhanna. *Breakfall* (N). London: Agora Books, 2023. [Chicago, Ill.]

Smelter, Lisa. *A Second Chance for Happiness* (N). Tampa, Fla.: Gatekeeper Press, 2023. [Iowa]

Smith, Cynthia Leitich. *Harvest House* (juv). Somerville, Mass.: Candlewick Press, 2023. [Kan.]

Smith, Ian K. *The Overnights* (N). NY: Amistad, 2023. [Chicago, Ill.]

Smith, Julie Fudge. *The Beast Keepers* (N). Newark, Ohio: Boyle & Dalton, 2023. [Ohio]

Smith, S.L. *A Party to Murder* (N). St. Paul, Minn.: Sightline Press, 2023. [St. Paul, Minn.]

Smith, Troy D. *Grassland Elegy* (N). S.l.: Cane Hollow Press, 2023. [Kan.]

Smolens, John. *A Cold, Hard Prayer* (N). East Lansing: Michigan State U P, 2023. [Mich.]

Sneider, Martin. *Shelf Life* (N). NY: Forefront Books, 2023. [St. Louis, Mo.]

Snelling Lauraine. *Fields of Bounty* (N). Minneapolis: Bethany House, 2023. [Neb.]

Snowe, Jaqueline. *Snowed in for Christmas* (N). NY: Forever, 2023. [Ill.]

Soderborg, Sondra. *Sky Ropes* (juv). San Francisco: Chronicle Books, 2023. [Mich.]

Sorensen, Karla. *The Best Laid Plans* (N). Seattle: Montlake, 2023. [Mich.]

Sortino, Anna. *Give Me a Sign* (juv). NY: G.P. Putnam's Sons, 2023. [Ill.]

Sparkes, Jo. *The Honey Tree* (N). S.l.: Oscar Press, 2023. [Mo.]

Sparks, Nance. *Starting Over* (N). Valley Falls, N.Y.: Bold Strokes Books, 2023. [Minn.]

Spredemann, Jennifer. *A Widower's Amish Courtship* (N). S.l.: Blessed Publishing, 2023. [Ind.]

Sprinkle, Deborah. *The Case of Mistaken Identity* (N). Morrilton, Ark.: Scrivenings Press, 2022. [Washington, Mo.]

———. *The Case of the Innocent Husband* (N). Morrilton, Ark.: Scrivenings Press, 2022. [Washington, Mo.]

Spufford, Francis. *Cahokia Jazz* (N). London: Faber & Faber, 2023. [Cahokia, Ill.]

St. John, Anna. *Doomed by Blooms* (N). S.l.: Level Best Books, 2023. [Kan.]

Stage, William. *A Friend of King Neptune* (N). St. Louis, Mo.: Floppinfish Publishing, 2023. [Ill.; St. Louis, Mo.]

Stanislav, Lorri. *Maddox's Dream* (juv). Kansas City, Mo.: VarietyKC, 2023. [Kansas City, Mo.]

Steele, Mindy. *The Flower Quilter* (N). Uhrichsville, Ohio: Barbour Publishing, 2023. [Ind.]

Steil, Ellen Won. *Fortune* (N). Seattle: Lake Union Publishing, 2023. [Iowa]

Stelljes, Roger. *The Snow Graves* (N). London: Bookouture, 2023. [Minn.]

———. *Their Lost Souls* (N). London: Bookouture, 2023. [Minn.]

Stone, Kyla. *The Hope We Keep* (N). Atlanta, Ga.: Paper Moon Press, 2023. [Mich.]

———. *The World We Burn* (N). Atlanta, Ga.: Paper Moon Press, 2023. [Mich.]

Stover, Sharee. *Fatal Artifacts* (N). Berne, Ind.: Annie's, 2023. [Neb.]

———. *Seeking Justice* (N). Toronto: Love Inspired Suspense, 2023. [S.D.]

Strachan, Robin. *The Irish Book Club of Dublin (Ohio)* (N). Kenmore, Wash.: Camel Press, 2023. [Dublin, Ohio]

Stradal, J. Ryan. *Saturday Night at the Lakeside Supper Club* (N). NY: Viking, 2023. [Minn]

Stradiotto, Susan. *Golden Orchid* (N). Eden Prairie, Minn.: Bronzewood Books, 2023. [Minneapolis, Minn.]

Stuart, Douglas T. *Fair Game* (N). Cambridge: Vanguard Press, 2023. [St. Louis, Mo.]

Stupnik, Cynthia Anne Frank. *Where Two Rivers Meet* (N). Berwyn Heights, Md.: Heritage Books, 2023. [Clearwater, Minn.]

Svoboda, Terese. *Dog on Fire* (N). Lincoln: U Nebraska P, 2023. [Midwest]

Swinarski, Claire. *What Happened to Rachel Riley?* (juv). NY: Quill Tree, 2023. [Madison, Wis.]

Sylvaine, Angela. *Frost Bite* (juv). S.l.: Dark Matter Ink, 2023. [N.D.]

Tahir, Rana. *Stranger Things* (juv). NY: Random House Children's Books, 2023. [Ind.]

Tanamachi, Cara. *The Second You're Single* (N). NY: St. Martin's Griffin, 2023. [Chicago, Ill.]

Tavares, Matt. *Hoops* (juv). Somerville, Mass.: Candlewick Press, 2023. [Ind.]

Taylor, Brandon. *The Late Americans* (N). NY: Riverhead Books, 2023. [Iowa City, Iowa]

Theisen, Allen. *Angry Water* (N). Burnsville, Minn.: Kirk House Publishers, 2023. [Wis.]

Thelen, Chris G. *Islands of Deception* (N). Birmingham, Ala.: Blackstone Publishing Group, 2023. [Beaver Island, Mich.]

Tichelaar, Tyler R. *Odin's Eye* (N). Marquette, Mich.: Marquette Fiction, 2023. [Marquette, Mich.]

Toalson, R.L. *The First Magnificent Summer* (juv). NY: Aladdin, 2023. [Ohio]

Todd, Susan see Weedman, Roz

Tomforde, Liz. *Caught Up* (N). London: Hodder & Stoughton, 2023. [Chicago, Ill.]

———. *Mile High* (N). London: Hodder & Stoughton, 2023. [Chicago, Ill.]

———. *The Right Move* (N). London: Hodder & Stoughton, 2023. [Chicago, Ill.]

Toon, Paige. *Only Love Can Hurt Like This* (N). NY: G.P. Putnam's Sons, 2023. [Ind.]

Torday, Daniel. *The 12th Commandment* (N). NY: St. Martin's Press, 2023. [Ohio]

Trumbo, Kari. *Bullseye Bride* (N). S.l.: Inked in Faith Publications, 2023. [Deadwood, S.D.]

Turkot, Joseph A. *The Rain* (N). Ashland, Or.: Blackstone Publishing, 2023. [S.D.]

Underhill, Edward. *Always the Almost* (juv). NY: Wednesday Books, 2023. [Wis.]

Undlin, Lindsey. *Spiral* (N). Nashville, Tenn.: Idun, 2023. [N.D.]

Valen, Christopher. *No Way to Die* (N). Tucson, Ariz.: Santa Rita Press, 2023. [St. Paul, Minn.]

Van Buren, M.J. *The Coroner Had No Comment* (N). S.l.: Kaw Valley Spring, 2023. [Topeka, Kan.]

Van Dam, C.K. *Lone Tree Claim* (N). S.l.: Pasque Publishing, 2023. [Dak.]

VanAlstine, Mary. *Deny Me, the Nightshade Boy* (N). S.l.: Dreaming in Color, 2023. [St. Paul, Minn.]

VanderLugt, Dana. *Enemies in the Orchard* (juv). Grand Rapids, Mich.: Zonderkidz, 2023. [Mich.]

VanDerSys, Robyn. *Black Hills Fall 2* (N). S.l.: Raventhorne Books, 2023. [S.D.]

VanHorn, Kellie. *Dangerous Desert Abduction* (N). Toronto: Love Inspired, 2023. [N.D.]

Varni, Holly. *On Moonberry Lake* (N). Grand Rapids, Mich.: Revell, 2023. [Minn.]

Vaun, Missouri. *Forever's Promise* (N). Valley Falls, N.Y.: Bold Strokes Books, 2023. [Kan.]

Vaz, Katherine. *Above the Salt* (N). NY: Flatiron Books, 2023. [Ill.]

Vick, Rod. *A Phantom Comes Home for Christmas* (N). Mukwonago, Wis.: Laikituk Creek Publishing, 2023. [Mukwonago, Wis.]

Viets, Elaine. *The Dead of Night* (N). Edinburgh: Severn House, 2023. [Mo.]

Vigne, Antoine. *Tout s'écoule* (N). Paris: Bartillat, 2023. [Detroit, Mich.]

Vincenz, Kathleen. *The Christmas Surprise* (juv). S.l.: Squirrels at the Door Publishing, 2023. [Wis.]

Von Schrader, Eric. *A Universe Revealed* (N). Carpinteria, Calif.: ABSOM Books, 2023. [St. Louis, Mo.]

Wall, Robyn G. *Tinker's Dam* (N). Parker, Colo.: Outskirts Press, 2023. [Ind.]

Warren, Susan May. *Creed* (N). Minnetonka, Minn.: Soli Deo Gloria Press, 2023. [Minn.]

———. *Fraser* (N). Minnetonka, Minn.: Soli Deo Gloria Press, 2023. [Minn.]

Weaver, Will. *Power & Light* (N). Minneapolis: Calumet Editions, 2023. [N.D.]

Weber, Ella. *The Dell Diaries* (N). S.l.: Latah Books, 2023. [Neb.]

Weber, Frank F. *The Haunted House of Hillman* (N). Pierz, Minn.: Moon Finder Press, 2023. [Minn.]

Weedman, Roz and Susan Todd. *Poppy and Mary Deliver the Goods* (N). Traverse City, Mich.: Mission Point Press, 2023. [Frankenmuth, Mich.]

Wees, Alyssa. *Nocturne* (N). NY: Del Rey Books, 2023. [Chicago, Ill.]

Weiner, Steve. *Duck Island* (N). Vancouver: New Star Books, 2023. [Wis.]

Welch, Margaret. *Till Then* (N). Danbury, Conn.: Guideposts, 2023. [Ohio]

Welch, Susan. *A Thread So Fine* (N). Chicago: Muse Literary, 2023. [St. Paul, Minn.]

Wells, S.I. *A Christmas Hometown Reunion* (N). S.l.: Stay Thirsty Publishing, 2023. [Iowa]

Welsh-Huggins, Andrew. *The End of the Road* (N). NY: Mysterious Press, 2023. [Ohio]

Wemlinger, John. *The Road to Empire* (N). Traverse City, Mich.: Mission Point Press, 2023. [Empire, Mich.]

Wendelboe, C.M. *Death under the Deluge* (N). Farmington, Me.: Encircle Publications, 2023. [S.D.]

Wenner, Jody. *The Mortician's Wife* (N). Adams Basin, N.Y.: Wild Rose Press, 2023. [Minn.]

Westerman, Gwen. *Songs, Blood Deep* (P). Duluth, Minn.: Holy Cow! Press, 2023. [Minn.]

Whicker, Mike. *Valentin's Secret* (N). S.l.: Walküre, 2023. [Evansville, Ind.]

White, Robb T. *Full-Tilt Boogie* (N). Cleveland, Ohio: Boxing World, 2023. [Youngstown, Ohio]

Wietgrefe, Gary. *Dakota Country Poems* (P). Rapid City, S.D.: GWW Books, 2023. [S.D.]

Williams, Katie. *My Murder* (N). NY: Riverhead Books, 2023. [Mich.]

Williams, Tennessee. *Caterpillar Dogs* (S). NY: New Directions, 2023.

Willis, Jason Lee. *The Alchemist's Stone* (N). Austin, Minn.: Fos Pointe Publishing, 2023. [Minn.]

———. *The Firehandler* (N). Mapleton, Minn.: Lura Publications, 2023. [Minn.]

———. *The Wintermaker* (N). Mapleton, Minn.: Lura Publications, 2023. [Minn.]

Wilson, L. Lamar. *Hemingway's Boys Are* (P). Hemingway Review, 43 (Fall 2023), 125.

Wilson, Nina. *House One* (N). Mesa, Ariz.: Cactus Moon Publications, 2023. [Iowa]

Wilson, Sariah. *The Hollywood Jinx* (N). Seattle: Montlake, 2023. [Ohio]

Windholz, Anne M. *Air Like Champagne* (N). Bartlett, Ill.: Aeolian Press, 2023. [Victoria, Kan.]

Winfrey, Kerry. *Faking Christmas* (N). NY: Berkley Books, 2023. [Ohio]

Winnette, Colin. *Users* (N). NY: Soft Skull Press, 2023. [Chicago, Ill.]

Winter-Swink, Sally. *To Share Love Again* (N). Murrells Inlet, S.C.: Covenant Books, 2023. [Iowa]

Winters, E.L. *Mythmatched* (N). S.l.: Scribe Hive Publishing, 2023. [Wis.]

Wiseman, Beth. *Hopefully Ever After* (N). Grand Rapids, Mich.: Zondervan, 2023. [Ind.]

Withers, Ellen E. *Show Me Betrayal* (N). Morrilton, Ark.: Scrivenings Press, 2023. [Mexico, Mo.]

Witwer, Michael. *Vivian Van Tassel and the Secret of Midnight Lake* (juv). NY: Aladdin Books, 2023. [Wis.]

Wolfe, Laura. *The In-Laws* (N). London: Bookouture, 2023. [Mich.]

———. *Prom Queen* (N). London: Bookouture, 2023. [Mich.]

Woo, Sung J. *Deep Roots* (N). Marlboro, N.J.: Agora Books, 2023. [Minneapolis, Minn.]

Woodling, D.B. *The Immortal Detective* (N). Brentwood, Tenn.: CamCat Books, 2023. [Kansas City, Mo.]

Woodsmall, Cindy. *Until Then* (N). Carol Stream, Ill.: Tyndale House, 2023. [Ohio]

Wright, Jamie Jo. *The Lost Boys of Barlowe Theater* (N). Minneapolis: Bethany House, 2023. [Wis.]

———. *The Vanishing at Castle Moreau* (N). Minneapolis: Bethany House, 2023. [Wis.]

Wyatt, Merrill. *Tangled up in Mayhem* (juv). NY: Margaret K. McElderry Books, 2023. [Sandusky, Ohio]

Wynters, Erica. *Marigolds, Mischief, and Murder* (N). S.l.: Gemma Halliday Publishing, 2023. [Ill.]

Zacharias, Pete. *The Man Trapped by Shadows* (N). Seattle: Thomas & Mercer, 2023. [Minn.]

Zafris, Nancy. *Black Road* (N). S.l.: Unbridled Books, 2023. [Ohio]

Zeineddine, Ghassan. *Dearborn* (S). Portland, Or.: Tin House, 2023. [Dearborn, Mich.]

Zelke-Windau, Marilyn. *Beneath the Southern Crux* (P). Tucson, Ariz.: Water's Edge Press, 2023.

Zimmerman, Laura. *Just Do This One Thing for Me* (juv). NY: Dutton, 2023. [Wis.]

Secondary Sources

General

Beasecker, Robert, ed. Annual Bibliography of Midwestern Literature*: 2021* (bibl). *MidAmerica*, 50 (2023), 162–214.

———, ed. Index to the Serial Publications of the Society for the Study of Midwestern Literature (bibl). *Midwestern Miscellany*, 51 (Spr.-Fall 2023), 4–296.

Hantke, Steffen. Machines in the Garden: De-Gothicizing the American Pastoral in Tales from the Loop (crit). *Journal of Popular Film and Television*, 51 (3) 2023, 131–37. [Midwest]

Hayner Genealogy & Local History Library. *Local Authors* (bibl; biog). Alton, Ill.: The Library, 2023. [Alton, Ill.]

Kohn, Mary and Trevin Garcia. A New Majority: Latinx English in Southwest Kansas (lang). *English World-Wide*, 44 (3) 2023, 351–80. [Kansas]

Kroucheva, Katerina. *Schlachthof und Kulturpoetik: Die Stockyards von Chicago in amerikanischer und europäischer Literatur, Wissenschaft und Populärkultur* (crit). Göttingen: Wallstein Verlag, 2023. [Chicago, Ill.]

Monaco, Pamela. What's New in Midwestern Nonfiction: A Review Essay (rev). *MidAmerica*, 50 (2023), 149–53.

Nesbitt, Monica. Phonological Emergence and Social Reorganization: Developing a Nasal /æ/ System in Lansing, Michigan (lang). *Language Variation and Change*, 35 (Oct. 2023), 273–97. [Michigan]

Norris, Keenan. *Chi Boy: Native Sons and Chicago Reckonings* (crit; M). Columbus,

Ohio: Mad Creek Books, 2023. [Chicago, Ill.]

O'Hagan, Malcolm E. *A Literary Odyssey: The Founding of the American Writers Museum* (gen). Chicago: American Writers Museum, 2023. [Chicago, Ill.]

Sears, Jeff. Rural, Urban, and Suburban Regionalism: A Review Essay (rev). *MidAmerica*, 50 (2023), 145–48.

Seaton, James E., Jr. The Midwest in American Drama: A Review Essay (rev). *MidAmerica*, 50 (2023), 154–61.

Smiley, Jane. *The Questions That Matter Most: Reading, Writing, and the Exercise of Freedom* (crit; M). Berkeley, Calif.: Heyday, 2023.

Wagel, Kristin Elizabeth. Rhetoric-Remembrance-Race-Region: Contemporary Stories of Abolition and the Making of Race in the Upper Midwest (crit). Ph.D. Dissertation, U Wisconsin-Milwaukee, 2023.

Zimmerman, Marc. *Mexican and Chicano Literature in Chicago: Transplanting Early Roots to the Barrios and Beyond* (crit). Chicago: LACASA Chicago Books, 2023. [Chicago, Ill.]

Addams, Jane (1860–1935)

Class, Claire Marie. Dynamic Reading: Suspicion, Sociology, and Urgency in Ida B. Wells's Antilynching Campaign (crit). *Criticism*, 65 (Win. 2023), 79–101.

Levine, Caroline. Nuts and Bolts: Collective Action, the Divestment Movement, and Jane Addams (crit). *Victorian Literature and Culture*, 51 (Win. 2023), 591–604.

Shields, Patricia M., Maurice Hamington, and Joseph Soeters, eds. *The Oxford Handbook of Jane Addams* (crit). NY: Oxford U P, 2023.

Algren, Nelson (1909–1981)

Boggs, Colleen Glenney. *American Hunger* vs. *America Eats*: Richard Wright and the Racial Politics of Lifestyle Writing (crit).

American Literary History, 35 (Win. 2023), 1638–64.

Cowie, Doug. Discovering *The Man with the Golden Arm* by Nelson Algren (crit). *Journal of American Studies*, 57 (Dec. 2023), 742–44.

Anderson, Margaret (1886–1973)

Baggett, Holly A. *Making No Compromise: Margaret Anderson, Jane Heap, and the Little Review* (crit). DeKalb: Northern Illinois U P, 2023.

Anderson, Sherwood (1876–1941)

Achilles, Jochen. Normative Crisis in Regionalist American Short Fiction (crit). *Journal of the Short Story in English*, 80–81 (Spr. 2023), 25–44.

Gazzaz, Rasha. Sherwood Anderson's *Winesburg, Ohio*: The Fragmented Self and Experience within the Context of War and the Uncanny Midwest (crit). *MidAmerica*, 50 (2023), 110–20.

Ichinose, Shimpei. Reconsidering Midwestern Author Sherwood Anderson: Columbus' Representations and the Society of American Indians (crit). *Midwest Quarterly*, 64 (Win. 2023), 155–68.

McCracken, David. William James's Metaphysical Revelation in Sherwood Anderson's "Tandy" (crit). *Explicator*, 81 (July-Dec. 2023), 136–41.

Zolotariov, Elena. "Black and Red Laughter": Subverting Whiteness in Hemingway's *The Torrents of Spring* (crit). *Hemingway Review*, 43 (Fall 2023), 67–86.

Baum, L. Frank (1856–1919)

Bunch, Ryan. *Oz and the Musical: Performing the American Fairy Tale* (crit). NY: Oxford U P, 2023.

Massachi, Dina Schiff, ed. *The Characters of Oz: Essays on Their Adaption and Transformation* (crit). Jefferson, N.C.: McFarland & Co., 2023.

Pugh, Tison. *Queer Oz: L. Frank Baum's Trans Tales and Other Astounding Adventures in Sex and Gender* (crit). Jackson: U P Mississippi, 2023.

Riley, Michael O'Neal. *The First Edition of The Wonderful Wizard of Oz: A New Bibliographic Description* (bibl). Milledgeville, Ga.: Pamani, 2023.

Shierry, Addison. Well Enough Alone: An Exploration of Feminine Solitude in Four American Novels (crit). Ph.D. Dissertation, U Texas-Dallas, 2023.

Tripp, Colleen. "Coach, I Got a Feeling We're Not in Kansas Anymore": *Ted Lasso* and the Heartland Mythos (crit). *Journal of American Culture*, 46 (Dec. 2023), 343–52.

Zheng, Lukun, Huiqiang Zheng, and Chandra Kundu. Authorship Attribution via Occupancy-Problem-Type Indices (crit). *Journal of Quantitative Linguistics*, 30 (Feb. 2023), 27–41.

Bellow, Saul (1915–2005)

Dean, Andrew. "You Had to Be a Crank to Insist on Being Right": Saul Bellow's Comedy (crit). *Studies in the Novel*, 55 (Sum. 2023), 148–66.

Lönhardt, Timea. Saül Bellow: La résistance à la modernité: Étude comparative des romans et des écrits critiques belloviens publiés après 1970 (crit). Thèse de Doctorat, Université Bordeaux Montaigne, 2023.

Marrouchi, Ramzi. *Madness and Subversion in Saul Bellow's Later Novels: A Deconstructive Perspective* (crit). NY: Peter Lang, 2023.

Newman, Judie. Saul Bellow in Utah: "Leaving the Yellow House" (crit). *Studies in the American Short Story*, 4 (1) 2023, 69–76.

Teymouri, Tohid, Zahra Jannessari Ladani, and Pyeaam Abbasi. Writing Space and Death Experience in Saul Bellow's

Novels (crit). *Critique*, 64 (2) 2023, 257–69.

Vanheste, Jeroen. No Pills, But Letters. Saul Bellow's *Herzog*: The Recovery of a Depressed Academic (crit). *Journal of Medical Humanities*, 44 (June 2023), 129–44.

Berryman, John (1914–1972)

Spaide, Christopher. You Can Never Be Sure (rev). *American Literary History*, 35 (Win. 2023), 1825–42.

Bierce, Ambrose (1842–1914?)

Corstorphine, Kevin. The Vanishing South: Race and the Ecogothic in Ambrose Bierce and Charles Chesnutt (crit). *Studies in American Fiction*, 50 (Spr.-Fall 2023), 55–73.

Manning, Paul. Somewhere in the Outer Darkness: Locating the Frontier (Eco) Gothic of Ambrose Bierce (crit). *Horror Studies*, 14 (2) 2023, 185–203.

Melbye, David. Two Divergent Cinematic Readings of Enslavement in "An Occurrence at Owl Creek Bridge" (crit). *Short Film Studies*, 13 (Mar. 2023), 35–48.

Black Elk (1863–1950)

Kelderman, Frank. Black Elk Faces East: Beb Vuyk, Cultural Translation, and John G. Neihardt's *Black Elk Speaks* (crit). *Journal of Transnational American Studies*, 14 (2) 2023, 7–27.

Bly, Robert (1926–2021)

Hodd, Thomas. Robert Bly in New Brunswick: The Cross-Border Poetics of Allan Cooper (crit). *American Review of Canadian Studies*, 53 (June 2023), 192–203.

Borden, Mary (1886–1968)

Brasme, Isabelle. *Writers at War: Exploring the Prose of Ford Madox Ford, Mary*

Sinclair, Siegfried Sassoon and Mary Borden (crit). NY: Routledge, 2023.

Boyle, Kay (1902–1992)

Grogan, Christine. Kay Boyle and the "Jewel of Inconsistencies" (crit). *ANQ*, 36 (Oct.-Dec. 2023), 588–92.

Bradbury, Ray (1920–2012)

Aronoff, Eric. Aliens, Anthropologists, and American Indians: Ray Bradbury's *The Martian Chronicles*, Culture, and Difference in Midcentury US Modernism (crit). *Modern Fiction Studies*, 69 (Sum. 2023), 309–40.

Bohovyk, Oksana and Andrii Bezrukov. Narrating Conspiracy Theories: A Paradoxical Ethics of Otherness, Propaganda and Mistrust (crit). *Enthymema: Rivista Internazionale di Critica, Teoria e Filosofia della Letteratura*, 34 (Sept. 2023), 164–79.

Eller, Jonathan R., ed. *Remembrance: Selected Correspondence of Ray Bradbury* (corr). NY: Simon & Schuster, 2023.

Lim, Suk Won. Understanding Media in *Fahrenheit 451*: Re-Reading Bradbury's Novel through the Lens of Marshall McLuhan's Media Theory (crit). *Extrapolation*, 64 (Sum. 2023), 149–66.

McCracken, David. "Isn't This the Ending of *Fahrenheit 451*?": The Intertextual Intersection of *Fahrenheit 451*, *Fight Club*, and *Adjustment Day* (crit). *ANQ*, 36 (Apr. 2023), 264–69.

Bromfield, Louis (1896–1956)

Bachelder, Thomas. *An Agitated Existence: Louis Bromfield, Conservation's Enigma* (biog). S.l.: S.n., 2023.

Sommer, Tine. Middlebrow Affective Mapping: Reading Modern Motherhood in Louis Bromfield's *Mrs. Parkington* (crit). *College Literature*, 50 (Win. 2023), 34–56.

Brooks, Gwendolyn (1917–2000)

Conrad, Rachel. "To Take My Freedom Is to Take My Breath": Lillian Myricks and Young Black Poets' Poetics of Freedom (crit). *Children's Literature Association Quarterly*, 47 (Win. 2023), 357–69.

Ellefson, Philip. Kitchenette Folks: Gwendolyn Brooks's *Maud Martha* and the Remodeling of the Novel (crit). *MELUS*, 48 (Fall 2023), 141–62.

Hunter, Walt. *The American House Poem, 1945–2021* (crit). Oxford: Oxford U P, 2023.

Taylor, Jonathon W. Revolutionary Spaces: Julia Kristeva, Gwendolyn Brooks, and a Post-Pandemic Path Ahead in Dominique Morisseau's *Pipeline* (crit). *Theatre Symposium*, 30 (2023), 40–54.

Wiman, Christian. One Wants a Teller (crit). *Commonweal*, 150 (May 2023), 62–63.

Burchfield, Charles E. (1893–1967)

Estes, Ben, ed. *The Sphinx and the Milky Way: Selections from the Journals of Charles Burchfield* (crit). Brooklyn, N.Y.: Song Cave, 2023.

Weekly, Nancy. *Charles E. Burchfield: A Lifetime of Themes* (crit). Buffalo, N.Y.: Burchfield Penney Art Center, 2023.

Burnett, William Riley (1899–1982)

Blanc, Jean-Noël. *Polarville: Images de la Ville dans le Roman Policier* (crit). Lyon: Presses Universitaires de Lyon, 2023.

Burroughs, William S. (1914–1997)

Bolin, John. "Anathema to the Spirit the Beats Are Remembered For": A Review of *Anti-Humanism in the Counterculture* (rev). *Journal of Modern Literature*, 46 (Win. 2023), 180–84.

Campbell, Bonnie Jo (b. 1962)

DuRose, Lisa, Ross K. Tangedal, and Andy Oler, eds. *Michigan Salvage: The Fiction of*

Bonnie Jo Campbell (crit). East Lansing: Michigan State U P, 2023.

Carter, Vincent O. (1924–1983)

Zocco, Gianna. Provincialising Europe "from the Inside": James Baldwin's and Vincent O. Carter's Writings about Switzerland (crit). *CompLit: Journal of European Literature, Arts and Society*, 2 (6) 2023, 255–56.

Castillo, Ana (b. 1953)

Hakobyan, Liana. Decolonial Healing and Epistemic Disobedience in Ana Castillo's *So Far from God* (crit). *Chiricú Journal: Latina/o Literatures, Arts, and Cultures*, 7 (Spr. 2023), 5–31.

Kasparian-Le Fèvre, Méliné. Les fruist du désert: L'écriture de la nourriture chez Ana Castillo, Sandra Cisneros et Pat Mora (crit). Thèse de Doctorat, Université Bordeaux Montaigne, 2023.

Lule, Liliana. "Wherever I Go I Carry Home on My Back": Notions of Belonging in Ana Castillo's *Sapogonia* (crit). *MidAmerica*, 50 (2023), 100–09.

Romanowski, Arne. Decolonial Spaces of Belonging in Chicana and Ukrainian-German Creative Nonfiction (crit). *Confluencia: Revista Hispánica de Cultura y Literatura*, 39 (Spr. 2023), 79–90.

Spencer, Andrew M. Catholicism as Environmental Protest in Rudolfo Anaya's *Bless Me, Ultima* and Ana Castillo's *So Far from God* (crit). *MELUS*, 48 (Win. 2023), 165–82.

Cather, Willa (1873–1947)

Bintrim, Timothy W. and Scott Riner. "Long-Cellared Wine": "Double Birthday," Edward J. H. O'Brien, and the Best American Short Stories Series (crit). *Willa Cather Review*, 64 (Spr. 2023), 15–23.

Burris, Patti. A Lost Wetland (crit). *Willa Cather Review*, 64 (Win. 2023), 32–34.

Clere, Sarah. Lost Ladies on Page and Screen (crit). *Willa Cather Review*, 64 (Win. 2023), 12–13.

———. Willa Cather and the Sisterhood of the Pulitzer (crit). *Willa Cather Review*, 64 (Fall 2023), 11–17.

Dunbier, Lonnie Pierson. Lost Lady Found (crit). *Willa Cather Review*, 64 (Win. 2023), 30–31.

Durrans, Stéphanie. Le langage poétique de Willa Cather: Une étude du temps et de la mémoire dans l'oeuvre de Willa Cather (crit). Thèse de Doctorat, Université Bordeaux Montaigne, 2023.

———. Elia Peattie and Willa Cather: Influence and Shared Vision (crit). *Willa Cather Review*, 64 (Spr. 2023), 3–8.

Flannigan, John H. A Tongue-Tied Generation Goes to War: Cather's Claude Wheeler and Tarkington's *Ramsey Milholland* (crit). *Willa Cather Review*, 64 (Fall 2023), 18–24.

Gustke, Charmion. The Odalisque and *A Lost Lady*: A Rereading through the Lens of Whiteness (crit). *Willa Cather Review*, 64 (Win. 2023), 8–9.

Hamilton, Erika K. When Mountains Fall: *A Lost Lady* in Colorado (crit). *Willa Cather Review*, 64 (Win. 2023), 19–21.

Kundu, Gautam. F. Scott Fitzgerald and Willa Cather: A Literary Relationship in Letters (crit). *ANQ*, 36 (Apr.-Sept. 2023), 400–10.

Mackas, Maria. Cather's Universal Appeal and Enduring Relevance: How She Inspires Today's Multicultural Writers (crit). *Willa Cather Review*, 64 (Spr. 2023), 24–29.

Murphy, Joseph C. A Museum without Walls: Willa Cather and John La Farge at *McClure's* (crit). *Willa Cather Review*, 64 (Fall 2023), 25–31.

Olin-Ammentorp, Julie. Niel and Marian (crit). *Willa Cather Review*, 64 (Win. 2023), 4–6.

Palmer, Daryl W. Willa Cather's Multiverse: Boy Prototypes in "The Way of the World," "The Treasure of Far Island," "The Enchanted Bluff," and *A Lost Lady* (crit). *Willa Cather Review*, 64 (Win. 2023), 23–29.

Rau, Emily J. Confronting Indigenous Erasure in *A Lost Lady* (crit). *Willa Cather Review*, 64 (Win. 2023), 6–7.

Rohy, Valerie. On the Divide: Reading Cather Against the Binary (crit). *Arizona Quarterly*, 79 (Win. 2023), 1–21.

Siporin, Steve. "A Gold Slipper" and a Pullman Sleeper: Willa Cather's Adaptation of a Modern Urban Legend (crit). *Willa Cather Review*, 64 (Fall 2023), 2–10.

Siraganian, Lisa. Stateless Regionalism and Corporate Power: Willa Cather's Public Relations Novel (crit). *American Literary History*, 35 (Spr. 2023), 126–42.

Smith, Elaine. Reading *A Lost Lady* with Older Eyes (crit). *Willa Cather Review*, 64 (Win. 2023), 21–22.

Sommer, Tine. How Houses Move Us: Atmospheric Practices in *The Professor's House* (1925) (crit). *Home Cultures*, 20 (Mar. 2023), 1–17.

Stout, Janis. Loving Lost Ladies (crit). *Willa Cather Review*, 64 (Win. 2023), 2–4.

Swift, John. Niel, the Prophet Samuel, and the Woman of Endor (crit). *Willa Cather Review*, 64 (Win. 2023), 16–17.

———. Puzzle and Passion: The Case of Willa Cather and Mary Roberts Rinehart (crit). *Willa Cather Review*, 64 (Spr. 2023), 9–14.

Taylor, Benjamin. *Chasing Bright Medusas: A Life of Willa Cather* (biog; crit). NY: Viking, 2023.

Thacker, Robert. "Nebraska: The End of the First Cycle" and *A Lost Lady* (crit). *Willa Cather Review*, 64 (Win. 2023), 18–19.

Van Wienen, Mark W. *A Lost Lady* at 100: Imperial Dreams, Indigenous Nightmare (crit). *Willa Cather Review*, 64 (Win. 2023), 10–11.

Wade, Sarah. Care Communities in *A Lost Lady* (crit). *Willa Cather Review*, 64 (Win. 2023), 35–39.

Wells, Elizabeth. Lost Lading: Freight in Willa Cather's *A Lost Lady* (crit). *Willa Cather Review*, 64 (Win. 2023), 14–15.

Zahorski, Alexandra. Willa Cather: Mouvement et culture (crit). Thèse de Doctorat, Université Bordeaux Montaigne, 2023.

Chesnutt, Charles W. (1858–1932)

Bentley, Nancy. The Novel, the *Demos*, and Genres of the Human (crit). *American Literary History*, 35 (Spr. 2023), 53–66.

Corstorphine, Kevin. The Vanishing South: Race and the Ecogothic in Ambrose Bierce and Charles Chesnutt (crit). *Studies in American Fiction*, 50 (Spr.-Fall 2023), 55–73.

O'Donoghue, James. Dropping Voices: Southern Black Agrarian Revolt in Charles Chesnutt's Fiction (crit). *Journal of Working Class Studies*, 8 (June 2023), 97–115.

Stone, Aaron J. Toward a Black Vernacular Sexology (crit). *GLQ: A Journal of Lesbian and Gay Studies*, 29 (Jan. 2023), 27–42.

Utphall, Jamie. Pain Management in Nineteenth-Century American Literature (crit). Ph.D. Dissertation, Ohio State U, 2023.

Chopin, Kate (1850–1904)

Abril Hernández, Ana. "The Voice of the Sea Speaks to the Soul": Voicing Silence in Kate Chopin's *The Awakening* and in Rebecca Migdal's Graphic Adaptation (crit). *ES Review: Spanish Journal of English Studies*, 44 (2023), 187–212.

Sun, Lu and Yunjie Wei. Achieving Humanity through Animality: A Study of the Birds in Kate Chopin's *The Awakening* (crit). *Journal of Language, Literature and Culture*, 70 (Apr. 2023), 38–48.

Cisneros, Sandra (b. 1954)

Kasparian-Le Fèvre, Méliné. Les fruist du désert: L'écriture de la nourriture chez Ana Castillo, Sandra Cisneros et Pat Mora (crit). Thèse de Doctorat, Université Bordeaux Montaigne, 2023.

Clemens, Samuel L. (1835–1910)

Ben-Daniels, Faith. Studying Mark Twain's *The Diaries of Adam and Eve* from a Ghanaian Context (crit). *Mark Twain Annual*, 21 (2023), 143–55.

Bird, John. "Like Setting Down on a Kag of Powder and Touching It Off Just to See Where You'll Go to": Reflections on Forty Years of Teaching *Huckleberry Finn* (crit). *Mark Twain Annual*, 21 (2023), 135–42.

Cavitch, Max. Mark Twain, the Talking Cure, and Literary Form (crit). *American Literary History*, 35 (Fall 2023), 1183–1205.

Fagan, Joshua. Mark Twain's *Connecticut Yankee*, William Morris, and the Problem of Late-Victorian Medievalism (crit). *Mark Twain Annual*, 21 (2023), 20.39.

Finger, Stanley. *Mark Twain, Dr. Oliver Wendell Holmes, and the Head Readers: Literature, Humor, and Faddish Phrenology* (crit). Cambridge: Cambridge U P, 2023.

Höll, Davina. Migration in Times of Pandemic: Mark Twain's "3,000 Years Among the Microbes" and the Prospect of Planetary Health (crit). *Journal of Transnational American Studies*, 14 (2) 2023, 141–64.

Jenn, Ronald. La traduction de la rhétorique enfantine chez Mark Twain (crit). Thèse de Doctorat, Université Bordeaux Montaigne, 2023.

Khazaeenezhad, Bahareh and Sara Taheri. A Comparative Study of Persian Translations of *The Adventures of*

Huckleberry Finn: Cultural Gain and Loss in Focus (crit; lang). *International Journal of Foreign Language Teaching and Research*, 11 (Apr. 2023), 11–26.

Machor, James L. *The Mercurial Mark Twain(s): Reception History, Audience Engagement, and Iconic Authorship* (crit). NY: Routledge, 2023.

McNamara, Megan. "Only Dead Men Can Tell the Truth in This World": The Growth of Mark Twain's Anger (crit). *Mark Twain Annual*, 21 (2023), 80–94.

Manning, Alan and Nicole Amare. Mark Twain's Early Contributions to Fantasy and Science Fiction and "Mormon" Narratives of Reconciliation (crit). *Mark Twain Annual*, 21 (2023), 40–60.

Moreno, Richard. *Frontier Fake News: Nevada's Sagebrush Humorists and Hoaxsters* (crit). Reno: U Nevada P, 2023.

Morris, Linda A. Susy Clemens: The Final Years (biog). *Mark Twain Annual*, 21 (2023), 61–79.

Murray, Seth. The Stakes of Stormfield: On Mark Twain's Vision of Heaven (crit). *Mark Twain Annual*, 21 (2023), 1–19.

Myrick, Leslie Diane and Gary Scharnhorst. *Cartoons and Caricatures of Mark Twain in Context: Reformer and Social Critic, 1869–1910* (crit). Tuscaloosa: U Alabama P, 2023.

Oliver, Jacob S. Judgment, Trust, and Common Sense in American Literature (crit). Ph.D. Dissertation, U Washington, 2023.

Scharnhorst, Gary and Leslie Diane Myrick, eds. *Mark Twain and the Critics, 1891–1910: Selected Notices of the Late Writings* (crit). Jefferson, N.C.: McFarland & Co., 2023.

Seybold, Matt. The Twain Doctrine (crit). *Mark Twain Annual*, 21 (2023), 95–116.

Shan, Xueqi. The Influence of Alexandre Dumas in Mark Twain's *Adventures of*

Huckleberry Finn (crit). *ANQ*, 36 (Apr. 2023), 218–21.

Sharma, Seema. Why I Still Teach Mark Twain in the Twenty-First-Century Indian Classroom (crit). *Mark Twain Annual*, 21 (2023), 117–22.

Sloane, David E.E. Comic Attack: Mark Twain and the N-Word in the Classroom (crit). *Mark Twain Annual*, 21 (2023), 123–34.

Snedecor, Barbara E. *Gravity: Selected Letters of Olivia Langdon Clemens* (corr). Columbia: U Missouri P, 2023.

Cooper, James Fenimore (1789–1851)

Lindquist, Andy. "Is a Nation to Be Sold Like the Skin of a Beaver!": James Fenimore Cooper's *The Prairie* and the Dilemma of Countersovereignty (crit). *Early American Literature*, 58 (1) 2023, 125–54.

Wegener, Signe O. *James Fenimore Cooper: A Companion* (biog; crit). Jefferson, N.C.: McFarland & Co., 2023.

Coover, Robert (1932–2024)

Rocha, Nilo Ferreira da. *A narrativa de metaficção: Teoria e crítica* (crit). Bahia: P55 Edição, 2023.

Cortez, Carlos (1923–2005)

Cumpián, Carlos and David Ranney, eds. *Coyote's Song: Collected Poetry and Selected Art* (biog; crit; P). Chicago: Charles H. Kerr Publishing Co., 2023.

Crane, Hart (1899–1932)

Hoffmeyer, John. The Architectonics of Hope: Fragments of Life and Text in Walter Benjamin and Hart Crane (crit). *Comparative Literature*, 75 (Sept. 2023), 348–72.

Miller, Christopher Patrick. American Tramps: Transient Gesture and Lyric Form in Hart Crane (crit). *Twentieth Century Literature*, 69 (Mar. 2023), 1–28.

Wallace, Nadira Clare. "Exploiting magnificence": Hart Crane versus T. S. Eliot on the Matter of Diction (crit). *Textual Practice*, 37 (Mar. 2023), 373–92.

Crothers, Rachel (1878–1958)

Huang, Amy B. On Memory and Movement (crit). *Eighteenth-Century Studies*, 57 (Fall 2023), 21–31.

Cunningham, Michael (b. 1952)

Alkhayat, Marwa. Towards a Feminization of Time in Michael Cunningham's *The Hours* (1998) and Sahar Al-Mouji's *The Musk of the Hill* (2017) (crit). *Women's Studies*, 52 (Apr.-May 2023), 339–61.

Dos Passos, John (1896–1970)

King, Zachary Murphy. Modernism under the Microscope: The Reception and Translation of Marcel Proust, John Dos Passos and James Joyce in Soviet Russia, 1922–1942 (crit). Ph.D. Dissertation, U Chicago, 2023.

Vasconcelos, Bernardo de, ed. *Thoughts in Time: Dos Passos Revisited/Reflexões no Tempo: Dos Passos Revisitado* (crit). Funchal, Portugal: Direção Regional da Cultura; 2023.

Dove, Rita (b. 1952)

Roy, Lekha. *Towards Post-Blackness: A Critical Study of Rita Dove's Poetry* (crit). NY: Peter Lang, 2023.

Dreiser, Theodore (1871–1945)

Lyle, Megan Cole. Fossil-Fueled Naturalism and Pastoral Optimism in the Novels of Dreiser, Norris, and Sinclair (crit). *Studies in American Naturalism*, 18 (Sum. 2023), 1–30.

McNeilly, Sam. The Forces of Fossil Capital: *Sister Carrie* and American Literary Naturalism's Industrial Middle-Class Ideology (crit). *Textual Practice*, 37 (June 2023), 867–86.

Ng, Kenny K.K. Cosmopolitanism from Below: Union Film's Adaptation of World Classics (crit). *Positions: Asia Critique*, 31 (Aug. 2023), 623–48.

Totten, Gary. Naturalism and the New Woman: Theodore Dreiser's *Sister Carrie* and Grant Allen's *The Woman Who Did* (crit). *Studies in American Naturalism*, 18 (Sum. 2023), 31–52.

Dylan, Bob (b. 1941)

Barnett, Christopher B. *Bob Dylan and the Spheres of Existence* (crit). Lanham, Md.: Lexington Books/Fortress Academic, 2023.

Cara, Ana C. On the High Art of Folk Poetry: What Jorge Luis Borges and Bob Dylan Have in Common (crit). *Journal of Transnational American Studies*, 14 (2) 2023, 419–32.

Davidson, Mark A. and Parker Fishel, eds. *Bob Dylan: Mixing up the Medicine* (biog; crit). East Hampton, N.Y.: Callaway, 2023.

Goodwin, Opher. *Bob Dylan: 1962–1970* (crit). Tewkesbury: Sonicbond Publishing, 2023.

Goss, Nina. Today and Tomorrow and Yesterday, Too: *Rough and Rowdy Ways /* "Murder Most Foul" (2020), Bob Dylan, and Late Style Studies (crit). *Aktualitet: Litteratur, Kultur og Medier*, 17 (3) 2023, 4–15.

Graves, Matthew, Pierluigi Lanfranchi, and Claudio Milanesi, eds. *Bob Dylan et le Mythe* (crit). Aix-en-Provence: Presses Universitaires de Provence, 2023.

Mai, Anne-Marie. Time Slots in Dylan's Oeuvre (crit). *Aktualitet: Litteratur, Kultur og Medier*, 17 (3) 2023, 31–42.

Metsa, Paul. *Blood in the Tracks: The Minnesota Musicians behind Dylan's Masterpiece* (crit). Minneapolis: U Minnesota P, 2023.

Miles, K.G. *Bob Dylan in Minnesota: Troubadour Tales from Duluth, Hibbing and Dinkytown* (biog). Carmarthen: McNidder & Grace, 2023.

——— and Jeff Towns. *Bob Dylan and Dylan Thomas: The Two Dylans* (crit). Carmarthen: McNidder and Grace, 2023.

Murphy, Nancy. *Times a-Changin': Flexible Meter as Self-Expression in Singer-Songwriter Music* (crit). NY: Oxford U P, 2023.

Reginio, Robert. Oh, Help Me in My Weakness: Entreaties and the Dissolution of Communal Time in *John Wesley Harding* (crit). *Aktualitet: Litteratur, Kultur og Medier*, 17 (3) 2023, 16–30.

Roberts, Brian Russell. Nothing Synthetic about It: Translating Bob Dylan's Domestic and International Civil Wars (crit). *Journal of Transnational American Studies*, 14 (2) 2023, 371–95.

Sato, Yoshiaki. The Ever-Changin' Times and Myth of Bob Dylan (crit). *Journal of Transnational American Studies*, 14 (2) 2023, 433–43.

Scarberry-García, Susan. On a Trail of Bells: Bob Dylans "Chimes of Freedom" (crit). *Aktualitet: Litteratur, Kultur og Medier*, 17 (1) 2023, 1–12.

Tsika, Noah. *I'm Not There* (biog; crit). Austin: U Texas P, 2023.

Erdrich, Louise (b. 1954)

Ayuso, Mónica G. Toward a Broader Definition of the Unrealistic: Louise Erdrich's *Future Home of the Living God* and Ernesto Quiñonez's *Taína* (crit). *Journal of the Fantastic in the Arts*, 34 (3) 2023, 28–42.

Chen, Qianqian and Joan Qionglin Tan. Voice Battle to be a Saint in *Love Medicine* (crit). *Orbis Litterarum*, 78 (June 2023), 235–46.

Coulouma, Flore. Territory, Sovereignty, and the Law: Defining Indian Country in Louise Erdrich's Fiction (crit). *Ranam:*

Recherches Anglaises et Nord-Américaines, 57 (2023), 91–109.

Faison, Elisa. The Design Unraveling: Salvaging the Past in Louise Erdrich's *Future Home of the Living God* (crit). *Extrapolation,* 64 (Win. 2023), 357–72.

Gheytasi, Sajjad and Mohsen Hanif. A Theory for Cultural Resistance: The Cases of L. M. Silko's *Ceremony* and L. Erdrich's *Tracks* (crit). *Interdisciplinary Literary Studies,* 25 (3) 2023, 378–402.

Hegeman, Susan. Human Rights and the Novel After UNDRIP: On Louise Erdrich's Justice Trilogy (crit). *College Literature,* 50 (Spr.-Sum. 2023), 410–31.

Ibarrola-Armendariz, Aitor. El Trauma Colectivo y el Papel de la Reparación en Louise Erdrich (crit). *ALPHA: Revista de Artes, Letras y Filosofia,* 56 (July 2023), 49–69.

Markasović, Valentina. An Ecofeminist Reading of Fleur And Lulu in Louise Erdrich's Novel *Tracks* (crit). *Anafora,* 10 (1) 2023, 79–108.

Olsen, Ida. Collapse and Reversed Extinction: Beyond Inherited Epistemologies of Species Loss in Louise Erdrich's *Future Home of the Living God* (crit). *Ecozon@: European Journal of Literature, Culture and Environment,* 14 (2) 2023, 6–19.

Rodi Risbert, Marinella and Laurie Vickroy. Repairing Historical Trauma in Louise Erdrich's *The Plague of Doves* (crit). *American Indian Quarterly,* 47 (Fall 2023), 297–323.

Smith, Cortney. The Suspense Novel as Persuasion: Survivance and Subversion in Louise Erdrich's *The Round House* (crit). *Studies in American Indian Literatures,* 35 (Spr.-Sum. 2023), 20–38.

Stanley, B. Jamieson. "Cornmeal Pancakes to Stave Off the Apocalypse": Ordinary Food in "Poison" and *Future Home of the Living God* (crit). *ISLE: Interdisciplinary*

Studies in Literature and Environment, 30 (Win. 2023), 826–45.

Eugenides, Jeffrey (b. 1960)

Morris, Christopher. The Silkworms of Eugenides and Derrida (crit). *Textual Practice,* 37 (June 2023), 959–75.

Schmidt, Kerstin. Relations with/to the Text: Four Plays on the Move (crit). *Journal of Contemporary Drama in English,* 11 (2) 2023, 332–42.

Farrell, James T. (1904–1979)

Vials, Christopher. Antifascist Narrative and the Politics of Optimism (crit). *American Literary History,* 35 (Spr. 2023), 158–72.

Ferber, Edna (1885–1968)

Clere, Sarah. Willa Cather and the Sisterhood of the Pulitzer (crit). *Willa Cather Review,* 64 (Fall 2023), 11–17.

Moulton, Erica L. The Motion-Picture Rights Contract: Legal Foundations and Trade Practices in the Studio Era (crit). *Film History,* 35 (Spr. 2023), 104–27.

Fitzgerald, F. Scott (1896–1940)

Alexander, Jeanne M., comp. Current Bibliography (bibl). *F. Scott Fitzgerald Review,* 21 (2023), 290–95.

Bate, Jonathan. Allegories of the Extractive Economy: Wagner, Conrad, Fitzgerald (crit). *F. Scott Fitzgerald Review,* 21 (2023), 27–53.

Bayat, Narges and Ali Taghizadeh. An Analysis of Amory Blaine's Affective Masculinity in Scott Fitzgerald's *This Side of Paradise* (crit). *Critical Literary Studies,* 5 (Spr.-Sum. 2023), 15–29.

Bedjaoui, Ahmed. *Francis Scott Fitzgerald et ses contemporains face à Hollywood* (biog; crit). Alger: Casbah Éditions, 2023.

Blazek, William, David W. Ullrich, and Kirk Curnutt, eds. *F. Scott Fitzgerald's The Beautiful and Damned: New Critical*

Essays (crit). Baton Rouge: Louisiana State U P, 2023.

Bruccoli, Matthew J. Memories from "A Moving-Around Life": An Interview with Scottie Fitzgerald (I). *F. Scott Fitzgerald Review*, 21 (2023), 186–235.

Burke, Mary M., et al. Death from a Thousand Cuts: a Roundtable on the 1937 Gatsby Condensation (crit; pub). *F. Scott Fitzgerald Review*, 21 (2023), 171–85.

Culbreath, Verdie. Towards a Literary History of the Rest Cure (1866–1932) (crit). Ph.D. Dissertation, Cornell U, 2023.

Curnutt, Kirk. Editor's Note (crit). *F. Scott Fitzgerald Review*, 21 (2023), vi–xix.

Daniel, Anne Margaret. Extra, Extra: The 1937 Newspaper Condensation of *The Great Gatsby* (crit; pub). *F. Scott Fitzgerald Review*, 21 (2023), 74–79.

———, ed. *The Great Gatsby*: The Sunday Novel … Complete in This Issue, 23 May 1937 [by F. Scott Fitzgerald] (pub). *F. Scott Fitzgerald Review*, 21 (2023), 80–170.

Fahy, Thomas. Class, Gender, and Train Travel in F. Scott Fitzgerald's "A Short Trip Home" (crit). *Studies in the American Short Story*, 4 (1) 2023), 18–35.

Furlich, Emily G. Bringing Queerness to the Surface: Truman Capote's November 1971 Screenplay Adaptation of F. Scott Fitzgerald's *The Great Gatsby* (crit). *Journal of Screenwriting*, 14 (1) 2023, 7–21.

Garnett, Robert R. *Taking Things Hard: The Trials of F. Scott Fitzgerald* (biog; crit). Baton Rouge: Louisiana State U P, 2023.

Kundu, Gautam. F. Scott Fitzgerald and Willa Cather: A Literary Relationship in Letters (crit). *ANQ*, 36 (Apr.-Sept. 2023), 400–10.

Krystal, Arthur. *Some Unfinished Chaos: The Lives of F. Scott Fitzgerald* (biog). Charlottesville: U Virginia P, 2023.

Mitchell, Alexandra and Jennifer Nolan, eds. *The Complete Magazine Stories of F. Scott Fitzgerald, 1921–1924* (crit; pub; S). Edinburgh: Edinburgh U P, 2023.

Nowlin, Michael, ed. *The Cambridge Companion to F. Scott Fitzgerald*. 2nd edition. Cambridge: Cambridge U P, 2023.

Oh, Seung Ah. Crossing the Queensboro Bridge: Gatsby, Automobiles, and Immigrant Mobility in Chang-rae Lee's *Native Speaker* (crit). *Explicator*, 81 (Jan.-June 2023), 41–45.

Park, Katharine. A Historical Tour from Great Neck to West Egg (crit). *F. Scott Fitzgerald Review*, 21 (2023), 1–26.

Parker, Robert Dale. Recentering "Crazy Indian Blood": Reversion to Type in "Bernice Bobs Her Hair" (crit). *F. Scott Fitzgerald Review*, 21 (2023), 54–73.

Rohrkemper, John. F. Scott Fitzgerald: Uncomfortable Superstar, Diligent Professional: A Review Essay (rev). *MidAmerica*, 50 (2023), 137–44.

Senn, Farrah R. Characteristically Fitzgerald: Propriety in Morphing Cultural Contexts in F. Scott Fitzgerald's "Thank You for the Light" (crit). *Studies in the American Short Story*, 4 (2) 2023, 138–60.

Shierry, Addison. Well Enough Alone: An Exploration of Feminine Solitude in Four American Novels (crit). Ph.D. Dissertation, U Texas-Dallas, 2023.

Snyder, Robert Lance. American Literary Noir? Donald E. Westlake's *Ordo* (crit). *Studies in the American Short Story*, 4 (2) 2023, 190–202.

Vujošević, Vladimir. The Paraleptic Effect (crit). *Primerjalna Književnost*, 46 (3) 2023, 61–79.

Warzycki, Bartosz. Selected Cultural Elements and Allusions in Five Polish Translations of F. Scott Fitzgerald's *The Great Gatsby* (crit; lang). *Beyond Philology*, 20 (2) 2023, 127–55.

West, James L.W., III. *Business Is Good: F. Scott Fitzgerald, Professional Writer* (crit). University Park: Pennsylvania State U P, 2023.

——— and Edmund Wilson, eds. *The Last Tycoon: An Unfinished Novel [by] F. Scott Fitzgerald* (crit; pub). NY: Scribner, 2023.

Fitzgerald, Zelda Sayre (1900–1948)

Bruccoli, Matthew J. Memories from "A Moving-Around Life": An Interview with Scottie Fitzgerald (I). *F. Scott Fitzgerald Review*, 21 (2023), 186–235.

Flint, Stephanie M. Our "Hideous Progeny": Monstrous Womanhood at the Advent of the Film Sequel in American Cinema, Literature, and Popular Culture (crit). Ph.D. Dissertation, Florida Atlantic U, 2023.

Novo, Vanesa Vázquez. Zelda Sayre Fitzgerald's Artistic Aspirations and Frustrations: An Analysis of Her Short Stories and Novels (crit). Tesis Doctoral, Universidade da Coruña, 2023.

Franzen, Jonathan (b. 1959)

Ahn, Sunyoung. The End of History in Jonathan Franzen's *The Corrections* (crit). *Explicator*, 81 (July-Dec. 2023), 155–58.

Galow, Timothy W. *Understanding Jonathan Franzen* (crit). Columbia: U South Carolina P, 2023.

Gibson, L. Freedom *Reread* (crit). NY: Columbia U P, 2023.

Gaiman, Neil (b. 1960)

Anjirbag, Michelle Anya. No Country for Old Women: Age, Power, and Beauty in Neil Gaiman's Fantasies (crit). *Marvels & Tales: Journal of Fairy-Tale Studies*, 37 (1) 2023, 3–20.

Carroll, Shiloh. *The Medieval Worlds of Neil Gaiman: From* Beowulf *to* Sleeping Beauty (crit). Iowa City: U Iowa P, 2023.

Giannini, Erin and Amanda Taylor, eds. *Deciphering Good Omens: Nice and Accurate Essays on the Novel and Television Series* (crit). Jefferson, N.C.: McFarland & Co., 2023.

Hume, Kathryn. What Is Punch That They Are Mindful of Him? Neil Gaiman, Ben Aaronovitch, and Russell Hoban (crit). *Critique*, 64 (4) 2023, 647–58.

Kérchy, Anna. Conceptualizing the Embodied Cognition of Uncertainty in Two Terrifying Tales: Lucy Lane Clifford's "The New Mother" and Neil Gaiman's *Coraline* (crit). *Marvels & Tales: Journal of Fairy-Tale Studies*, 37 (2) 2023, 217–40.

Wight, Linda. "Somebody to Love": The Queer Possibilities of Amazon Prime's *Good Omens* (crit). *Journal of the Fantastic in the Arts*, 34 (1) 2023, 211–37.

Gardner, John (1933–1982)

Metcalf, Josephine and Laura Skinner. Reading America, Reading Rodriguez: Exploring American Literature at an English Prison Book Group (crit). *Journal of American Studies*, 57 (Dec. 2023), 700–24.

Gass, William H. (1924–2017)

Gaskill, Nicholas. How Blue Is Read: Language and Sensation in Literature and Philosophy (crit). *Philosophy and Literature*, 47 (Oct. 2023), 294–309.

Glaspell, Susan (1876–1948)

Alberola Crespo, Nieves. *Susan Glaspell: Teatro, vanguardia y humor (1917–1918)* (crit). València: Universitat de València, 2023.

Gainor, J. Ellen, ed. *Susan Glaspell in Context* (crit). Cambridge: Cambridge U P, 2023.

Jamali, Ali. Theories of the Gaze Crossing Feminisms: *Trifles* as a Site to Ponder the Fundamentals (crit). *Critical Literary Studies*, 5 (Spr.-Sum. 2023), 31–45.

Kang, Meeyoung. The Aesthetics of Affect in Susan Glaspell's *Trifles* (crit). *Interdisciplinary Literary Studies*, 25 (2) 2023, 216–34.

Goines, Donald (1938–1974)

Manditch-Prottas, Zachary. Never Die Alone: Donald Goines, Black Iconicity, and Série Noire (crit). *MELUS*, 48 (Win. 2023), 1–26.

Haldeman-Julius, Emanuel (1889–1951)

Le Brech, Goulven. *Little Blue Books: Histoire de l'éditeur le plus rocambolesque du monde* (biog; crit). Paris: L'Échappée, 2023.

Hall, Donald (1928–2018)

Cheseldine, Lucy. Talking Modernism: Donald Hall's *Paris Review* Interviews (crit). *Essays in Criticism*, 73 (Jan. 2023), 76–94.

Hall, James Norman (1887–1951)

Aizier, Gonzague. *Après la tourmente: Sur les traces de James Norman Hall au-delà des Révoltés de la Bounty* (biog). Tahitai: Editions 'Ura, 2023.

Hamilton, Virginia (1934–2002)

Rizzuto, Lauren. "Good Cause for Living": Environmental Justice in Virginia Hamilton's *M. C. Higgins, the Great* (crit). *International Research in Children's Literature*, 16 (Oct. 2023), 281–93.

Hansberry, Lorraine (1930–1965)

Bailey, Peter J., ed. *Critical Insights: A Raisin in the Sun* (crit). Hackensack, N.J.: Salem Press, 2023.

Colbert, Soyica Diggs. Lorraine Hansberry and Miriam Makeba's Affirmative Movements in History (crit). *American Literature*, 95 (Mar. 2023), 135–50.

Grant, Carl A. *Examining Lorraine Hansberry's* A Raisin in the Sun *as Counternarrative: Understanding the Black Family and Black Students* (crit). NY: Routledge, 2023.

Herode, Yuvraj Nimbaji. *Dramatic Movement of African American Women: The Intersections of Race, Gender, and Class* (crit). London: Anthem Press, 2023.

Kastleman, Rebecca R. Reforming the Chorus: Insurgent Collectivities in Hansberry's Smug Bohemia (crit). *American Quarterly*, 75 (Dec. 2023), 859–74.

Sharma, Aakash. The Generational Question in *A Raisin in the Sun*: A Critical Analysis (crit). *Creative Saplings*, 1 (Feb. 2023), 21–30.

Hayden, Robert (1913–1980)

Tolle, Yeshua G.B. Under the Sign of the Middle Passage: Black Solidarity Reimagined (crit). *Texas Studies in Literature and Language*, 65 (Sum. 2023), 115–39.

Heap, Jane (1883–1964)

Baggett, Holly A. *Making No Compromise: Margaret Anderson, Jane Heap, and the Little Review* (crit). DeKalb: Northern Illinois U P, 2023.

Heinlein, Robert A. (1907–1988)

Sandberg, Eric. China Miéville: Radical SF, Nostalgic Utopianism, and the Politics of the Past (crit). *CEA Critic*, 85 (July 2023), 174–86.

Schryer, Stephen. Neoliberal World Reduction: Robert Heinlein and Milton Friedman's Free-Market Utopias (crit). *Science Fiction Studies*, 50 (July 2023), 175–96.

Hemingway, Ernest (1899–1961)

Abouddahab, Rédouane. Hemingway's Posthumous Fiction and Nabokov's *Lolita*: A Cross-Textual Reading (crit). *Ostrava Journal of English Philology*, 15 (1) 2023, 5–22.

Beegel, Susan. Remembering Charles M. "Tod" Oliver: Founding Editor, *The Hemingway Review*, 1932–2022 (M). *Hemingway Review*, 43 (Fall 2023), 10–13.

Bevilacqua, Thomas and Robert K. Elder. *Mythbusting Hemingway: Debunking Hemingway Myths and Celebrating the Extraordinary Stories of His Life* (biog). Essex, Conn.: Lyons Press, 2023.

Borkiewicz, Klaudia. On the Verge of the Here and Now: Madness, Paranoia and Improvisation of the Present in Hemingway's "A Pursuit Race" (crit). *Critical Survey*, 35 (3) 2023, 96–110.

Bostian, Lisa Michelle. Hemingway's Curse Reimagined: A Depth Psychological Analysis of His Fiction (crit). Ph.D. Dissertation, Pacifica Graduate Institute, 2023.

Brenner, Gerry. Interpreting (Mostly) Hemingway's *in our time* Vignettes (crit). *Studies in the American Short Story*, 4 (2) 2023, 114–37.

Chakravertty, Tania. *Ernest Hemingway and the Fluidity of Gender: A Socio-Cultural Analysis of Selected Works* (crit). NY: Routledge, 2023.

Curnutt, Kirk. The Early Years of the *Hemingway Review* (1981–1992): An Interview with Charles M. ("Tod") Oliver (I). *Hemingway Review*, 43 (Fall 2023), 14–20.

Daiker, Donald A. Hemingway's Nick Adams and His Lost "Indian Girl" (crit). *Hemingway Review*, 42 (Spr. 2023), 8–24.

Eby, Carl P. *Reading Hemingway's* The Garden of Eden: *Glossary and Commentary* (crit). Kent, Ohio: Kent State U P, 2023.

Feng, Wei. Gangster Cinema on a Vaudeville Stage: George's Mediated Perception of Reality in Ernest Hemingway's "The Killers" (crit). *CEA Critic*, 85 (Mar. 2023), 14–30.

Haigh, Jennifer. PEN/Hemingway Keynote Address (crit). *Hemingway Review*, 43 (Fall 2023), 21–26.

Herlihy-Mera, Jeffrey. *The Sun Also Rises*: A Pilgrimage Novel (crit). *Hemingway Review*, 42 (Spr. 2023), 25–55.

Hingley, Lillian. Theodor Adorno's Comments on Ernest Hemingway (crit). *Notes and Queries*, 70 (Dec. 2023, 315–16.

Köseman, Zennure. *Ernest Hemingway and the Short Story* (crit). Washington, D.C.: Academica Press, 2023.

Kübler, Marina. *White Male Disability in Modernist Literature: Reading Lawrence, Hemingway, and Faulkner* (crit). Boston: Brill Academic, 2023.

Lehofer, Morgan. "Intellectual Evasion" or "The Spirit of Tragedy"?: Re-thinking Race in Hemingway's *The Sun Also Rises* (crit). *Hemingway Review*, 43 (Fall 2023), 52–66.

Maksudyan, Nazan. The Fall of a City: Refugees, Exodus and Exile in Ernest Hemingway's Istanbul, 1922 (crit). *Journal of European Studies*, 53 (Sept. 2023), 234–52.

Marshall, Ian. Constructions of Race and Revolution in Ernest Hemingway's "The Porter" (crit). *Hemingway Review*, 43 (Fall 2023), 110–24.

——— and Margaret E. Wright-Cleveland. Hemingway in Black and White: An Introduction (crit). *Hemingway Review*, 43 (Fall 2023), 27–37.

Martin, Eileen and Greer Rising. Pen and Sword: The Symbiosis between Ernest Hemingway and Maj. Gen. Buck Lanham (biog; crit). *Military Review*, Sept.-Oct. 2023, 8–16.

Miller, D. Quentin. "Injustice Everywhere": Confronting Race and Racism in Hemingway's *The Sun Also Rises* (crit). *Hemingway Review*, 43 (Fall 2023), 38–51.

Nebot-Deneuville, Laëtitia. Travel and Transgression in Northern Italy in *Glimpses of the Moon* (1922) by Edith Wharton and *Across the River and into the Trees* (1950) by Ernest Hemingway (crit). *Journal of American Studies of Turkey*, 59 (Spr. 2023), 69–89.

Norris, Marcos Antonio. *Hemingway and Agamben: Finding Religion without God* (crit). Edinburgh: Edinburgh U P, 2023.

———. Reading "On the Quai at Smyrna" and "A Natural History of the Dead" in Consideration of Hemingway's Anti-Humanism (crit). *Hemingway Review*, 42 (Spr. 2023), 75–90.

Orent, Monika. Translating Emotions: Emotive Aspect in Ernest Hemingway's *For Whom the Bell Tolls* and Its Polish Translation by Bronisław Zieliński (crit; lang). *Beyond Philology*, 20 (2) 2023, 97–125.

Palmer, Katherine, et al. "The Truest Sentence That You Know": Four True Sentences by Ernest Hemingway (crit). *MidAmerica*, 50 (2023), 79–99.

Pastor, Aaren. "I'm a Girl. But Now I'm a Boy Too": Dildonics and Prosthetic Gender in Ernest Hemingway's *The Garden of Eden* (crit). *Modern Fiction Studies*, 69 (Win. 2023), 687–706.

Paul, Steve and Kelli A. Larson, eds. Current Bibliography (bibl). *Hemingway Review*, 42 (Spr. 2023), 129–41.

———. Current Bibliography (bibl). *Hemingway Review*, 43 (Fall 2023), 146–55.

Pottle, Russ. Hemingway's Slang in Lyndsay Faye's *The Paragon Hotel* (crit). *Hemingway Review*, 42 (Spr. 2023), 105–12.

Preece, Felicia M. Making Geography Come Alive: Hemingway and Representing Space in Mid-Century America. Ph.D. Dissertation, Wayne State U, 2023.

Reisinger, Richard. Rifles and Broad Shoulders: *For Whom the Bell Tolls* and Hemingway's Shifting Perspective on Gender (crit). *South Atlantic Review*, 43 (Fall 2023), 38–51.

Selden, Sarah. "Pure Literature Is Today Doomed": Hemingway's Modernism and *the transatlantic review* (crit). *Hemingway Review*, 42 (Spr. 2023), 56–74.

Sion, Ng Lay. Teaching "Indian Camp" in the Japanese Classroom (crit). *Teaching American Literature*, 13 (Spr. 2023), 65–75.

Srilatha, G. *Hemingway and Ecocriticism* (crit). London: Academica Press, 2023.

Thayer, Frances Anne. Ernest Hemingway: The Sustainable Effect of Creative Writing as a Therapeutic Technology Infused by Cubism (crit). Ph.D. Dissertation, Salve Regina U, 2023.

Tyler, Lisa. "The Gallantry of the Aging Machine": Ernest Hemingway's Colonel Cantwell and Masculine Aging in Modernist Literature (crit). *Polish Journal of English Studies*, 9 (2) 2023, 57–76.

Vanderwall, Eric. They've All Gone to Look for America": Perpetual Exile in Ernest Hemingway's *In Our Time* (crit). *Hemingway Review*, 42 (Spr. 2023), 91–104.

Ward, J.A. "The Blue Hotel" and "The Killers" (crit). *CEA Critic*, 85 (Mar. 2023), 87–88.

Weaver, Russell. *The Moral World of* The Sun Also Rises (crit). NY: Peter Lang, 2023.

Wright-Cleveland, Margaret E. The Disappearance of Krebs: Hemingway's "Soldier's Home" as a Critique of Whiteness (crit). *Hemingway Review*, 43 (Fall 2023), 87–109.

Wyatt, David. "Have Sure Tried": Hemingway's Unfaltering Career (crit). *American Literary History*, 35 (Win. 2023), 1843–62.

Zolotariov, Elena. "Black and Red Laughter": Subverting Whiteness in Hemingway's *The Torrents of Spring* (crit). *Hemingway Review*, 43 (Fall 2023), 67–86.

Howells, William Dean (1837–1920)

Benack, Carolin. On the History of Choice: William Dean Howells and the Roots of the Neoliberal Individual (crit). *ELH: English Literary History*, 90 (Win. 2023), 1099–1122.

Emmert, Scott D. A Great Modern American Story: "Editha" by William Dean Howells (crit). *MidAmerica*, 50 (2023), 26–37.

Howland, Bette (1937–2017)

Ellis, Nina. The Short Autofictions of Eve Babitz, Lucia Berlin and Bette Howland (crit). *Critique*, 64 (5) 2023, 776–89.

Hughes, Langston (1902–1967)

Chagas, Gabriel. *Pérolas negras na periferia: Personagens femininas de Langston Hughes e Lima Barreto* (crit). Campinas, SP: Pontes Editores, 2023.

Dimakis, Athanasios. "Ma soul's a Witness for de Waldorf-Astoria!" Langston Hughes's Poetic Hotel Advertisement (crit). *Explicator*, 81 (July-Dec. 2023), 128–31.

Ford, Mark. Daddy, Ain't You Heard? (rev). *London Review of Books*, 45 (16 Nov. 2023), 35–36.

Kutzinski, Vera M. and Anthony Reed, eds. *Langston Hughes in Context* (crit). Cambridge: Cambridge U P, 2023.

Layne, Louisa Olufsen. "Let us look at the immediate background of this young poet": Langston Hughes and the Sociological Critique of Taste (crit). *African American Review*, 56 (Spr.-Sum. 2023), 27–42.

Lewis, Bethany P. Diverse Experiences in Children's Literature: Langston Hughes (crit). *Reading Teacher*, 77 (July-Aug. 2023), 16–23.

Murray, Joshua M. Taken by the Sea Wind: Langston Hughes and the Currents of Black Identity (crit). *Atlantic Studies*, 20 (June 2023), 277–91.

Schormová, Františka. Tractors and Translators: Langston Hughes in Cold War Czechoslovakia (crit). *PMLA*, 138 (May 2023), 519–33.

Jones, James (1921–1977)

Moore, M.J. *Star-Crossed Lovers: James Jones, Lowney Handey, and the Birth of From Here to Eternity* (biog; crit). NY: Heliotrope Books, 2023.

Kahf, Mohja (b. 1967)

Abduljabbar, Dima Abdulmajeed. *Thawrah des Odalisques* at the Matisse Retrospective: Henri Matisse's Odalisques from the Metamorphosis of Painting to the Transmogrification of Poetry(crit). *Interventions: International Journal of Postcolonial Studies*, 25 (4) 2023), 540–61.

Lane, Rose Wilder (1886–1968)

Koupal, Nancy Tystad, ed. *Pioneer Girl: The Path into Fiction* (crit; pub). Pierre: South Dakota Historical Society Press, 2023.

Larsen, Nella (1891–1964)

Caputi, Celia R. Belated Epiphanies: Intersectionality and Education in Virginia Woolf's *The Voyage Out* and Nella Larsen's *Quicksand* (crit). *Woolf Studies Annual*, 29 (2023), 5–26.

Chen, Hsiao-Wen. Black Cosmofeminism: Commodity, Sexuality, and the Transnational Mixed-Race Subject in Nella Larsen's *Quicksand* (crit). *Journal of Modern Literature*, 46 (Sum. 2023), 146–66.

Delsandro, Erica Gene and Jennifer Mitchell. Fraught Intimacies: Toward the Impossibility of Women's Kinship (crit). *Feminist Modernist Studies*, 6 (1) 2023, 6–11.

Hsu, Hsuan L. Race, Urban Heat, and the Aesthetics of Thermoception (crit).

American Literary History, 35 (Sum. 2023), 769–94.

Hutchinson, George. New Light on Nella Larsen's Denmark (biog; crit). *ANQ*, 36 (Apr. 2023), 411–14.

Venkatesh, Vidya. Around Talk: Affect, Triviality, and Possibility in Marcel Proust, Henry James, and Nella Larsen (crit). Ph.D. Dissertation, King's College, Cambridge, 2023.

Ziering, Anna. "Anything Might Happen": Spatial Metaphor, Instability, and Escape in Nella Larsen's *Passing* (crit). *Arizona Quarterly*, 79 (Sum. 2023), 115–40.

Lee, Rebecca (b. 1967)

Reisner, Philipp. Lutheranism in the Contemporary American Short Story (crit). *Studies in the American Short Story*, 4 (1) 2023, 55–68.

Leopold, Aldo (1886–1948)

Irr, Caren. The Multispecies We: Democracy and Pronouns in the Environmental Novel (crit). *American Literary History*, 35 (Spr. 2023), 276–89.

Paliewicz, Nicholas S. Thinking Like a Copper Mine: An Ecological Approach to Corporate Ethos and Prosōpon (crit). *Rhetoric Society Quarterly*, 53 (2) 2023, 231–46.

Lewis, Sinclair (1885–1951)

Bembridge, Steven. Sinclair Lewis's *Elmer Gantry*: A Study of the Fundamentalist-Modernist Controversy (crit). *Christianity & Literature*, 72 (Mar. 2023), 34–52.

Beretta, Francesca G. Pavese's Border Multilingualism: The Homeric *Nekyia* and Beyond (crit). *MLN*, 138 (Jan. 2023), 90–116.

Lovelace, Maud Hart (1892–1980)

Cleere, Eileen. Girls on Fire: Mary Elizabeth Braddon's *Lady Audley's Secret* (1861), Maud Hart Lovelace's *Betsy and Tacy Go Downtown* (1943), and the Adolescent Sublimation of Victorian Sensation (crit). *Children's Literature Association Quarterly*, 48 (Fall 2023), 280–301.

Ma, Ling (b. 1983)

Barr, Allan H. From "Thoughts on March 8" to "Gap" and "The Sufferings of Liping": Mate Selection and Marriage in Three Works by Yan'an Authors (crit). *Nan Nü: Men, Women, and Gender in China*, 25 (1) 2023, 103–51.

De Mul, Sarah. The Politics and Poetics of the Women's Millennial Workplace Novel: The Trope of Burnout in Kikuko Tsumura's *There's No Such Thing as an Easy Job* (2015) and Ling Ma's *Severance* (2018) (crit). *Literature & Aesthetics*, 33 (2) 2023, 6–18.

Fan, Christopher T. Semiperipherality and the Taiwanese American Novel (crit). *College Literature*, 50 (Spr.-Sum. 2023), 212–36.

Kayışcı Akkoyun, Burcu. Urban Apocalypse, Global Precarity, and Uncanny Liminality in Colson Whitehead's *Zone One* and Ling Ma's *Severance* (crit). *Critique*, 64 (2) 2023, 282–95.

Marcus, Sara. Novels of Democratic Exhaustion (crit). *American Literary History*, 35 (Spr. 2023), 364–73.

Ong, Amanda. How to Imagine the End of the World: Narratives of Disaster in Speculative Fiction (crit). Ph.D. Dissertation, U Wisconsin, 2023.

Park, Heejoo. Unsettling Genres: On Supernatural Outbreak Narratives in Ling Ma's *Severance* and Silvia Moreno-Garcia's *Certain Dark Things* (crit). *MELUS*, 48 (Fall 2023), 50–72.

Robitaille, Iana W. Alien Domesticity: Settler-Capitalist Invasion and the Limits of Representation in Ling Ma's *Severance* (crit). *Studies in the Novel*, 55 (Fall 2023), 289–306.

Sulimma, Maria. "To Live in a City Is to Consume Its Offerings": Speculative Fiction and Gentrification in Ling Ma's *Severance* (2018) (crit). *Journal of Urban Cultural Studies*, 10 (1) 2023, 95–112.

Malcolm X (1925–1965)

Bichler, Gabriele Aïsha. *By any means necessary?! Analogien und Differenzen im Denken von Frantz Fanon und Malcolm X: Ein ethnopsychoanalytisch-biografischer Zugang* (crit). Wiesbaden: Springer VS, 2023.

Corbman, Marjorie. *Divine Rage: Malcom X's Challenge to Christians* (crit). Maryknoll, N.Y.: Orbis Books, 2023.

Mamet, David (b. 1947)

Saunders, Graham. #MeToo Pinter and David Mamet's *Oleanna* (crit). *Harold Pinter Review*, 7 (1) 2023, 3–22.

Mandel, Emily St. John (b. 1979)

Gadpaille, Michelle. Pandemic, Prophecy, and Politics in Mary Shelley and Emily St. John Mandel (crit). *Central European Journal of Canadian Studies*, 18 (1) 2023, 19–38.

Herren, Graley. The Prospero of Wonderland; or, Miranda Carroll, Author of Station Eleven (crit). *Comparative Drama*, 57 (Sum.-Fall 2023), 139–64.

Manfred, Frederick (1912–1994)

Way, Ginny. Frederick and Maryanna Manfred House, Luverne, Rock County (biog). *Minnesota History*, 68 (Win. 2022-2023), 119.

Mengestu, Dinaw (b. 1978)

Studniarz, Slawomir. Postcolonialism Goes Queer: Concealments and Disclosures in Dinaw Mengestu's *All Our Names* (crit). *African American Review*, 56 (Spr.-Sum. 2023), 89–101.

Micheaux, Oscar (1884–1951)

Martin, Michael T. "That's the Difference, I Am Fully Engaged with Art": Renée Baker on the Practice of Scoring Silent Film and the Matter of "Race Movies" (crit). *Black Camera*, 14 (Spr. 2023), 7–48.

Miller, Arthur (1915–2005)

Atlas, Marilyn Judith. Additional "Attention Must Be Paid": Linda Loman's Nylon Stockings and the Politics of Womanhood in *Death of a Salesman* (crit). *MidAmerica*, 50 (2023), 121–36.

Moore, Lorrie (b. 1957)

Castelli, Alberto. The Melancholy of the Second-Person Narrator (crit). *Confluencia: Revista Hispánica de Cultura y Literatura*, 38 (Spr. 2023), 41–59.

Sehgal, Parul. Mortal Coil (rev). *New Yorker*, 99 (19 June 2023), 65–67.

Morris, Wright (1910–1998)

Kochin, Michael S. "Life as Literature": Wright Morris's *Love Among the Cannibals* (crit). *Textual Practice*, 37 (Mar. 2023), 357–72.

Morrison, Toni (1931–2019)

Abe, Kodai. Afro-Asian Antagonism and the Long Korean War (crit). *American Literature*, 95 (Dec. 2023), 701–28.

Abeygunawardana, Melanie. Yes, Pain, But What Else? Racial Liberalism and Late-Style Morrison (crit). *Representations*, 161 (2023), 20–40.

Alameroo, Asma Ali Abdullh. Confronting the Shadow Side to Heal the Black Self: Southern Black Female Writers Theorize Blackness, Love, Beauty, and Spirit (crit). Ph.D. Dissertation, Indiana U of Pennsylvania, 2023.

Araújo, Eliza. *Morrison, Angelou e Evaristo: Mulheres negras e escrita revolucionária* (crit). Campinas, SP: Pontes Editores, 2023

Atieh, Majda. Aging as an Epistemology of Sustainability: Reimagined Designs in Toni Morrison's *Paradise* (crit). *Polish Journal of English Studies*, 9 (2) 2023, 128–49.

Balfour, Katharine Lawrence. *Toni Morrison: Imagining Freedom* (crit). NY: Oxford U P, 2023.

Beks, Neske. *De kleine Morrison: Een wegwijzer in het lezen van haar werk vanuit Zwart perspectief* (crit). Amsterdam: Uitgeverij Atlas Contact, 2023.

Blanchette, Sarah. Black Girlhood Persists: Pecola's Persistence as Non/Child in Toni Morrison's *The Bluest Eye* (crit). *Women's Studies*, 52 (July 2023), 566–85.

Brown, Lauren M. Basements, Bars, and Burials: Exploring Exceptionalist Fantasy and Violence in Toni Morrison's *Home* (crit). *Studies in the Novel*, 55 (Spr. 2023), 37–57.

Bystrov, Yakiv and Nataliya Telegina. Jazz Music and Intermedial References in Toni Morrison's *Love* (crit). *Forum for Modern Language Studies*, 59 (Oct. 2023), 513–29.

Collins, Corrine, et al. Forum: "After Morrison" (crit). *Women's Studies*, 52 (Mar. 2023), 161–72.

Drake, Simone. On Foremothers, Muses, and Black Feminist Theorizing (crit). *Women's Studies*, 52 (Mar. 2023), 210–26.

Edwards, Brent Hayes. Other Afterlives (crit). *PMLA*, 138 (Mar. 2023), 233–40.

El Helou, Rachelle. La vulnérabilité dans la fiction de Toni Morrison: De l'aliénation à la reconstruction identitaire par le langage (crit). Thèse de Doctorat, Université Côte d'Azur, 2023.

Evans, Shari. Narrating the Self and Other: Trauma, Language, and the Empathic Listener in Toni Morrison's *A Mercy* (crit). *MELUS*, 48 (Spr. 2023), 142–69.

Fagan, Allison. Secondary Agency: Toni Morrison, Toni Cade Bambara, and the Making of *Those Bones Are Not My Child* (crit). *Tulsa Studies in Women's Literature*, 42 (Spr. 2023), 135–56.

Franklin, Kelly. Black Girlhood Remixed: Reimagining, Redressing, and Redeeming Black Girlhood Studies with Toni Morrison (crit). *Journal of Ethnic American Literature*, 13 (2023), 57–82.

Goldberg, Jess A. Living after, and before, the End of the World: Toni Morrison's *Beloved* and N.K. Jemisin's *Broken Earth* (crit). *Women's Studies*, 52 (Mar. 2023), 173–91.

Goodhead, Dokubo Melford. The Education of Milkman Dead: The Bildungsroman as Aesthetic Cycle in Toni Morrison's *Song of Solomon* (crit). *African American Review*, 56 (Spr.-Sum. 2023), 43–56.

Gruesser, John C. and Norlisha Crawford. The Shadow That Poe Casts: An Interview with Maurice Carlos Ruffin (crit; I). *Poe Studies*, 56 (2023), 41–59.

Harris, Allison N. Indian Removal and the Plantation South: Cherokee Present-Absence in Three Neo-Slave Narratives (crit). *MELUS*, 48 (Win. 2023), 139–64.

Haytock, Jennifer. Structural Racism and Just War Theory in Post-World War II America: Susan Choi and Toni Morrison on Violence, Imagination, and Human Flourishing (crit). *LIT: Literature Interpretation Theory*, 34 (1) 2023, 30–46.

Hiro, Molly. *The Emperor Jones* and the Moral Meanings of the Black Past (crit). *Arizona Quarterly*, 79 (Spr. 2023), 23–50.

Khanam, Shadma. *Art of Black Aesthetics in the Novels of Toni Morrison* (crit). New Delhi: Rudra Publishers, 2023.

Kirton, Jenny. "No Future to Be Had": Journeying toward Death in Toni Morrison's *Song of Solomon* (crit). *MELUS*, 48 (Win. 2023), 183–205.

Kumar, Ajit and Rafseena M. *Toni Morrison: Literary Perspectives and Critical Interpretations* (crit). New Delhi: Vitasta, 2023.

Li, Qianqian. Women-Centered Diaspora in Toni Morrison's *A Mercy* (crit). *Women's Studies*, 52 (Apr.-May 2023), 320–38.

Mhlambi, Innocentia J. Black Liberation Politics and Quagmires in Trans-Atlantic Black Operas (crit). *Journal of the African Literature Association*, 17 (1) 2023, 112–31.

Mosalla Nejad, Afshin, Hassan Shahabi, and Shahram Raeisi Sistani. The Racial Myth of the Black Violence: A Žižekian Study of Toni Morrison's *The Bluest Eye, Sula,* and *Beloved* (crit). *Critical Literary Studies*, 5 (May 2023), 135–48, 228.

Owusu, Portia. Of Life and Death: African Cultural Worldviews and Black American Survival in Toni Morrison's *Song of Solomon* and Amiri Baraka's *Slave Ship* (crit). *Comparative Literature Studies*, 60 (1) 2023, 73–94.

Patil, Manisha. *Playing with Darkness: A Study of Toni Morrison's Early Novels from Postcolonial Perspective* (crit). New Delhi: Authorspress, 2023.

Pereira, Jane Cely Marques do Nascimento and Márcia Tavares Silva. A relação entre os espaços físicos e a representação feminina negra no romance o olho mais azul, de Toni Morrison: uma análise interseccional da trajetória de Pecola Breedlove (crit). *ERAS: European Review of Artistic Studies*, 14 (1) 2023, 45–66.

Porro, Simona. Enchantment as a Subversive Force in Toni Morrison's *God Help the Child* (crit). *Annali di Ca' Foscari: Serie Occidentale*, 57 (Sept. 2023), 261–72.

Pyon, Kevin. Between Psychoanalysis and History: The Cultural Legacy of Toni Morrison in Modern Black Horror (crit). *Women's Studies*, 52 (Mar. 2023), 246–65.

Reames, Kelly L. and Linda Wagner-Martin, eds. *The Bloomsbury Handbook to Toni Morrison* (crit). London: Bloomsbury Academic, 2023.

Roy, Keidrick. The Fugitive Covenant: Reconstructing the Social Contract *This Side of Paradise* (crit). *ELH: English Literary History*, 90 (Spr. 2023), 273–308.

Schindler, Melissa E. From the Margin to the Fold: The Imprint of Toni Morrison on the Writing of Akwaeke Emezi (crit). *Women's Studies*, 52 (Mar. 2023), 227–45.

Scott, Robert. Fear and (Black Self-) Loathing: Teaching *The Bluest Eye* (crit). *Teaching American Literature*, 13 (Spr. 2023), 30–35.

Sharp, Ryan. The Unspeakable in Cornelius Eady's *Brutal Imagination* (crit). *Women's Studies*, 52 (Mar. 2023), 192–209.

Thorsson, Courtney. *The Sisterhood: How a Network of Black Women Writers Changed American Culture* (crit). NY: Columbia U P, 2023.

Wehling-Giorgi, Katrin. Unspeakable Things Spoken: Transgenerational Trauma, Fractured Bodies and Visual Tropes in Toni Morrison, Elsa Morante and Elena Ferrante's Works (crit). *Romance Studies*, 41 (1) 2023, 248–66.

Whitt, Richard J. Trauma, Mind Style, and Unreliable Narration in Toni Morrison's *Home* (crit). *Style*, 57 (2) 2023, 187–204.

Witzling, David. Toni Morrison's Authorial Audience and the Properties of Black-Centered Imaginative History (crit). *Narrative*, 31 (May 2023), 159–78.

Zhang, Dora. The Mark of the Detail: Universalism, Type, Difference (crit). *Modern Language Quarterly*, 84 (June 2023), 147–68.

Muir, John (1838–1914)

Jacob, Sam. Rerouting Russian America: Decontinentalized Alaska, Archipelagic

Poetics, and Speaking Glaciers (crit). *ISLE: Interdisciplinary Studies in Literature and Environment*, 30 (Win. 2023), 931–51.

King, Dean. *Guardians of the Valley: John Muir and the Friendship That Saved Yosemite* (biog). NY: Scribner, 2023.

Mukerjee, Bharati (1940–2017)

Chattopadhyay, Shrimoyee. Non-Conforming Women in Neoliberal Cities: Re-thinking Empowerment in Contemporary Diaspora Fiction and Film (crit). Ph.D. Dissertation, U Debrecen, 2023.

Gautam, Reena. *A Study of Selected Novels of Bharati Mukherjee and Uma Parmeswaran* (crit). Delhi: ABS Books, 2023.

Maxey, Ruth. Animals in the Writing of Bharati Mukherjee (crit). *ARIEL: A Review of International English Literature*, 54 (Jan. 2023), 55–71.

Satyan, Urmi. *Cultural Sentiments and Diaspora Sensibilities: Reflections on the Select Anthologies by Bharati Mukherjee and Chitra Banerjee Divakaruni* (crit). Jaipur: Yking Books, 2023.

Neihardt, John G. (1881–1973)

Kelderman, Frank. Black Elk Faces East: Beb Vuyk, Cultural Translation, and John G. Neihardt's *Black Elk Speaks* (crit). *Journal of Transnational American Studies*, 14 (2) 2023, 7–27.

Nguyen, Bich Minh (b. 1974)

Stewart, Sophia. Author Profile: Family Ties. *Publishers Weekly*, 270 (22 May 2023), 33–34.

Niedecker, Lorine (1903–1970)

Kuhn, John. Clipping Easter's Wing: Lorine Niedecker and the Metaphysical Lyric (crit). *Modern Philology*, 121 (Nov. 2023), 192–213.

Norris, Frank (1870–1902)

Lyle, Megan Cole. Fossil-Fueled Naturalism and Pastoral Optimism in the Novels of Dreiser, Norris, and Sinclair (crit). *Studies in American Naturalism*, 18 (Sum. 2023), 1–30.

Wolff, Nathan. "It's People in the Swamp": Du Bois against the Democracy of Things (crit). *American Literary History*, 35 (Spr. 2023), 81–96.

Oates, Joyce Carol (b. 1938)

Aviv, Rachel. Personal Statement: Joyce Carol Oates's Relentless Search for a Self (biog; crit). *New Yorker*, 99 (27 Nov. 2023), 26–37.

Chatterjee, Srirupa and Swathi Krishna S. Roads, Misogyny, and the Rape Culture in Joyce Carol Oates' *Rape: A Love Story* and Cara Hoffman's *So Much Pretty* (crit). *LIT: Literature Interpretation Theory*, 34 (3) 2023, 196–219.

Dalyan, Mustafa Fatih. Not-Quite-Humans in Contemporary Western Culture: Oates's *Zombie*, Burton's *Edward Scissorhands* and Lessing's *The Fifth Child* (crit). Ph.D. Dissertation, Dokuz Eylül Üniversitesi, 2023.

Kostopoulos, Sharon P. Moving from Pathological to Productive Melancholia: Daughters Who Survive Loss in Joyce Carol Oates's Short Fiction (crit). Ph.D. Dissertation, Edith Cowan U, 2023.

Marquette, Caroline. L'écriture du corps dans la fiction de Joyce Carol Oates: Une dynamique des fluides (crit). Thèse de Doctorat, Université Bordeaux Montaigne, 2023.

Oliver, Mary (1935–2019)

Bazregarzadeh, Elmira. Affective Turn or Ecological Turn: Mary Oliver's Poetry Revisited (crit). *Anafora*, 10 (1) 2023, 109–25.

Olsen, Tillie (1912–2007)

Lance, Stephanie. Fabricant, It's What's for Dinner: Tracing Industrialized Slaughter through Upton Sinclair's *The Jungle*, Tillie Olsen's *Yonnondio: From the Thirties*, and David Mitchell's *Cloud Atlas* (crit). *Studies in the Fantastic*, 15 (Fall 2023), 57–93.

McCune, Louise. Tillie Olsen's Reproductive Aesthetics (crit). *ELH: English Literary History*, 90 (Fall 2023), 883–907.

Peattie, Elia W. (1862–1935)

Durrans, Stéphanie. Elia Peattie and Willa Cather: Influence and Shared Vision (crit). *Willa Cather Review*, 64 (Spr. 2023), 3–8.

Pinckney, Darryl (b. 1953)

Gilmore, Leigh. Desperation, Revenge, and Memoir: The Year in the US (crit). *Biography: An Interdisciplinary Quarterly*, 46 (1) 2023, 93–96.

Pokagon, Simon (1830–1899)

Morseau, Blaire, ed. *As Sacred to Us: Simon Pokagon's Birch Bark Stories in Their Contexts* (crit). East Lansing, Mich.: Michigan State U P, 2023.

Wisecup, Kelly. Toward a Bibliography of Birch Bark: The 2023 Annual Meeting Keynote (bibl; crit). *Papers of the Bibliographical Society of America*, 117 (Dec. 2023), 421–40.

Powers, Richard (b. 1957)

Butter, Stella. The Mercurial Effects of Abstract Reflection: Troubling Hegemonic Cultures of Knowledge in Ted Chiang's Short Math Fiction and Richard Powers's Maximalist Arboreal Novel (crit). *Anglia: Zeitschrift für Englische Philologie*, 141 (4) 2023, 522–53.

McMain, Emma M. and J.T. Torres. Saviors, Nurturers, or Magically Insane: A Braided Reading of White Women Characters in Three Ecological Narratives (crit). *Feminist Media Studies*, 23 (June 2023), 1643–58.

Sugiyama, Kazutaka. The Survival of Specters: Hauntology and Richard Powers's *The Overstory* (crit). *Studies in the Novel*, 55 (Sum. 2023), 210–32.

Vermeulen, Pieter. Forests as Markets: *The Overstory*, Neoliberalism, and Other Fictions of Spontaneous Order (crit). *Environmental Humanities*, 15 (July 2023), 142–61.

Ramanujan, A. K. (1929–1993)

Dwivedi, A.N. *The Poetic Art of A.K. Ramanujan* (crit). Delhi: B.R. Publishing, 2023.

Richter, Conrad (1890–1968)

Cotugno, Marianne. Awakening Ecological Consciousness in Conrad Richter's *Ohio Trilogy* (crit). *CEA Critic*, 85 (July 2023), 119–33.

Rivera, Tomás (1935–1984)

Caminero-Santangelo, Marta. Imagining a Latino Heartland: Migrant Placemaking, Corridos of the Midwest, and Tomás Rivera (crit). *MELUS*, 48 (Sum. 2023), 52–78.

Penman-Lomeli, Andrea. Debt, Time, and Dreams: Failing to Arrive in Tomás Rivera's *… y no se lo tragó la tierra* (crit). *MELUS*, 48 (Sum. 2023), 119–41.

Valella, Daniel. Crystal City's "Alien" Farmworkers: Tomás Rivera's *. . y no se lo tragó la tierra* and the Shared Histories of Chicanx and Japanese American Detention (crit). *MELUS*, 48 (Spr. 2023), 115–41.

Robinson, Marilynne (b. 1943)

Anand, Aswathi Velayathikode and Srirupa Chatterjee. The Female Prophet and Religious Re-Visioning in Marilynne

Robinson's *Lila* (crit). *ANQ*, 36 (Apr.-Sept. 2023), 444–53.

Cusveller, B.S. *Van waarde zijn: Kennismaking met het denken van Marilynne Robinson* (crit). Amsterdam: Buijten & Schipperheijn Motief, 2023.

Douglas, Christopher. What If God is a "Pagan Amalgam": Marilynne Robinson and Historical Bible Scholarship (crit). *Literature and Theology*, 37 (June 2023), 67–92.

Ghosal, Nilanjana and Srirupa Chatterjee. Fictive Kinship in Marilynne Robinson's *Gilead* (crit). *ANQ*, 36 (Mar. 2023), 137–40.

Gibson, Ian. Wishful Thinking: Loss and the Overcoming of Loss in Marilynne Robinson's *Housekeeping* (crit). *Christianity & Literature*, 72 (Mar. 2023), 53–72.

Kemp, Ryan S. *Marilynne Robinson's Worldly Gospel: A Philosophical Account of Her Christian Vision* (crit). London: Bloomsbury Academic, 2023.

Sorensen, Thomas. Reading for Atmosphere: A Pedagogical Approach (crit). *PMLA*, 138 (Jan. 2023), 188–93.

Yothers, Brian. Radical Immanence: An Interview with Marilynne Robinson (I). *Leviathan: A Journal of Melville Studies*, 25 (Oct. 2023), 63–69.

Rodríguez, Luis J. (b.1954)

Metcalf, Josephine and Laura Skinner. Reading America, Reading Rodríguez: Exploring American Literature at an English Prison Book Group (crit). *Journal of American Studies*, 57 (Dec. 2023), 700–24.

Roethke, Theodore (1908–1963)

Mondal, Pradip. *Dealing with Dilemma: An Existentialist Study of Select Poems by William Carlos Williams, Robinson Jeffers and Theodore Roethke* (crit). Jaipur: Aadi Publications, 2023.

Rølvaag, O. E. (1876–1931)

Langum, Virginia. Prairie Madness: Mental Illness and Norwegian Immigration to North America in the Late Nineteenth and Early Twentieth Centuries (crit). *Literature and Medicine*, 41 (Spr. 2023), 207–29.

Mureşan, Ioana-Andreea. *The Quest for Identity in Norwegian-American Immigrant Narratives: Correspondences with the Romanian Immigrant Experience in America* (crit). Cluj-Napoca: Presa Universitară Clujeană, 2023.

Sandburg, Carl (1878–1967)

Anderson, Robin. *Uncommon Sanctuary: Carl Sandburg Home National Historic Site: Spring into Summer* (biog). Flat Rock, N.C.: Mountain Page Press, 2022.

Ponsatí-Murlà, Oriol. "Un poeta hispánico se asoma a la lírica norteamericana": Una conferència inèdita d'Agustí Bartra a la Wesleyan University (crit). *Revista de Lenguas y Literaturas Catalana, Gallega y Vasca*, 28 (2023), 63–85.

Sandoz, Mari (1896–1966)

Bartelt, Guillermo. *Defamiliarization in Mari Sandoz's* Crazy Horse (crit). Lewiston, N.Y.: Edwin Mellen Press, 2023.

Santos, Bienvenido N. (1911–1996)

Dickey, Paul E. *Bienvenido N. Santos: An Illustrated Bibliography* (bibl). Omaha, Neb.: Dickey Books, 2023.

Seiffert, Marjorie Allen (1885–1970)

Gillette, Meg. Midlife Selfhood in the Poetry of Marjorie Allen Seiffert (crit). *MidAmerica*, 50 (2023), 14–25.

Shapiro, Karl (1913–2000)

Carruthers, A.J. What Anticriticism Is (after Karl Shapiro) (crit). *Symplokē: A Journal for the Intermingling of Literary, Cultural and Theoretical Scholarship*, 31 (1–2) 2023, 253–71.

Shepard, Sam (1943–2017)

Fernández-Caparrós, Ana. Horses and Cowboys on the Contemporary American Stage: The Horse as Prop in Sam Shepard's *Kicking a Dead Horse* and Sarah Ruhl's *Late: A Cowboy Song* (crit). *Studies in Theatre and Performance*, 43 (1) 2023, 91–107.

Greenfield, Robert. *True West: Sam Shepard's Life, Work, and Times* (biog; crit). NY: Crown, 2023.

Zimmerman, Guy. Shepard's Political Economy: Curse of the Starving Class in Neoliberal Capitalism (crit). *Modern Drama*, 66 (Dec. 2023), 477–95.

Sinclair, Upton (1878–1968)

Banerjee, Mita. Hygiene, Whiteness and Immigration: Upton Sinclair and the "Jungle" of the American Health Care System (crit). *Journal of Transnational American Studies*, 14 (2) 2023, 165–91.

Lyle, Megan Cole. Fossil-Fueled Naturalism and Pastoral Optimism in the Novels of Dreiser, Norris, and Sinclair (crit). *Studies in American Naturalism*, 18 (Sum. 2023), 1–30.

Stegner, Wallace (1909–1993)

Tharaud, Jerome. Western Salvage: Scarcity, Settler Colonialism, and Adaptation in Wallace Stegner's *Wolf Willow* (crit). *ISLE: Interdisciplinary Studies in Literature and Environment*, 30 (Sum. 2023), 406–25.

Stowe, Harriet Beecher (1811–1896)

Allukian, Kristin. *Slavery, Capitalism, and Women's Literature: Economic Insights of American Women Writers, 1852–1869* (crit). Athens: U Georgia P, 2023.

Atassi, Sami H. Revolting Laughter: Antebellum America Satire and the Reformation of Terror (crit). Ph.D. Dissertation, Indiana U, 2023.

Garvey, Ellen Gruber. Little-Known Documents: "The Captain's Story" (crit). *PMLA*, 138 (Oct. 2023), 1165–71.

Kowalski, Philip J. "Our Country Neighbors": Harriet Beecher Stowe's Domestication of Nature (crit). *Children's Literature Association Quarterly*, 48 (Fall 2023), 302–22.

Martinez, Rosa. Ellen Craft's "Spanish" Masquerade: Racially (Mis)Reading Hispanicism in Her Cross-Dressing, Feigning Disability, and Running to Sea (crit). *Journal of American Studies*, 57 (Dec. 2023), 637–76.

O'Loughlin, Jim. "It Was Left for Others to Speak": *Uncle Tom's Cabin* and the Civil War (crit). *ANQ*, 36 (Apr.-Sept. 2023), 377–84.

Wakefield, Hannah. Dismantling the Sentimental in Harriet Beecher Stowe's *Dred: A Tale of the Great Dismal Swamp* (crit). *Arizona Quarterly*, 79 (Win. 2023), 99–128.

Tarkington, Booth (1869–1946)

Flannigan, John H. A Tongue-Tied Generation Goes to War: Cather's Claude Wheeler and Tarkington's *Ramsey Milholland* (crit). *Willa Cather Review*, 64 (Fall 2023), 18–24.

Terkel, Studs (1912–2008)

Frisch, Michael. Studs Terkel's *Hard Times: An Oral History of the Great Depression* (crit). *Journal of American Studies*, 57 (Dec. 2023), 744–46.

Van Allsburg, Chris (b. 1949)

Putz, Nastassia. The Making of "Magic" (crit). *Trains*, 83 (Dec. 2023), 18–25.

Van Vechten, Carl (1880–1964)

Orringer, Nelson R. Roots of Lorca's Black Poetry in Van Vechten's Vision of the

African American Spiritual (crit). *Diagonal: An Ibero-American Music Review*, 8 (1) 2023, 53–74.

Sinha, Ajay J. *Photo-Attractions: An Indian Dancer, and American Photographer, and a German Camera* (crit). New Brunswick, N.J.: Rutgers U P, 2023.

Volpicelli, Robert. Countee Cullen's Harlem Decadence (crit). *PMLA*, 138 (Oct. 2023), 1078–93.

Vonnegut, Kurt (1922–2007)

Augello, Chuck. *Talking Vonnegut: Centennial Interviews and Essays* (crit; I). Jefferson, N.C.: McFarland & Co., 2023.

Clough, William. Re-Vision of History: Historiographic Metafiction in Kurt Vonnegut's *Mother Night* and Salman Rushdie's *Midnight's Children* (crit). *CEA Critic*, 85 (Mar. 2023), 1–13.

Hernández García, Maria Luisa. Escribir después del horror: El tiempo dislocado en la novela Matadero cinco de Kurt Vonnegut (crit). *Tropelías: Revista de Teoría de la Literatura y Literatura Comparada*, 40 (2023), 413–28.

López Guzmán, David. The Gospel from Outer Space: Apocalypse, America, and Science Fiction in the Novels of Kurt Vonnegut (crit). Tesis Doctoral, Universidad Complutense de Madrid, 2023.

Martín Párraga, Javier. *Vulnerabilidad y trauma tecnológico en la narrativa de Kurt Vonnegut* (crit). Granada: Editorial Comares, 2023.

Raj, Ankit and Nagendra Kumar. Finding "Bluebeard" in Kurt Vonnegut's *Bluebeard* (crit). *ANQ*, 36 (Mar. 2023), 132–36.

———. The Painter and the Muse: On Archetypes, Complexes and the Anti-Jungian Quest for Mother in Kurt Vonnegut's *Bluebeard* (crit). *Partial Answers: Journal of Literature and the*

History of Ideas, 21 (June 2023), 279–302.

Wallace, David Foster (1962–2008)

Bowlby, Ewan. The Theology of Attention in *The Fault in Our Stars*: John Green's Novel Contribution to "Thinking About Suffering" (crit). *Journal of Religion and Popular Culture*, 35 (Apr. 2023), 36–49.

Carver, Beci. Tennis as Literary Technique (crit). *Textual Practice*, 37 (June 2023), 919–40.

Chase, Greg. "Pointing at Shadows": Wallace, Wittgenstein, and the Problem of Putting Pain into Words (crit). *Critique*, 64 (2) 2023, 182–94.

Fernández-Santiago, Miriam. Post-Postmodernist Esthetics of Irrelevance: Textual Disability as Narrative Prosthesis (The Lin/Wallace Connection) (crit). *Critique*, 64 (2) 2023, 270–81.

Gonzalez, César. What Is Water? Exploring Ethical Ontology in the Work of David Foster Wallace (crit). Ph.D. Dissertation, Southern Connecticut State U, 2023.

Langroudi, Narjess Jafari. Nietzsche's *amor afati* in David Foster Wallace's *Infinite Jest* (crit). *Folia Linguistica et Litteraria*, 44 (2023), 133–48.

Lee, Shuyu. Leaving Class Behind? Social Mobility and Meritocratic Individualism in *The Pale King* (crit). *Orbis Litterarum*, 78 (Apr. 2023), 129–43.

———. Ontologies of Alterity: Free Gift, Social Reproduction, and Affect in David Foster Wallace's *The Pale King* (crit). *Partial Answers: Journal of Literature and the History of Ideas*, 21 (June 2023), 343–66.

Lekesizalin, Ferma. Enjoying the Symptom: David Foster Wallace's *Brief Interviews with Hideous Men* (crit). *Journal of Literary Studies*, 39 (2023), unpaginated.

López Sande, Sergio. Literature beyond Solipsism: Self-Consciousness, Empathy and the Other in the Short Fiction of David Foster Wallace (crit). Ph.D. Dissertation, Universidade de Santiago de Compostela, 2023.

Matthews, Edward. Limitations of Postmodern Irony: How David Foster Wallace Writes a Superior Critique of American Consumerism in *Infinite Jest* Compared with Bret Easton Ellis's *American Psycho* (crit). *Critique*, 64 (5) 2023, 808–18.

Rajendran, Punnya. Towards an Ethics of Reading: Syntax and Self-Care in Depression Narratives (crit). *Critique*, 64 (5) 2023, 737–48.

Van de Ven, Inge and Ties Van Gemert. Resisting Attention Economies: Wallace, Voskuil, and the Ethics of Noise (crit). *Diacritics*, 51 (3) 2023, 60–80.

Yu, Timothy. David Foster Wallace, Both Professional and Not (crit). *English Studies*, 104 (Apr. 2023), 305–28.

Wallace, Lew (1827–1905)

Bronson, Peter. *The Man Who Saved Cincinnati* (biog). Milford, Ohio: Chilidog Press, 2023.

Ware, Chris (b. 1967)

Baldanzi, Jessica. *Bodies and Boundaries in Graphic Fiction: Reading Female and Nonbinary Characters* (crit). London: Routledge, 2023.

Eckhoff-Heindl, Nina. *Comics begreifen: Ästhetische Erfahrung durch visuell-taktiles Erzählen in Chris Wares Building Stories* (crit). Berlin: Dietrich Reimer Verlag, 2023.

Fraser, Benjamin. Chris Ware's *Building Stories* Jigsaw Puzzle (2021) (crit). *Journal of Urban Cultural Studies,* 10 (1) 2023, 3–13.

Samolsky, Russell. The Book of Ashes: Authorial Instructions, Incorporations, and House Rules in *Jimmy Corrigan: The Smartest Kid on Earth* (crit). *Narrative*, 31 (May 2023), 179–97.

Wescott, Glenway (1901–1987)

Kindig, Patrick. Glenway Wescott's Narratives of Queer Drift (crit). *GLQ: A Journal of Lesbian and Gay Studies*, 29 (Apr. 2023), 215–36.

Wilder, Laura Ingalls (1867–1957)

Koupal, Nancy Tystad, ed. *Pioneer Girl: The Path into Fiction* (crit; pub). Pierre: South Dakota Historical Society Press, 2023.

Miller, Robynne Elizabeth and J.D. Rushmore. *Tennessee Wildcat: On the Trail of Laura Ingalls Wilder's Mr. Edwards* (crit). Portland, Or.: Practical Pioneer Press, 2023.

Wilder, Thornton (1897–1975)

Abbotson, Susan C., et al. Responses to DeGrazia [Thornton Wilder: Why Here? Why Now?] (crit). *Thornton Wilder Journal*, 4 (Oct. 2023), 149–99.

Coleman, Troy. The Uncoupling of Humanity Aboard the *Pullman Car Hiawatha* (crit). *Thornton Wilder Journal*, 4 (Oct. 2023), 200–22.

DeGrazia, Emilio. Thornton Wilder: Why Here? Why Now? (crit). *Thornton Wilder Journal*, 4 (Oct. 2023), 137–48.

Gontarski, S.E. Wilder's Joyce: Inspiration, Borrowing, Appropriation, Plagiarism (crit). *ABEI Journal: The Brazilian Journal of Irish Studies*, 25 (June 2023), 29–46.

Haberli, Nina. *The Skin of Our Teeth*, Phoenix Theatre Ensemble, Nyack, New York (crit). *Thornton Wilder Journal*, 4 (June 2023), 116–22.

Hamlett, Bonnie Georgette. Recent Thornton Wilder Research and Scholarship (bibl). *Thornton Wilder Journal*, 4 (Oct. 2023), 245–52.

Kelly, Joshua. *Our Town*, American Players Theatre, Spring Green, Wisconsin (crit). *Thornton Wilder Journal*, 4 (Oct. 2023), 265–71.

Kelty, Shawna Mefferd. *Our Town*, Pendragon Theatre, Saranac Lake, New York (crit). *Thornton Wilder Journal*, 4 (Oct. 2023), 271–77.

Kyle, Brenton. *Our Town*, Arvada Center for the Arts and Humanities, Arvada, Colorado (crit). *Thornton Wilder Journal*, 4 (June 2023), 123–28.

McIntyre, John P. Thornton Wilder on Inculturation (crit). *Thornton Wilder Journal*, 4 (June 2023), 77–85.

Martocello, Charles. The Last Yeoman: An American Historicist Reading of Act 1 of *The Skin of Our Teeth* (crit). *Thornton Wilder Journal*, 4 (Oct. 2023), 223–44.

Mayo, Chelsea. *Our Town*, Center Stage, Baltimore, Maryland (crit). *Thornton Wilder Journal*, 4 (June 2023), 108–15.

Regen, Haas. *Lunar Eclipse*, by Donald Margulies, Shakespeare & Company, Lenox, Massachusetts (crit). *Thornton Wilder Journal*, 4 (Oct. 2023), 259–64.

Roessel, David and Eva Leaverton, eds. *A Sapphic Ode* by Thornton Wilder: A Previously Unpublished Playlet (crit; D). *Thornton Wilder Journal*, 4 (June 2023), 1–11

Rojcewicz, Stephen J. Literary Attacks on Thornton Wilder (crit). *Thornton Wilder Journal*, 4 (June 2023), 46–76.

Scharff, Jill Savage. Trumpet: Revisiting and Reimagining Thornton Wilder's *The Trumpet Shall Sound* (crit). *Thornton Wilder Journal*, 4 (June 2023), 86–107.

Sedacca, Alyssa. Ancient Greece and 1920s America: A New Historicist Approach to Thornton Wilder's *The Woman of Andros* (crit). *Thornton Wilder Journal*, 4 (June 2023), 12–28.

Simonetti, Paolo. Women and Literature in Thornton Wilder's *The Ides of March* (crit). *Thornton Wilder Journal*, 4 (June 2023), 29–45.

Sterbenk, Eric. *Our Town*, Syracuse Stage, Syracuse, New York (crit). *Thornton Wilder Journal*, 4 (June 2023), 128–35.

Williams, Tennessee (1911–1983)

Besse, Olivier. Mythes et structures chez Tennessee Williams... et Dieu dans tout çà ? (crit). Thèse de Doctorat, Université Bordeaux Montaigne, 2023.

Cep, Casey. Becoming Tennessee: A Portrait of the Playwright as a Young Artist (rev). *New Yorker*, 99 (10 & 17 July 2023), 74–77.

Feldman, Alex. "The World's Wildest and Loveliest Populated Places": Visions of the Tropic Imaginary in Tennessee Williams, John Huston, and Herman Melville (crit). *Partial Answers: Journal of Literature and the History of Ideas*, 21 (Jan. 2023), 25–51.

Mertens, Mahlu. De enscenering van bet autobiografisch geheugen in Tennessee Williams' *The Glass Menagerie* (1945) (crit). *Spiegel der Letteren*, 65 (2–3) 2023, 237–56.

Özcan, Duygu Beste Başer. Shattering Normalcy: Disability and Queerness in Tennessee Williams's *One Arm* (crit). *Modern Drama*, 66 (Mar.2023), 48–70.

Rodriguez, Kaitlyn Farrell. The Kindness of Strangers: Eugenics and Tennessee Williams's *A Streetcar Named Desire* (crit). *Modern Drama*, 66 (Mar.2023), 1–21.

Saddik, Annette J. Exploring the Line between Creation and Creator in Mabou Mines's *Glass Guignol: The Brother and Sister Play* (crit). *Journal of Contemporary Drama in English*, 11 (2) 2023, 298–307.

Sakai, Takashi. *Onnagata*, Grotesque Beauty, and Aging: Reading Tennessee Williams's Kabuki-Inspired Plays (crit). *Modern Drama*, 66 (Mar. 2023), 26–47.

Schoenberger, Nancy. *Blanche: The Life and Times of Tennessee Williams's Greatest Creation* (crit). NY: Harper, 2023.

Toledo, Luis Marcio Arnaut de. A Dialética Apocalíptica de Tennessee Williams em *The Chalky White Substance* (crit).

Remate de Males: Revista do Departamento de Teoria Literária, 43 (July-Dec. 2023), 494–515.

Wolfe, Toya (b. 1981)

Hunt, D. Bradford. In Conversation: Author Toya Wolfe and Historian D. Bradford Hunt (I). *Newberry Magazine*, no. 21 (Fall-Winter 2023), 26–29.

Woodrell, Daniel (b. 1953)

Achilles, Jochen. Normative Crisis in Regionalist American Short Fiction (crit). *Journal of the Short Story in English*, 80–81 (Spr. 2023), 25–44.

Woolson, Constance Fenimore (1840–1894)

Brehm, Victoria. *Constance Fenimore Woolson's Subversive Politics* (crit). Lanham, Md.: Lexington Books, 2023.

Wright, Harold Bell (1872–1944)

Han, John J. *Harold Bell Wright's Ozarks: Photos with Notes* (biog). Allahabad: Cyberwit.net, 2023.

Wright, Richard (1908–1960)

Boggs, Colleen Glenney. *American Hunger* vs. *America Eats*: Richard Wright and the Racial Politics of Lifestyle Writing (crit). *American Literary History*, 35 (Win. 2023), 1638–64.

Bousquet, Florian. Bigger and Bessie on Nambi E. Kelley's Stage: Adapting *Native Son*'s Genre and Gender for the Twenty-First Century (crit). *Palimpsest: A Journal of Women, Gender, and the Black International*, 12 (1) 2023, 66–82.

Brown, Donald. Embracing What He Was "Taught to Shun": Tracing Richard Wright's Recommitment to His Grandmother's Seventh-Day Adventist Faith (biog; crit). *Christianity & Literature*, 72 (Dec. 2023), 601–19.

Daniels, Devin William. Everybody's Statistical Record: Richard Wright and the Determinations of Late Naturalism (crit). *Representations*, 164 (Fall 2023), 115–36.

Direkoglu, Daniel. American Agony: Richard Wright's Language of Pain in *Black Boy (American Hunger)* (crit). *University of Toronto Quarterly*, 92 (Nov. 2023), 633–60.

Green, Tara T. Revisioning Richard Wright's Bessie (crit). *Palimpsest: A Journal of Women, Gender, and the Black International*, 12 (1) 2023, 18–30.

Hawkes, Delisa D. More Than a Black Rat Sonofab----: Animality in Defining Americanness and the Human in Nambi E. Kelley's *Native Son* (crit). *Palimpsest: A Journal of Women, Gender, and the Black International*, 12 (1) 2023, 83–98.

Hawthorne, Tasha. Playwright Nambi Kelley Finds the Love: Adapting Richard Wright's *Native Son* for the Stage (crit). *Palimpsest: A Journal of Women, Gender, and the Black International*, 12 (1) 2023, 114–23.

Jarman, Cody. "No Theme, No Message, No Thought": The Redressive Politics of *Their Eyes Were Watching God* and the Harlem Renaissance (crit). *MELUS*, 48 (Sum. 2023), 99–118.

Johnston-Levy, Taylor. Whiteness and the Affective Economy of Happy Antiracism in *Native Son* and *Meridian* (crit). *Twentieth Century Literature*, 69 (June 2023), 147–76.

Jones, Douglas A. Repetition and Value in Richard Wright's *Man Who Lived Underground* (crit). *American Literature*, 95 (Mar. 2023), 123–34.

Lester, Neal A. "This Is a Man's World": Richard Wright Just Won't Give a Sistah a Break in "Long Black Song" (crit). *Palimpsest: A Journal of Women, Gender, and the Black International*, 12 (1) 2023, 50–65.

McClain, Kathryn J. Engaging with an Imperfect Past: Simultaneity and the Many Stories within Director Rashid Johnson's *Native Son* (crit). *Adaptation: The Journal of Literature on Screen Studies*, 16 (Mar.2023), 63–78.

Manigault-Bryant, James. Seeing "The Death of Mann" (crit). *Mississippi Quarterly*, 76 (1) 2023, 89–112.

Marchi, Lisa. Homes: A Quartet (crit). *Zeitschrift für Anglistik und Amerikanistik*, 71 (1) 2023, 27–40.

Nero, Charles I. Redeeming Bigger Thomas: Rashid Johnson and Suzan-Lori Parks's "Woke" *Native Son* (crit). *Palimpsest: A Journal of Women, Gender, and the Black International*, 12 (1) 2023, 99–113.

Shiraki, Mitsuyoshi. Narratives within Protest: Richard Wright's Genres (crit). Ph.D. Dissertation, SUNY Buffalo, 2023.

Steiner, Michael C. Richard Wright, the Warmth of Other Suns, and Chicago's Impact on a Southern Migrant to the Black Metropolis, 1927–1937 (crit). *MidAmerica*, 50 (2023), 60–78.

Washington, Sondra Bickham. Uncle Tom's Daughter: Sarah versus the Enduring Misogyny of Wright's "Long Black Song" (crit). *Palimpsest: A Journal of Women, Gender, and the Black International*, 12 (1) 2023, 35–49.

Wyatt, Edith (1873–1958)

Ruhlmann, Ellyn. Revisiting Edith Wyatt: A New Woman's View of Chicago's Melting Pot (crit). *MidAmerica*, 50 (2023), 38–59.

Zelazny, Roger (1937–1995)

Anisimova, Olga Vladimirovna and Inna Makarova. Mythopoetic Images of Irish Mythology in American Fantasy (the Case of Roger Zelazny's "Chronicles of Amber"-Corwin Cycle) (crit). *Litera* [Slovak Republic], 4 (2023), 92–101.

Zitkala-Ša (1876–1938)

Brown, Elizabeth C. Middle Passages: Lessons in Racial Subjection at the Hampton Institute and Carlisle Indian Industrial School (crit). *American Quarterly*, 75 (Dec. 2023), 707–30.

Roger Bresnahan

Winner of the 2026 MidAmerica Award
for distinguished contributions to the study of midwestern literature

and

Margaret (Peggy) Rozga

Winner of the 2026 Mark Twain Award
for distinguished contributions to midwestern literature

These awards will be presented at the Society's 54th annual meeting, Kellogg
Hotel and Conference Center, Michigan State University, May 28–29, 2026.

Society for the Study of

MIDWESTERN LITERATURE

2026 Symposium of Scholars and Creative Writers

CALL FOR PROPOSALS · papers/posters · panels · round tables

LITERARY CRITICISM or CREATIVE WRITING or PEDAGOGY

See ssml.org for submission instructions.

DEADLINE February 15, 2026

QUESTIONS Jeff Hotz (jhotz@esu.edu)

MAY 28–29 2026

WRITING THE MIDWEST

Kellogg Hotel and Convention Center · East Lansing, MI

CFP: Reading and Writing the Midwest

Recent essays in popular publications such as *The Atlantic*, *The New York Times*, and *Psychology Today* have sounded the alarm that college students today cannot read. Is this true? The Society for the Study of Midwestern Literature calls for proposals for an upcoming issue of its peer-reviewed journal *Midwestern Miscellany* devoted to the topic of Reading and Writing the Midwest, to be guest-edited by Rachael Price (Abraham Baldwin Agricultural College) and Catherine Clifford (Hastings College).

Successful essays will describe a specific challenge in the classroom and/or a successful classroom activity or assignment; evaluate a theory of reading, writing, literacy, or pedagogy; or examine a text or historical moment related to literacy in the Midwest. Please send proposals (max. 300 words) and short CV to Catherine Clifford (cat.clifford@hastings.edu) and Rachael Price (rprice @abac.edu) by March 1, 2026. Finished essays should be 3,000-6,000 words.

Topics may include, but are not limited to, the following:

- Classroom exercises or lesson plans that engage Midwestern students in reading and/or writing
- Midwestern texts that engage students or promote specific reading skills
- Writing about the Midwest or place
- Responses to think pieces about university students and reading and/or writing
- Debates about early reading instruction (such as the Science of Reading and/or Whole Language reading)
- Theories of literacy, as they apply to midwestern classrooms and/or texts
- Theories of composition, including multimodal composition and accessibility, as they apply to midwestern classrooms and/or texts
- Use of generative AI in higher ed classrooms
- Theories of evaluation, such as anti-racist or equity-minded grading, in higher ed
- Debates about school choice, charter schools, or parents' rights bills in the Midwest

*AI-generated image of Midwestern higher ed classroom with laptops.

New Perspectives on Midwestern Working-Class Literature

The Society for the Study of Midwestern Literature invites essay proposals for an upcoming issue of its peer-reviewed journal *Midwestern Miscellany* on the topic of Midwestern Working-Class Literature, to be guest edited by Marilyn Atlas (atlas@ohio.edu). *Midwestern working-class literature* is a genre of writing that focuses on the lives and experiences of working-class people living in the American Midwest, exploring themes of industrial and farm labor, economic hardship, community struggle, and social issues prevalent in the region.

Douglas Wixson, in *Worker-Writer in America* (1994), demonstrates a tradition of twentieth-century Midwestern literary radicalism. Writers in this tradition include notable authors such as Hamlin Garland (*Main-Travelled Roads*), Upton Sinclair (*The Jungle*), Richard Wright (*Native Son*), Theodore Dreiser (*Sister Carrie*), Tillie Olsen (*Tell Me a Riddle*), Toni Morrison (*The Bluest Eye*), and Sanora Babb (*whose names are unknown*). But the field has expanded to include previously ignored communities and print forms, such as hobo newspapers and Heartland Marxist magazines, as well.

For this issue, SSML seeks new and diverse approaches to the study of Midwestern working-class literature. Potential contributors are invited to propose creative topics on well-known writers/texts or to expand or challenge the established history or conventions of working-class literature in the Midwest. Questions might include, but are not limited to, the following: What is the role of the working-class writer in working-class literature? Is this literature diverse, hybrid, or experimental? How has the literary representation of labor changed over time?

Please send queries and/or proposals to Marilyn Atlas (atlas@ohio.edu) by March 1, 2026. Proposals should be no more than 700 words and should be accompanied by a recent CV. (Finished essays should be 3,000-6,000 words.)

Call for Proposals

The Society for the Study of Midwestern Literature invites essay proposals for a forthcoming issue of the peer-reviewed journal Midwestern Miscellany on the topic of Midwestern Drama, to be guest-edited by Marilyn Atlas (atlas@ohio.edu).

Recent years have seen a resurgence of interest in Midwestern drama. In 2022, for example, Marcia Noe published *Three Midwestern Playwrights: How Floyd Dell, George Cram Cook, and Susan Glaspell Transformed American Theatre*, a critical work highlighting the importance of the Midwest in forging Modernist American theater. Several classic Midwestern plays have recently been revived or reevaluated, such as Lorraine Hansberry's *The Sign in Sidney Brustein's Window* (New York) and Arthur Miller's *All My Sons* (London), with its radical color-blind casting and earthy toned, "Midwest" staging. And Noah Diaz's *You Will Get Sick* (performed at the Steppenwolf in Chicago 2025) shows us something hilarious and brilliant about Midwesterners and the contemporary Midwest economic scene. It is time for scholars to weigh in again and reinterpret Midwest drama from a fresh perspective.

Contributors may address any aspect of Midwestern drama (i.e., drama set or performed in the Midwest), but topics might include the following:

- Still little-known Midwest dramatists that ought to be getting attention
- Important Midwestern plays that have been ignored or forgotten
- Verse dramas (such as Harriet Monroe's) that deserve a second look
- Contemporary Midwestern drama, troupes, or theatre spaces
- Dramatists or plays that challenge traditional conceptions or narratives of the Midwest
- New theoretical or critical approaches to well-known Midwestern plays or dramatists
- Revivals of Midwestern plays

Please send queries and/or proposals to Marilyn Atlas (atlas@ohio.edu) by March 1, 2026. Proposals should be no more than 700 words and should be accompanied by a recent CV. (Finished essays should be 3,000-6,000 words.)

Image: Screenshot of trailer for Noah Diaz's *You Will Get Sick*, Steppenwolf Theatre (Chicago, IL), June 5 to July 20, 2025 (Andrew Boyce, scenic design).